Hunger
Sean Kelly

Hunger
Sean Kelly
The autobiography

PELOTON PUBLISHING

First published in paperback in Great Britain in 2015
by Peloton Publishing
© 2013 Sean Kelly / Peloton Publishing

First published in hardback in 2013

Typeset by Peloton Publishing
Printed and bound by SS Media

Cover design by Peloton Publishing
Artwork by Simon Scarsbrook

Peloton Publishing Ltd
Registered in England
2 Gaddesden Lane, Redbourn, St Albans, Herts AL3 7NP
Registered company number: 7353619
www.seankellybook.com

ISBN 978-0-9932899-0-3

The story of my life on a bike.

To everyone who played a part along the way.

Contents

Foreword
by Sir Bradley Wiggins
The 2012 Tour de France winner

From my earliest days of being interested in cycling, Sean Kelly was constantly there. He wasn't one of the riders who you only saw racing in July at the Tour de France, he was winning races and getting places week in and week out.

Cycling Weekly was the only reference we had in Britain at the time, before Twitter, the internet and Eurosport covering cycling, and Sean always seemed to be winning. So from the age of eight or nine I was reading about him, all through the season.

I remember watching Channel Four as a kid, and Richard Keys, who was presenting in those days, always made a lot of Sean, whether it was the Tour, the Kellogg's city centre criteriums or the Kellogg's Tour of Britain. And there was one Nissan Classic when he made a huge impression on me, the day in 1991 when he went away with Sean Yates over St Patrick's hill in Cork, in the wind and rain. It made an incredible photo on the back of *Cycling Weekly*. I cut out the poster and put it on my wall.

As a kid, I liked proper working-class heroes and that's what Sean was. He still is. A farmer's son from Ireland. Perhaps it's because we were working class that he became a hero but I could look at someone like Sean and think, 'I could do that one day.'

When I was a kid, my heroes were Sean Kelly, Sean Yates and Miguel Indurain. No kid could compare themselves to Indurain because he was a machine, but you could see a bit of yourself in Kelly and Yates. They had no critics, they made no enemies.

When I got a bit older, and won the individual pursuit at the World Junior Track Championships, I got to meet Sean Kelly for the first time, and he was exactly the same as he'd seemed on television. He totally lived up to my expectations of him as my childhood hero. He was down to earth, treating everyone the same no matter who they were, whether it was Eddy Merckx or some kid like me from Kilburn.

These are qualities you find in the best working-class heroes. They know they are someone but they don't act as if they are someone.

I'd put Sean in that category along with England's World Cup-winning captain Bobby Moore, Tommy Simpson – who I never met, but who I feel I know from reading interviews, the books and the archive stuff – Indurain, Yates obviously, and the boxer Henry Cooper, who I did get to meet. You never hear anyone say a bad word about any of these guys. They were and are gentlemen who transcend their sports.

However much I admire it, I could never do what Sean Kelly did on a bike. He raced hard in every race he started, and won a lot – Paris-Nice seven times, Milan-San Remo twice, Paris-Roubaix twice, the Vuelta a España, four green jerseys and fourth overall at the Tour de France, medals at the World Championships.

Kelly just had such an appetite. You have to admire the fact that he was a hard, hard man. Even when he was at the top of his game he didn't live a lavish life. He spent most of his career based in a room in a house in Belgium, just doing his job 100 per cent.

I've only got to know Sean since he stopped racing, listening to his commentary on Eurosport and meeting him at the races. He's pretty much continued from where he was in cycling: utterly professional, never saying anything bad about anyone. Most surprising of all, for someone who was that hard and that good, he doesn't expect the riders of today to be like him. He's still as humble and modest as when he was racing.

He's been a role model for me and it's a shame there aren't more around who are like him.

Sir Bradley Wiggins

1. Poggio

Milan-San Remo, March 1992

What was I thinking as I plummeted down the descent of the Poggio in pursuit of Moreno Argentin? Was I really a man possessed, as they said? Had I abandoned all thoughts for my safety? Did I care whether I ended up toppling over the low wall and shattering through the roof of one of the glasshouses below?

None of this mattered. I was thinking of winning, nothing else. I was going to give everything to catch Argentin and win the race. If I finished the day lying on my face among the tomato plants and shards of glass, so be it.

Over the years the story of the 1992 Milan-San Remo has developed a life of its own. I've heard it said that my back wheel skidded around every corner and that I bounced off the walls on my way down, leaving scuff marks on the shoulders of my jersey. That wasn't the case. Perhaps people feel the need to embellish the drama. I don't. For me, it was more than dramatic enough.

TO SUCCEED IN BIKE RACING, you need something deep inside that drives you, a hunger that allows you to ignore the pain when it screams at you to ease up.

Every rider dreams of winning the biggest races but how many truly yearn for it? How many feel it in the pit of their stomach? The easiest thing in the world is to get so far and then pull back. It's not difficult to convince yourself that you've given everything but it takes something extra to push on until the stars dance in front of your eyes and your vision narrows to a thin strip of black. You can't do that unless you are hungry for victory. Ravenous for it. Even then, it might not be not enough. Much of the time there's someone stronger, with even more desire to win.

Bike racing hurts but going hungry hurts more.

The biggest single-day races on the cycling calendar are called the Classics. Of those, five have been elevated to an even greater status and are known as the Monuments. They are Milan-San Remo, the Tour of Flanders, Paris-Roubaix and Liège-Bastogne-Liège in the spring, and the Tour of Lombardy in autumn. These are the longest and most gruelling tests a professional cyclist can be subjected to. Each race has its own character and demands a different set of skills but they have one thing in common. They are all extremely difficult to win. They are long, gruelling, tactically-demanding. There are viciously steep hills or battered, cobbled roads to negotiate. And there's a pack of 200 riders all racing like dogs chasing a fox even though only a handful have a realistic hope of winning.

Only the very best riders have any chance. The winner will prove himself to be in excellent physical shape. Any niggling injury or tiny weakness will be ruthlessly exploited by the terrain and the opposition. And when the race comes down to the sharp end, when everyone is prepared to bare their teeth, it is the one who is prepared to bite that will win.

AS THE 1992 EDITION of Milan-San Remo approached, I was coming towards the end of my career. A couple of months short of my 36th birthday, I knew I had passed under the *flamme rouge*, the red flag that marks the final kilometre of all the major bike races. I could see the finishing straight.

With eight Monuments to my name, as well as one of cycling's Grand Tours, the Vuelta a España, I had nothing to prove to anyone. The days when the press conducted an inquest if I failed to show strongly in the Classics were passing. At the end of the previous season I had won the Tour of Lombardy, and a lot of people had seen it as my farewell to the big stage.

But I wasn't quite done yet. The old dog still had some bite.

Over the winter, I left the Dutch PDM team, one of the biggest squads in the world and my home for three seasons, to join a haphazard-looking mob sponsored by the Festina Watches company. To those on the outside, it probably looked like an old man grabbing at one last payday as he slid down the ladder towards retirement.

Changing teams had renewed my enthusiasm and sharpened my focus. For a start, I felt like I owed something to Miguel Rodriguez, the boss of the Festina company, because he was paying me a small fortune. He had offered me a handsome salary because he needed a big name to take his team to the next level. Festina had been a modest team but Rodriguez was an ambitious man. He wanted to make his team the best in the world and I could play a part in setting them on their way.

My salary wasn't dependent on performing well or winning races. Festina were paying for Sean Kelly and what I had done in the past. But I felt a duty to Rodriguez and, more importantly, to my own sense of self-respect. He was paying me to race my bike; he wasn't just adding to my pension fund.

I'd trained well during the winter and quickly found some good form in the early-season races. I'd also worked out that, of all the spring Classics, Milan-San Remo represented my best chance of delivering a big result for my new team. The Tour of Flanders had never been kind to me. Paris-Roubaix was too much of a lottery. Liège-Bastogne-Liège was too hilly and the explosive pace on the many Ardennes climbs would be too much for me now.

But Milan-San Remo offered an opportunity because it required a rider to have a clever mind and cunning in his heart as well as strong legs. Don't assume that meant the race would be easy because it wouldn't. The course was almost 300 kilometres long but the action is distilled into the final phase of the race, with a series of climbs along the Ligurian coastline sapping the legs and slowly whittling down the number in contention.

The race follows the rhythm of many Italian bike races. For a long time no one does anything at all, they just roll along at a casual pace, then suddenly it bursts into life and before you know it the attacks are going off and it's like standing in the middle of a firework display wondering what will go bang next.

The names of two of the key hills, the Cipressa and the Poggio, will be familiar to anyone who has followed the history of cycling. This is where the slow-burning Milan-San Remo ignites. In the thick of the action it's easy to miss the importance of each tiny mistake that adds up to inevitable defeat.

The pace is so high in the final two hours that every effort has to be judged to perfection. Just a few metres spent riding in the wind can be costly, as can getting caught in the wrong place in the bunch at the wrong time.

That's why it is a test of experience as much as one of strength. Having ridden Milan-San Remo more than a dozen times, I knew I could read the race well enough to be a factor, even if there were stronger climbers and faster sprinters in the field.

TIRRENO-ADRIATICO IS THE dress rehearsal for Milan-San Remo. It is a week-long stage race that takes the riders across Italy, from one coast to the other. It's also a week during which everyone watches everyone else for little clues. Who is in good shape? Who will be the men to watch at Milan-San Remo?

That week, Moreno Argentin made no effort to disguise his condition. He was in blistering form. The Italian was a former world champion who seemed to perform better as the races got longer and tougher. The way he attacked the climbs at Tirreno-Adriatico was breathtaking. He won three stages in a row, which had the rest of us shaking our heads. The press were convinced they were looking at the winner of Milan-San Remo. We were too. The way he was racing, it seemed he would make mincemeat of us on the Poggio because he looked untouchable.

I felt good during Tirreno-Adriatico but I hid away in the bunch. Not that anyone was studying me too closely. Although I had won the Tour of Lombardy the previous autumn, I was not at the top of anyone's list of favourites for Milan-San Remo.

Lombardy is a hard, prestigious, beautiful race but it comes at the end of a long season so for many of the riders enthusiasm is already on the wane and they are looking forward to taking a break. Milan-San Remo is at the start of a fresh campaign and everyone is feeling lively.

I didn't mind staying in the shadows. I didn't want to draw attention to myself. I wanted them to underestimate the old

warrior. The day before Milan-San Remo, I caught a sight of the
Italian sports paper *La Gazzetta dello Sport*. They had listed the
favourites for the race. Argentin stood alone, with five stars next
to his name. They gave me one star, probably for old times' sake.

The evening before the race, we sat around the dinner table
after we'd finished eating. The food in Italy always puts a smile on
a cyclist's face so there was a relaxed atmosphere in our team.

Acacio Da Silva, a livewire from Portugal, Tommy Wegmüller,
a solid and reliable Swiss, and Mauro Gianetti were among those
with me at the table. They were my friends as well as team-mates.
The mood was light-hearted.

One of the joys of being part of a professional cycling team
was the sense of camaraderie. I was never a big talker but I always
liked sitting round the dinner table, digesting the meal and listening to others tell their stories. The talk is always the same. Who's
going well, who's riding as if their back brake was permanently
on, who's getting paid how much, and who's got a new girlfriend.
There's always plenty of bravado and bluster and it's all got to be
taken with a pinch of salt. I've heard stories about myself that have
been exaggerated to the point where only my name was true.

Someone started to tell a tale about the 1979 Milan-San
Remo. Roger De Vlaeminck, the brilliant Belgian rider, had just
joined a team sponsored by Gis Gelati, an Italian ice cream maker.
The company had been owned by a flamboyant businessman. The
day before the race, he promised De Vlaeminck his Ferrari if he
won. Sure enough, De Vlaeminck won. After the race he took a
shower, collected the keys to the boss's Ferrari and drove his prize
all the way back to Belgium.

Cyclists love little more than a story about win bonuses and
fast cars. Acacio chirped up. 'Hey,' he said to the Italian represen-
tative of the Festina Watches firm, who had joined us for dinner,
'what do we get if we win tomorrow?'

The rep promised us a top-of-the-range Festina watch, worth
several thousand quid, which made Acacio even more excitable.

DURING TIRRENO-ADRIATICO I had crashed twice.
Neither was very serious but I had broken both my race bikes and

there wasn't time to get a replacement built up and sent to Italy. So I had to ride the first major Classic of the season on a bike that was half an inch too big for me, even with the saddle lowered.

There was no point worrying about that. I would cope, but I was obsessive about my tyres, knowing how technical the descents of the Cipressa and Poggio are. I wanted my tyres to be grippy and reliable, so I broke in a brand new pair of Vittoria CX tubular tyres during the final stage of Tirreno-Adriatico, just to take the sheen off the surface. Then I went to find our mechanic and asked him to glue them onto the rims with even more care than usual. I wanted them well stuck on.

The pattern of the race itself wasn't going to be a surprise to anyone. We knew Argentin would attack on the Poggio, which comes a few kilometres before the finish in San Remo.

The question was, would anyone be able to go with him? I had doubts about whether I could match his pace on the climb, particularly considering his form, so my strategy was simple. As far as possible, I would ignore the fireworks on the climb and save my effort for the descent. Instead of trying to match Argentin's attack, I would stay in the sweetspot, around a dozen places back in the bunch, where it's possible to stay out of the wind and preserve a bit of energy. I would wait and choose my moment.

Milan-San Remo is a test of patience and experience but it is easy to get carried along with all the excitement in the final hour. The Italians are very keen to attack on the climbs. They want to get their faces on television and although it is tempting to get drawn into a race with them, I knew I had to resist that.

Every acceleration and every second spent with my nose in the wind would put the needle in the red. The final hour of Milan-San Remo is one of the most intense hours of racing of the whole season. It's full-on all the way. There might be a brief chance to rest the legs for a few seconds by freewheeling round a corner but that's about it.

The climbs start with 250 kilometres covered. There are half a dozen of them, most of which are only little bumps compared to the mountains we climb in the big tours but after almost six hours in the saddle, and hit at such speed, they feel hard. The pace rises all the time and on the final two climbs, the Cipressa and the Poggio, it feels like we can't possibly go any harder.

Before the battle started, I dropped to the back of the bunch of riders and signalled for my team car to come up alongside me. I wanted to get my helmet. In those days it was not compulsory to wear one and I often went without but I had signed a pretty lucrative sponsorship deal with the manufacturer Brancale and I was due a big bonus if I won a Classic wearing their helmet. It was not the most attractive thing; it looked like my mother's old mixing bowl.

On one of the other small hills before the Cipressa I had a near-miss – one of those moments which makes or breaks a race. I was about 25th in line, on the left-hand side of the bunch, behind an Italian rider called Davide Cassani. He was moving up to the front and I was following him, benefitting from being in his slipstream. There wasn't a lot of room to pass the riders on our right as we were very close to the wall on the edge of the road.

There was a little scooter parked right on the side of the road, next to the wall. Cassani tried to flick round it but the rest of the riders were crammed shoulder to shoulder across the width of the road so there was nowhere for him to go. Instead, he clipped the scooter and went flying. In the blink of an eye, he was separated from his bike, which went spinning into the air and was about to fall directly on top of me.

Instinctively, I put my arm up and pushed the bike away. It was an extraordinary escape but those behind me were not so lucky. I heard the crash and knew that at least 20 guys would have been caught in it. That's one way to get rid of a few rivals and there was bound to be a favourite or two who were delayed with a tiring chase to get back to the front of the bunch. I am not superstitious and I don't believe in destiny but when I survived a moment like that I began to think it could perhaps be my day.

ARGENTIN ATTACKED on the Poggio, as we all knew he would. He went once, twice and finally got away the third time. It was a searing effort. A few riders tried to respond but they soon fell back. I was behind about ten riders, nestling in their slipstream, attempting to insulate myself from the irregular, uncomfortable changes of pace that would send the dial shooting into the red. But don't presume I was having an easy ride because I was following the wheels. The pace was very fast and so was my breathing. I wondered whether I'd be able to last to the top of the climb. And all the time, Argentin was pulling out a gap.

As we went over the top of the of the Poggio I heard a voice crackle over the race radio, which was being broadcast through a speaker on one of the official motorbikes. It told me Argentin had a lead of 15 seconds. That sounds small but with six kilometres to descend it was a nice advantage.

From the top of the Poggio we turned left and then plunged back down to sea level. The descent is very technical. The road is cut into the hillside and zig-zags all the way down, with many hairpin bends to negotiate. The gaps between the straights are filled with greenhouses, used by the locals to grow tomatoes and an array of vegetables. The only thing between me and a nasty fall was a little stone wall.

Argentin's team-mates from the Ariostea squad were doing a superb job for him. Rolf Sørensen was at the front of the bunch, blocking the chasers by cornering wide and steadily. As we went round the first bend I tried to duck underneath him but he closed me off. It wasn't a dodgy move, it was just clever riding to prevent me going in pursuit of Argentin.

It would have been easier to back off and wait for a clearer opportunity but I knew I had to get past Sørensen now or the gap would open too much. It took me a couple of attempts but eventually I got past. Sørensen left the door ajar, I made my move, he tried to discourage me again by moving across the road but I refused to be bullied and forced my way through.

Once I was ahead of Sørensen, with the road to myself, I could steer my way down the Poggio. Every now and then I caught a glimpse of Argentin's red and yellow jersey below me. As I entered one corner, I could see him on the road lower down.

The closer I got to the bottom, the more I knew I could push my luck. I braked later and more lightly, laid the bike over a little more and cut the corners more finely. But it was not a kamikaze descent. Everything was under control. I could hear the tyres squeaking beneath me but they weren't slipping away from me. And although the adrenaline was pumping through my veins I never gave myself a heart-stopping moment. And all the time, I was closing the gap.

Once I'd finished the descent and swung onto the main road that led into San Remo, I could see him clearly but I had to hammer across the gap in a big gear or else my momentum would be lost. I needed to catch him as soon as possible so I could grab a few moments to recover before we fought out the finish.

Closing the gap to his rear wheel, pushing that big gear on the flat road, really hurt my legs but I caught him just as we went under the red flag. When he turned round and saw me, he must have had the shock of his life. Victory must have seemed like it was in the bag. Now he had me to deal with.

For the first time since I squeezed past Sørensen, I looked over my shoulder. I wanted to make sure there was daylight behind me. There was a gap but I could see the herd galloping after us.

There wasn't much time to mess about or else the rest would catch us and my painful chase would be for nothing. Argentin turned to me and said, 'Tira' – meaning 'pull'. He wanted me to go to the front. I did my best acting. I didn't say anything, I just opened my mouth wide, to show how hard I was breathing.

I moved over a little so he had a clear view of the chasers behind us. This was an important moment. The sight of the big pack closing down on us made him panic so he carried on at a good pace. I wasn't bluffing him. The effort of closing the gap had almost exhausted me but I wanted to preserve what little energy I had for the sprint so I left him with little choice. He could take the risk of pressing on with me in his shadow, or slow down and try to lure me to the front, which might see us get caught.

I needed every second I could get to recover. My thighs were swollen and sore from six hours of pedalling, my calves were screaming after the chase but it's amazing how much it's possible to recover by lightening the gear a little and getting the breathing back under control.

Argentin opened up the sprint, because I gave him no choice.

He moved across the road to force me to go the long way round but I had enough strength to get past him. As I crossed the line, there was silence, apart from the roar which came from my own mouth. Thousands of Italians had just seen their boy beaten.

I'VE NEVER BEEN A sentimental soul. I don't recall ever feeling sorry for an opponent I'd beaten fair and square but on the podium that afternoon my own delight was tempered by a feeling of awkwardness. I felt that Argentin had lost in those circumstances. He was so strong – probably the strongest in the race – and he was racing in front of his home crowd, and he had victory in the palm of his hand. All he had to do was curl his fingers around it and keep it safe. Instead, I swiped the prize away from him.

I knew the clock was ticking on my own career. It was as if Old Father Time had been in the chase group but I had managed to hold him off one more time. How many days like this would I have left? It turned out to be the last big one. Perhaps that's why I remember it so vividly.

And the fearless pursuit on the Poggio certainly captured the imagination. Even now, more than 20 years later, people ask me about it. They want to know what I was thinking. Was I worried about crashing? Was I certain I could catch him?

What was I thinking? Well, it certainly wasn't the bonus I got for wearing a particular brand of helmet or the ten grand watch (which Acacio eventually got for us after several months and dozens of calls to Festina HQ). No, I was just thinking about catching my prey and satisfying my hunger.

2. A simple game

I can still remember the feeling I had the first time I raced a bike. The local races were held on Sunday afternoons and Tuesday evenings and the details are lost in the mists of time now so I can't remember which day in August 1970 my first race was on. But I can remember one thing vividly: pure fear.

I was 14 years old and I had entered a local handicap race organised by the Carrick Wheelers Road Club. My older brother, Joe, had been racing for a while and I wanted to try it for myself.

We cycled over to Carrickbeg, just south of Carrick-on-Suir, where the club held the races. On the way, Joe tried to give me some pointers but I wasn't listening. I already knew what I was going to do. Pedal like hell and not look back.

The race was beautifully simple. About 20 of us were split into groups according to age and ability. As one of the younger riders, and certainly one of the greenest, I was in the group that would be set off first. We were told we'd get a three-minute head start over the oldest, strongest boys.

We were told to race about three miles up the road and then, when we saw a man with a flag, turn around and race back again.

As soon as we were given the order to go, I stamped on the pedals. I didn't have a clue about drafting in another rider's slipstream. I had no idea about how to work efficiently with the other riders to share the pace-setting. I just put my back into it and pedalled as fast as I could. Almost immediately I left the other riders behind and was away on my own, with only the sound of my breathing, which was wild and desperate, for company.

After the turn for home, I saw the chasing group coming the

other way and assumed they were bearing down on me. This must be what it's like to be a hare fleeing the pack of dogs.

The terror got me up out of the saddle and I renewed my effort. The idea of being caught, of squandering the precious gift of a three-minute lead, was horrible. The idea of being beaten by Joe and hearing about it all the way home was even worse.

I didn't ease up for a second. I didn't dare.

At the finish, I was still clear of the rest. A quick glance round told me I had won my first ever race.

Someone clapped me on the back and told me there was no way I'd be getting a head start like that again.

Almost three minutes later, the main group with all the fast boys came in. They'd barely dented my advantage.

That rush of it all was so exciting. When it was over and my breathing had returned to normal I wanted to do it again. The fact I'd have to wait a week before racing again was agonising. I'd never enjoyed anything as much as this.

Of course, I had no idea then that cycling was to become my life. I was just happy to have discovered something that gave me such a thrill. I loved riding my bike more than I enjoyed school or working on the farm but racing was something else.

My horizons were limited growing up in rural Ireland. In one direction lay a life on the farm, following the changing seasons and tending to the animals, in the other was the building site. They were pretty much the only choices for a boy from the country, unless he happened to be good at school. And I wasn't any good at school.

I couldn't even picture a world in which I might be able to race a bike for a living. I'd rarely been as far as Dublin, let alone abroad. I also didn't consider myself gifted. There were others who were better than me, although most of them had the advantage of a couple of years on me. But I had strong legs, a robust constitution and a determination never to give up. Even when I was starting to tire, I could plough on through sheer bloody-mindedness and keep going long after others gave up.

Some of those qualities were in my genes but I don't believe I was born to ride a bike.

Discovering I was good at something drove me. The importance of hard work had been drilled into me at home but I couldn't apply it to the chores around the farm or the classroom. However, put me on a bike and I was away.

I followed a path that allowed me to make a living from professional cycling. A very good living. I was determined to make the best of it. At the start, the fear of having to return to the farm with my tail between my legs and admit to mother and father that I had failed pushed me on. I didn't want to hear father say: 'I told you so.'

Later on, the opportunity to earn good money made me very serious about cycling but still the main motivation was to do my best so that I wouldn't have to return to a life more ordinary.

I won some of the biggest bike races in the world – Milan-San Remo, Paris-Roubaix and Liège-Bastogne-Liège twice each and the Tour of Lombardy three times. I was the world's number one rider for five years in a row and won the Vuelta a España.

And although there are a couple of notable gaps – I never won the World Championships or the Tour de France – I am happy with my lot.

They named a square in Carrick-on-Suir after me and nicknamed me King Kelly. I didn't seek it but I liked being recognised for what I had achieved. I loved cycling, I liked winning and I enjoyed earning the money.

I am not a great one for reflecting or reminiscing. We can't change anything about the past. The way I look at things, I did what I thought was best at the time.

This is my story of the races I won and some I lost.

3. Life on the farm

Curraghduff

The lessons of life are not only taught, they are absorbed. I saw my mother and father work hard, and as soon as I could milk a cow, dig up vegetables or gather up the hay, I worked hard too.

I grew up on a farm at Curraghduff, not far from Carrick-on-Suir in County Waterford, near the border with County Tipperary. It's a long way to Tipperary, says the song, but when I was growing up it seemed a long way from everywhere.

The river is the border between Waterford and Tipperary and, although the people across the border tried to claim me when I was successful, I have always been a Waterford man. People still ask me now: 'What county are you really from?' It's not a matter of pride, it's a matter of fact. I was born in Waterford. There's a lot of rivalry between the two, and hurling and Gaelic football matches between teams from opposing counties would often end up in punch-ups. When I was the number one cyclist in the world there were heated arguments in pubs about where I was from.

Our farm was quite remote. There were not many neighbours nearby, so until I went to school that was my world, apart from trips to church or into town to go to the shops. We didn't have many visitors to the farm either, so it was a quiet upbringing.

My mother, Nellie, and father, Jack, were farm folk. They had grown up on farms as had their parents before them. Living in rural Ireland was simple. You had to make the land work for you by working the land.

My mother had been married before she married my father, to a man called Martin Power and they had a son, also called Martin. Mother's first husband died of a stroke and she later met Jack and they were married in 1950. I was born John James Kelly in 1956, a couple of years after Joe and before Vincent. Right from my earliest days I was called Sean. My father's name was also John but everyone called him Jack. That's just how it was in a lot of Irish families at the time: you were christened with one name and called by another.

Martin was technically my half-brother but as far as I was concerned, he was my brother. Although ours was a Catholic community there was no stigma that I knew of. Mother wasn't someone who'd get into a big conversation about things but she explained to me at some point, when I was old enough to understand, that my father was not Martin's father. It certainly wasn't a secret, but nor was it something that people made a big deal of.

The farm was not a big operation but it was more than enough to keep our family going, with the surplus being taken off to market to be sold. There were 35 acres of fields for crops and some cows, pigs, sheep and chickens.

There was always work to do. Lots of it. Mother and father would get up very early and they worked all day, had dinner and went to bed before getting up to do it all again. I can't remember either of them sitting down with nothing to do. We'd have our evening meal and afterwards there'd be more work. During the spring when the calves or lambs were due, we'd take turns to check on them through the night and help with the delivery.

Dinner time was sacrosanct and we had to be in to sit down round the kitchen table. Sometimes the meal was very simple, but there was always enough. During the busy times such as spring or harvest, when the farm's workload seemed to be never-ending, we had to make our own. I used to manage a boiled egg and toast but that was about my limit. It's fair to say I'm even worse in the kitchen now.

As soon as I could squeeze the udders I was sent out with a little stool and a bucket to milk the cows. I fed the chickens, mucked out the pigs, brought in the cows and took them out again. I sowed the seeds and dug up the vegetables.

Father embraced the rhythm of a farmer's life. He believed in the phrase that you reaped what you sowed because that was how he lived. Like mother, he was not a big talker. He was comfortable with other farmers and he could get into a discussion with them when he went to market but unless he had something to say, he remained silent. He believed in discipline and he was always giving out if our jobs were not done properly.

Life was dominated by three things: discipline, work and faith.

It was a Catholic household. Name me a house in rural Ireland in the late 1950s that wasn't. We believed and we went to mass on a Sunday. I never questioned the faith, not at home, nor at school and certainly not at church. I still have a faith but it is not as strong as it was. When I was young I believed in the miracles but I grew out of it. Cycling taught me there are no miracles.

The parlour at home was the room reserved for special occasions like Christmas, or a visit from the priest, which meant it was locked for 11 months of the year.

AT SCHOOL I WAS very quiet. I was shy but that wasn't the only reason I kept my mouth shut. I took after father. If I had nothing to say I didn't feel the need to fill the silence with blather.

School was not the highlight of my life. I went to the national school in Crehana, about a mile-and-a-half from home, and my favourite part of the day would be riding there and back on my bike.

In class, I rarely troubled the top of the leaderboard but I wasn't a bad lad. I got into the usual scraps and scrapes but rarely anything more serious than pinching apples. I only got into real bother on one or two occasions.

The most serious incident happened one summer's evening when I was about 12. There was a strange guy who lived out our way, a misfit who spent a lot of his time drinking in the pubs in town. We had this stupid idea that we'd throw stones at his car, so we hid in a ditch and pelted him when he drove past.

We did this in full view of the schoolmaster's house. He was in his garden and saw it all. The next morning our names were called out and we got the stick, which was a length of ash wood cane. We got five lashes on either side of the hand. I had to hold out my palm and take five blistering strikes, then turn my hand over and take it across the knuckles too. My fingers were raw afterwards and we feared getting the stick with good reason. It made me think twice before doing anything that might land me in trouble.

Another time there was a scuffle in one of the classrooms. Four of us were grappling, wrestling and brawling. We ended up against the window and someone's elbow went through the pane.

When the teacher asked the culprits to own up, no one confessed. I was pretty sure it wasn't my elbow that broke the glass so I was hoping to get out of it that way.

The teacher decided to hold a court case with the rest of the children forming the jury. The four of us had to make a statement and then answer questions from the other children about the incident. I can remember choosing my words carefully to avoid incriminating myself. In the end they decided that another boy and I were guilty because we'd been nearest the window when it broke. I felt that was unfair because four of us had been involved and we all should have taken the blame. When I got home, father was very angry with me and I got a couple of clatters.

JOE WAS THE GOLDEN BOY of the family. It wasn't that mother and father had a favourite, it's just that Joe barely put a foot wrong. He was good at school and he did his little work around the farm efficiently and with less complaining, which meant he was allowed a lot more leeway than me. Martin was a good bit older than us and had a job so he was spared the chores. Vincent was the youngest, so allowances were made for him too.

We learned a lot of useful lessons from father, particularly how to budget and save. Father lived according to the rhythm of the farm, knowing that in times of plenty you put a little something away for the days when there was not so much to spare. Joe took after father and was a saver too. Whenever he had some money he would save every shilling. He opened a bank account at a young age and started building himself a little nest egg. I followed the same routine, mainly because I didn't like looking across at Joe and seeing his pile of savings after I'd spent all my own money.

Joe wasn't tight or mean, but he was sensible, and it was a characteristic I was grateful to have adopted later in life. I saw plenty of riders who signed their first professional contract in the morning and had bought a BMW by the afternoon.

SPORT PLAYED A BIG PART in my life. I played Gaelic football and soccer and I had a competitive spirit that boiled over into the odd punch-up. From an early age I cycled to school on an old steel Raleigh bike. It was black, with straight handlebars and only one gear. The frame was so heavy it could have doubled as our farm's gate but to me it offered freedom and an escape route.

Joe was the first one to take to cycling in a serious way. He moved up to the Christian Brothers school in Carrick and one day they had a visit from the Carrick Wheelers club. He joined the club for a couple of rides at the weekend and found he was good at it.

At some point there was a row in the Carrick Wheelers club and a few guys split off to form a rival organisation. The Irish are never happier than when they are arguing and plotting against each other. Tony Ryan, who was my cycling mentor, and Dan Grant, the father of Linda, who I would later marry, were instrumental in the breakaway. They even pinched the old club's name, calling their new group the Carrick Wheelers Road Club. That was probably just to be provocative.

Joe started to do some local races and was good enough to compete further afield. For a while he showed a good deal of promise, as did Vincent at one time. Of course, whatever Joe did, I wanted to copy. I was always hassling father to let me join in but he'd see me disappearing from the farm on my bike for hours and the list of jobs to be done would keep going up. A number of times he put his foot down and told me that cycling had to come after the farm work was finished.

The problem with the farm was that nothing was ever finished. Even when every animal was fed and watered there was something to clean or mend. Then it was time to start again. As a teenager, I grew resentful of the animals, so dumb and needy. I cleaned up their shite, fed them and then there'd be some more shite to clean up. But father had me lined up to be a farmer. I don't think he ever intended having too much discussion about it but I was having big doubts. I realised I didn't have the patience for farming – not when there were so many other roads to explore.

The idea of making a living from riding a bike didn't occur to me. All sport in Ireland at that time was amateur. Sport was a hobby or a way to pass Sunday afternoon after church. It wasn't a job. Besides, showing a little bit of promise with the Carrick Wheelers didn't mean a thing. When I won the national junior road race in 1972, at the age of 16, father was quietly impressed but being the best junior in Ireland at that time was not exactly an indicator of future greatness.

People wondered where this aptitude for cycling came from. Joe, Vincent and I were all pretty good. We had an uncle Ned, who had been a pretty decent hurler, so the stories went, and there was a cousin who was a good athlete, but the affinity with the bike started with Joe. That said, the capacity for hard work was inherited from our parents.

I left school at 14. My time at Crehana National school was up and it was time to move on. I wasn't academic enough to follow Joe to the Christian Brothers school, so it looked like I'd be going to the technical school in Carrick, where they taught a skill that could be turned into a profession.

After I'd enrolled at the school, but before the first day, father got sick. He went to hospital and they found out he had an ulcer that needed surgery. It meant there'd be no one to work on the farm while he recovered. For five or six weeks, I took the place of father as best I could, working long days. Joe and Vincent chipped in a little but I did the bulk of it.

When father was back to full health, mother said to me: 'Right, tomorrow, you go to school.'

I was defiant. Having missed the first five weeks of the term, there was no way I was going. There was a big debate about it but I refused to budge. I was already not a good scholar; to start five weeks behind everyone else was definitely not something I wanted.

Father chipped in and said that if I left school I had two choices. I could either work full-time on the farm, or get a job.

One of the members of the cycling club, a guy called Martin Wall, got me a job as a bricklayer. I didn't mind the work. It required the same discipline as farming but you could see the rewards of your work. You put one brick down, made sure it was straight, and then placed another brick beside it. At the start of the day there was a pile of bricks and mortar and at the end of it you had a wall.

I stuck at the bricklaying for about 18 months but the cycling was already taking over and broadening my horizons. I knew my future lay elsewhere.

4. Amateur days

Cycling was my escape from the farm and it got me out of Ireland for the first time too. In June 1974, some of the best young riders in Ireland were invited to take a trip to Devon. A stage of the Tour de France was due to be held on the Plympton bypass near Plymouth and there were some races for junior riders being held nearby.

A guy called Frank Smith took us on that trip. We got the ferry from Dun Laoghaire to Holyhead and then squeezed ourselves, restless and hot, into the back of the car for the long drive to the south west of England.

We didn't pull up any trees at the races, that's for sure. We were so green. Usually the races in Ireland only had 20 or 25 riders, now we were up against fields of 70. The races we did at home were unsophisticated – we were very aggressive and tried to smash each other to pieces until the strongest guy won. We quickly found there was a bit more to bike racing than that.

Cycling was never on television in Ireland so we had no idea about tactics. The newspapers covered the Irish races, such as the Rás Tailteann, which was a big deal for the amateur riders. You might get a line in the paper saying that Eddy Merckx had won the Tour de France for the fourth time but that would be it, so my knowledge of the big Classics and tours was limited to what we read in the pages of the English magazine, *Cycling*.

Someone in the Carrick Wheelers would get hold of a copy which would have taken about three weeks to get across the Irish Sea. If you weren't quick it could be another week before it was your turn to have a look. I wasn't a great reader but I could sit for a while with a copy of *Cycling* and soak it all in.

Going to England by boat to race our bikes and seeing the Tour de France while we were there was so exciting to us but just getting out of Ireland for a few days was an adventure. I was keen to see what else life had to offer. Staying in a little bed and break-fast and ordering a full English breakfast in the morning made it feel like the holiday of a lifetime.

The sheer size of the Tour de France was mind-boggling, although you have to bear in mind that to a boy from Carrick the county fair seemed like a big deal. But I cannot honestly say I imagined one day being a part of the Tour.

The Tour de France was visiting England to promote a new ferry route between Plymouth and Roscoff. The businesses in Brittany saw the Tour as an opportunity to promote their trades to the English. It wasn't just the race that left an impression but everything that surrounded it. The cars had horns that sounded like they came from another world. And the vehicles that followed the bunch of cyclists was incredible. Later, of course, I realised that this was the publicity caravan – a fleet of cars and trucks advertis-ing all manner of exotic things. The companies being promoted were probably just like the businesses we had at home but it was all so different.

The trucks passed one by one until one grabbed our attention. It was full of pretty French girls throwing things to the spectators. We were more interested in the girls than what they were throwing but a load of strange-looking vegetables landed at our feet.

I know now that they were artichokes but at the time I had never seen one. We didn't grow artichokes on our farm. We looked at each other, wondering what the hell we were supposed to do with them, then one of the guys took a bite out of one like it was an apple.

Then came the race itself. The Tour de France was captivating. The pack of cyclists whizzed by, all in their brightly coloured jerseys on their gleaming, modern bikes. The whole thing certainly got my heart beating. But riding the Tour de France was beyond a fantasy for me. It seemed totally out of my reach. Being a good junior in Ireland was a world away from this.

I'VE ALWAYS BEEN MORE of a listener than a talker and in those days I did about 99 per cent listening. That's just the way I was. There's a story that has followed me around for years: that I once nodded in response to a question I was asked during a radio interview. I don't remember the incident, and it's probably one of those things that sounded so good it grew into a myth, but it does sum me up well. I found that I learned more from listening than I did from talking. I was also quite observant. In the races I tried to pay attention to the way the stronger riders moved. What did they do that made them better than me? By copying the good ones I began to improve.

In a very small way I began to make a name for myself. Winning the Irish junior championships seemed very important at the time but you couldn't escape the fact that only one rider from Ireland had ever gone to Europe and made a success of it, and that was Shay Elliot, who had an almost God-like status. There was no way I could put myself in the same bracket.

Towards the end of 1974 I began to make a few steps forward in the races at home but the level of competition in Europe was still daunting. We went to Munich for a junior championship and there were 150 riders on the start line. It was extremely intimidating. The start was like a stampede of buffalos and for the first 20 kilometres there were crashes everywhere. More than once I had my foot out of the toestraps and my heel on the floor trying to skid to a halt before I rode into a pile of guys and their bikes.

Another trip to Poland ended up being a waste of time. We didn't get any further than London. On the flight from Dublin to London someone had a newspaper and the guy from the Irish Cycling Federation looked at the classified results in the sports pages and noticed that the race we were flying out for had already happened. We landed in London and got the next flight home.

By 1975 I had become a regular in the Irish amateur team. We did the Girvan, a three-day stage race held in Scotland over the Easter weekend, as preparation for the Tour of Britain, one of the biggest amateur races in the world, which was sponsored by the Milk Marketing Board and known as the Milk Race. It was a fortnight long and the stages could be very difficult. The riders from the Soviet Union, East Germany, Czechoslovakia and Poland were strong enough to race as professionals – it was only the Iron Curtain that prevented them.

The Irish were minnows in comparison. And sometimes we didn't help ourselves. Irish cycling has always been a political world, divided into factions, often split along family lines. However, everyone more or less put their differences aside at the Milk Race. It was at the Tour of Ireland where war sometimes broke out.

Some of my team-mates in the Irish team were very good and some were horrible. There was a split in the middle of the team, with the McQuaid clan on one side and the Lally clan on the other. There were Pat and Keiron McQuaid, and Tony and Sean Lally, and I was in the middle, although I had one foot in the McQuaid camp partly because Jim McQuaid, the Irish team manager, had always been very supportive to me and partly because Pat took me under his wing.

Pat had the gift of the gab and he won friends easily with his charm but he was also a dominant character who had something to say about everything. Unlike a lot of fellows who did a lot of talking, it wasn't all blather. He was an experienced rider who had been around a bit and knew how the races worked.

The 1975 Milk Race was the first time anyone outside Ireland took notice of me. The race started the day after my 19th birthday and the opening few stages were a real education. The racing was tougher than anything I'd done before. Stage seven from Southport to Sheffield was a real killer: almost a hundred miles over Saddleworth Moor and Holme Moss, two back-breaking climbs in the Pennines, and on to Norfolk Park in Sheffield.

I got into a breakaway with a couple of very strong riders. One was Bernt Johansson, a Swede who was one of the favourites to win the race overall and who went on to win the road race at the Olympics the following year. The other was a Pole called Jan Trybala. We were away for a long time and had a big enough lead over the pack that we knew well before we arrived in Sheffield that we could fight out the finish between us.

On the run-in, I missed a few turns at the front. I was starting to feel tired but I was also trying to save the energy I did have for the sprint. Jim McQuaid rode up alongside me on a motorbike – the team managers often used motorbikes instead of cars in those days – and told me to stop co-operating with the other two.

Johansson and Trybala seemed to think the stage was between them anyway. As they took turns on the front, I sat in their slip-stream. They had a brief chat among themselves and although I couldn't hear what they were saying, it seemed that they had things carved up between them. Johansson stood to inherit the yellow jersey, so the logical arrangement was that Trybala could take the stage victory.

As we came into the park, I got on to Trybala's wheel. Johansson tried to bully me but I put my head down and attacked hard.

Despite the fatigue, I managed to hold on to win the stage, which didn't go down too well with the others. My rewards were a pint of ice cold milk, a bouquet of flowers and the threat of a smack in the mouth. Neither Johansson nor Trybala were happy with me but I kept my response short. Two words did it.

I can understand why they weren't happy. They didn't like the fact the Paddy had sat behind them before sprinting past them at the finish but my defence was that my team manager had told me not to work. It wasn't my fault that they underestimated me.

I rode well throughout the second week, even though I was getting tired as the race went on. With one stage to go, I was still lying third overall and looked set to finish on the podium.

Johansson was leading, and was out of my reach, but third place in the Milk Race would be seen as an extraordinary result back in Ireland.

The 12th and final stage was about 100 miles long, taking us from Morecambe to Blackpool. I punctured after 25 miles, just as the race was starting to heat up.

A couple of my team-mates stopped with me to help pace me back to the bunch once I'd had my wheel changed.

The problems started with a difficult wheel change. The rubber brake block was knocked out of position and it took a min-ute or so to get it sorted.

When I did get going, I realised my brake blocks were rubbing on the rim of the wheel, so I had to stop again to sort it out. Then my gears slipped on the climb and I fell. While all this was happening the bunch was getting away from us.

The course that day was very hard, up and down all the time, so it was hard to close the gap to the bunch.

Eventually I realised it was a hopeless cause. We didn't even reach the back of the convoy of cars following the bunch, which would at least have given us a chance to shelter in their slipstream for a while and catch our breath. Instead we battled on with empty road ahead of us.

By the time I arrived on the seafront in Blackpool I was ten minutes behind and had plummeted down the overall standings. A remarkable result turned into an anonymous one. It was very deflating because I was 19 and I had no idea what my career had in store. For all I knew, that could have been the best it ever got.

When I got back to Ireland there was quite a fuss. People were starting to talk about the Olympic Games, which were due to be held in Montreal the following year. My place in the Irish team seemed certain and people had started suggesting that I could go there and get a good result, perhaps even win a medal.

Later that summer, at the Tour of Ireland, the harmony in the Irish team was shattered. Racing on home soil, with Olympic places at stake, intensified the internal fighting. The rivalry between the McQuaids and the Lallys always simmered away but that week it boiled over.

Pat was wearing the yellow jersey when one of our riders, Alan McCormack, decided to pour fuel on an already volatile situation by attacking. The Lallys then refused to help chase so it was left to the rest of us to drag McCormack back.

By this time, Pat probably saw me as being one of his boys and that led to an offer that was to change the course of my entire career.

5. I'm Alan Owen

The 1975 Rapport Tour

One evening, a couple of days from the end of the Tour of Ireland, Pat and Keiron McQuaid came to my room with an idea. At the end of the season, we were going to ride the Rapport Toer in South Africa. It was hard ten-day stage race at the beginning of October that would help us prepare for the Olympic Games. While everyone else was winding down for winter, we would be racing on in the sunshine. The Rapport Toer would prolong our season, enabling us to rack up more racing miles, and it would shorten the winter.

There was only one snag.

Racing in South Africa was against the rules because of an international agreement that barred sportspeople from competing in the country in protest at the apartheid regime there. South Africa was split in two. Blacks and whites. I didn't follow politics but even I knew the word 'apartheid'. I also knew that if we got caught in South Africa, we'd be in trouble.

Pat was always a good salesman and he made the trip sound very attractive. He made his pitch while I listened. The weather would be great, all our expenses would be covered and the organisers had promised us a minibus and a string of free hotel rooms so we could go on a week's holiday afterwards.

Pat said we'd never get found out because we'd be racing under false names.

Famous last words.

We weren't the first people to go from Europe to South Africa to race. A Scottish rider called John Curran had been the year before, and the organisers invited him to put together a 'British' team. The team would be Curran, another Scottish rider called Henry Wilbraham, and three Irishmen – Pat and Keiron McQuaid and me.

I'd weighed things up and, convinced that we wouldn't get found out, decided to be part of the plot. In the mid-1970s, South Africa was a very, very long way from rural Ireland. News travelled much more slowly than now and, if we were racing under false names, who could possibly find out?

I wasn't totally without reservations but I didn't wrestle with my conscience for long before deciding to go to South Africa. I didn't know a lot about the situation there. I didn't sit down in the evenings to watch the news on television and I rarely read the papers, other than the sports pages. I certainly wouldn't have gone to the library in Carrick to read up on South African history and its politics. None of that was my business. For me, it was a bike racing trip.

To start with we kept everything secret, but gradually I told a couple of people in the club, and then my brother Joe.

Joe's reaction was what convinced me it would be okay.

'You're mad,' he said. 'You'll never get away with it.'

Joe always walked straight down the line, never straying one way or the other. He was naturally cautious, so his concern was almost an endorsement.

Mother and father were much more worried and tried to stop me from going. They were worried more about the danger than breaking the rules. Mother feared she'd never see me again.

Although the risk of being discovered seemed very slim, we still had to be careful about our plans. If anyone at the Irish Cycling Federation found out, we'd be in trouble before we even got on the plane. The McQuaids and I were in line for a place on the Irish team at the Olympic Games, so we couldn't just disappear off the face of the earth for three weeks without being noticed.

If anybody asked, we were off to Spain to train in the last of the warm weather before winter set in.

The final race before our adventure was on the last Sunday of September, in Enniscorthy. Everything was perfectly planned. Dan Grant took me to the race with my suitcase in the car boot. After the race, I went back to Dan's car and we drove a little further to meet Jim McQuaid. I put my bike and suitcase in Jim's car and we headed to Dublin to stay at the McQuaids' house for the night.

The following morning we got on a flight from Dublin to London before going on to Paris and finally Johannesburg. We were almost rumbled before we'd got out of Europe. A Scottish cycling official called Gerry McDaid was on the flight. Everyone knew Gerry because he was a judge at a lot of the amateur races. Fortunately we were scattered throughout the plane so McDaid didn't work out what was going on.

THE FIRST THING I NOTICED when we stepped off the plane in Johannesburg was how strong the sun felt on my face. The second thing to hit me was that I was short of breath because Johannesburg is at an altitude of 5,700 feet, which I had not experienced before.

And as we walked into the terminal building I noticed what apartheid really meant. The baggage handlers were black. The people mopping the toilet floor were black. All the passengers waiting in the departure lounge were white, as were the girls behind the check-in desks.

We were taken to a huge house owned by one of the men who sponsored the Rapport Toer and we stayed there a few days before the race started. We were told which roads we could train on and where it might not be safe. We stayed in the wealthier white areas and saw only glimpses of how the black people lived.

On the one hand there was such a lot to take in. I'd never seen anything like it. But on the other, I just accepted what I saw. This was how life was in South Africa. We lived our way in Ireland, they lived another way here. What was I going to do to change it?

THE FIVE OF US WERE to ride for a team sponsored by Mum for Men, which was a brand of deodorant spray. A couple of days before the race we were introduced to our team manager, Tommy Shardelow, a British ex-pat.

The organisers of the race knew that riders from outside South Africa risked getting into trouble if they were discovered taking part, so they were happy for us to be assigned false names.

Tommy told me my new name was Alan Owen. Pat was Jim Burns. We were told to refer to each other by our false names but I felt uncomfortable because I wasn't sure I'd remember what everyone was supposed to be called. I decided to keep it simple and avoid using names at all. I didn't talk much anyway, so nobody would notice any difference.

Tommy used our false names because as far as he was concerned that was who we were. He didn't know 'Sean Kelly' he knew 'Alan Owen'. Several times he called me Alan but I was ignoring him because I didn't realise straight away that he was talking to me.

We weren't the only riders from Europe there. The race was very popular with the French amateur clubs. Jean-François Pescheux, who is now part of the organisation that runs the Tour de France, was there, as was the American Jock Boyer of the Paris club ACBB, who rode with me on the Sem team years later.

From a sporting point of view, the Rapport Toer was fantastic. It was well organised and the stages were competitive. The hotels were more luxurious than anything I'd ever experienced and the countryside was stunning. We'd leave one town, race through the plains for a couple of hours and finish in another town. The alternative was training in the Irish drizzle. No comparison. Jim Burns, aka Pat McQuaid, won two stages and Alan Owen was eighth overall. Everything went perfectly.

Well, almost perfectly.

It was in Port Elizabeth that we ran into a spot of trouble. We had no idea that a journalist from the Daily Mail in London had been sniffing around the race.

Two British movie stars, Elizabeth Taylor and Richard Burton, were spending their second honeymoon in South Africa and had a huge press pack following their every move. They'd been to the game reserves and diamond mines and were now on their way to Port Elizabeth.

I later found out the journalist from the Mail was called John Hartdegen. He had spotted that a British team was taking part in a cycling race in South Africa and thought it might make a story.

One morning Tommy told us that a British journalist had been asking questions about us so we kept a low profile for a couple of days. But the journalist was persistent and asked if he could take a photograph of the Mum for Men team.

I didn't know this until later but Tommy had rounded up a group of five other riders and tried to convince the journalist that they were the Mum for Men team he wanted to photograph.

The journalist wasn't fooled because someone had spoken with a South African accent.

We didn't know it but over the next couple of days the journalist asked a photographer to get a snap of each of us in our Mum for Men jerseys. He then sent the photographs back to the British Cycling Federation to find out who the mystery riders were.

And that was when the game was up because the BCF identified one of the riders not as Jim Burns but as the Irish Olympic team hopeful Pat McQuaid.

One evening towards the end of the race, Pat called home. His wife said that someone from the Daily Mail had been on the phone asking where Pat was.

The mood was gloomy for an hour or so but Pat was quickly back into salesman's mode. We still had a stage or two to race and a week's holiday to look forward to. So what if we'd been found out? Why worry about it until we got home?

Pat was convinced our punishment would be light. A British rider who'd ridden the Rapport Toer in 1974, Arthur Metcalfe, had been discovered and banned for two years but everyone knew the British were tough on this sort of thing. He said that French riders who had raced in South Africa before had been suspended for a handful of weeks – a ban they served during the winter when there weren't any races anyway.

We were certain the Irish Cycling Federation would be lenient. They surely wouldn't weaken their chances of getting a result at the Olympic Games. At worst, we'd get a slap on the wrists.

The race finished and we headed off in the minibus for a tour round the game reserve at Kruger Park and into Swaziland. It was an unforgettable experience and for a few days we pushed to the back of our minds worries about what might await us.

The story got out and made quite a splash so we returned to Ireland by the back door and braced ourselves.

Mother was relieved I had got home in one piece. Father told me that I'd known the consequences of getting caught and now I'd have to face them, which was quite true.

Apparently the newspapers had been quite critical of us but I didn't read them.

For a while, nothing happened. Then a letter arrived at the club, addressed to me, informing me I was to be banned, although I'd be allowed to race again in early April.

John Lackey, the Irish team manager, selected me for the Tour of the North in Northern Ireland at Easter. It was my first race back and I won it. Everything was on course for Montreal.

Then it got political and they told us we were banned from the Olympic Games. I didn't find out why the case was re-opened or why they decided to punish us again.

I've often been asked what it felt like to miss the Olympics. At the time it was disappointing but there was no use shedding any tears about it. I had made the decision to travel to South Africa and I knew that there was a chance the consequences might be serious if we were caught. Nothing I did or said would change the decision to bar me from Montreal, so there wasn't any point wasting energy fighting it.

But there were times when I regretted missing the Games. I was still young and I had no idea how my career was going to turn out. The Olympics could have been the making of me – after all, it was Bernt Johansson who won the gold medal, and he was the one I'd outwitted in Sheffield to win a Milk Race stage.

Had I gone to Montreal and finished in the first ten I might have been tempted to remain as an amateur for another four years in the hope of winning a medal in 1980. Instead, the suspension forced my hand and set me on the path to France and, eventually, a professional career.

You could argue that going to South Africa was not so much the end of an Olympic dream but the start of something bigger.

6. Metz

1976

The Olympic Games were off the agenda so I had to work out an alternative. All the strongest amateur clubs were based in France, so I knew I had to go there. It wasn't that I was thinking of it as a stepping stone towards a professional contract but it was a move up from racing in Ireland.

I was still working on a building site in Ireland, which meant my bike spent days at a time propped against the wall at home. If I went to France, I would have the time to dedicate myself to cycling and see how much progress was possible.

I knew there would be opportunities for me. After I'd ridden the junior World Championships in 1975, a man called Alain Steinhof from Velo Club Metz-Woippy approached me and gave me his card. He said there was a place for me at his club any time I wanted it. I hadn't called.

John Lackey, the Irish team manager, and Johnny Morris, who was involved in cycling in Britain, had contacts all over the place and they followed up the lead for me. They got in touch with the president of VC Metz-Woippy, Aldo Bevigniani.

We agreed that I would go to Metz, in north-eastern France in June 1976, straight after the Milk Race, and spend the second half of the season there.

Breaking the news to my parents, mother in particular, was extremely tricky. I was never one for making grand announcements and we didn't talk things through in our house. Instead, important matters simmered away on the stove.

I knew they wouldn't be in favour of me going to France so, over a number of weeks, I softened them up. They could see no future in cycling. They wanted me to concentrate on my job on the building site and make a career for myself, although they accepted that cycling was taking over my life. The trips away with the Irish team and the stage races meant I was doing more racing than bricklaying. I was more interested in building form than houses.

I broke it to my parents gradually. I told them I was going to Britain for the Milk Race and then slipped in that I'd been invited to do some races in France afterwards. I made it sound like a short trip rather than tell them the plan was to stay there until the autumn. My plan was to get away with the minimum of fuss and discussion then, if it worked out well, call them to say I was staying a little while longer. There was no point making a big deal about it because there was a chance I might be on a plane home after a fortnight if I didn't measure up.

Mother asked a lot of questions. 'Where will you stay? What will you do for money? What will you eat? You can't survive on boiled egg and beans on toast for breakfast, lunch and supper.'

Father's objections were purely practical too. He knew my head wasn't in the clouds, dreaming of riches and stardom but he simply couldn't see a future for me in cycling. He urged me to stick at the bricklaying and get some qualifications, then I could continue with cycling once I had something solid to fall back on. These were reasonable enough concerns. They weren't in favour of the idea but they didn't tell me not to go.

I didn't have the answers to a lot of their questions but the uncertainty of what I was about to experience didn't worry me the way it would have concerned my father. I was quite happy to take whatever came my way. Father would have wanted some guarantees. Every time the subject came up at home, which was often, I gave them the spiel and said whatever needed to be said to stop them worrying about me.

Before I went to France, I rode the Milk Race for the second time. The opening week was unspectacular for me. The whole Irish team was not performing well. The evening before the sixth stage from Birmingham to Stoke-on-Trent, our manager Jim McQuaid offered £20 to the first Irishman to win a stage. The next day, with visions of that big, crisp note dancing before my eyes, I outsprinted the Polish rider Ryszard Szurkowski.

Once the Milk Race was over, I flew straight to Luxembourg where someone from Velo Club Metz-Woippy picked me up and took me to my new home.

VC Metz-Woippy took its name from the two neighbouring towns and was the dominant amateur club in the north-eastern region. The team's best riders competed in most of the top amateur races in France. Bevigniani, the club's president, was originally from Italy and he was passionate about cycling. He owned a transport company that sponsored the club but the cycling team fired his enthusiasm more than his business. He was a frustrated *directeur sportif* – the team manager who directs the riders in the races.

My home was some office space above the headquarters of another of the club's sponsors, a building firm on the outskirts of Metz. It was an empty office with some chipboard partitions put up to make some rooms. The best thing going for it was that it was rent-free. I lived there with a couple of riders from New Zealand. They had been in Metz since the start of the year and so they knew the lie of the land and the best places to train.

There was a small kitchen and a little bathroom but we couldn't escape the fact we were living in an office. We didn't have any blinds or curtains so we hung some bedsheets across the big plate-glass windows. They didn't do a great job of blocking out the light but at least that meant we were always up early for training.

Arriving in June was perfect for me. I was already race-fit after the Milk Race, the weather was great and the programme was packed. Through June, July and August I could race three times a week without any difficulty.

The two Kiwis had settled in okay but they hadn't made a great deal of effort learning to speak French so they were a bit cut off from the rest of the club's riders.

Living with a couple of guys who spoke English made it a lot easier for me to settle in, even though I was never really homesick. I spoke so little, it didn't really matter whether I knew the language or not. I was there to race, to win some money and do enough to avoid being sent home.

The standard of racing in France was high. Much higher than back at home. And the style of racing was something I was not used to either. Most of our races were criteriums – fast circuit races held in a town or village.

I learned quickly how to win money. We were paid a small allowance by the club, which was enough to eat well enough at home but not to go out to restaurants. That was probably deliberate. They paid us enough to live but not enough to indulge. That kept us lean, hungry and sober. There was no point giving us the cash so we could get a taste for rich food or beer.

Almost all our allowance money was spent on living expenses so the prizes we won in races made a big difference. In the bigger events and the stage races, we would pool all the winnings and divide it between the riders in the team. But the cash we won at the criterium races went straight in the back pocket. And me being a keen saver, that definitely sharpened my senses.

Winning races was good for the bank balance but often there was a wait before getting the money because the race organiser paid it to the French Cycling Federation, which then paid it on to the club, who would then pass it on to the rider. It could be six or eight weeks between winning a race and getting the money.

But if a rider won an intermediate sprint prize he got paid at the end of the night. Often there were two or three sprints per race, with prizes put up by the local butcher or baker. These intermediate sprints were called *primes*. Sometimes the money on offer for winning three *primes* was more than the prize for winning the actual race, so I quickly realised they were worth going for. Not only could I win more money but I'd get to take the cash home.

I learned fast. One word at a time, I picked up some French. The phrases that came to me first were the ones that could help me in the races.

My French team-mates pointed out which riders I needed to keep an eye on and I'd check with them when the sprint laps were coming up.

I'd see the board at the side of the road and notice the speed increase but to make sure I'd check with a team-mate.

'Sprint prime?'

'Oui.'

That was how I earned the nickname Monsieur Sprint Prime.

They liked to have a joke with the foreigners but I only fell for it once when they shouted at me to sprint for a non-existent prize at the end of one lap.

Some nights I'd head home with a fistful of francs. Officially, we were amateurs but from day one I made a good living with my prize money, the club's allowance and a healthy bonus system. During the first half-season in Metz, I won 15 races. The club was happy with me because I was winning and my team-mates were happy because they often got a share of the spoils. One of the club's members ran a butcher's shop and more than once, after a big victory, we were treated to some fine cuts of meat, which we'd take back to our makeshift flat and cook.

Life was simple. Being an amateur with one of the top clubs in France meant I could live almost like a professional would. I didn't have to work and so there was little to worry about except racing and training. And all the while, I was saving enough money to make father and Joe proud of me.

It can be tough to leave home and live away from everyone and everything you know but I never found it a problem. There weren't any mobile phones or computers in those days and we didn't have a phone in our office either. I wasn't one for writing letters – it might take me a fortnight to finish one – so weeks could go by without me being in touch with people at home.

Before I left Ireland, I had become friendly with Linda Grant so I'd cycle over to Bevigniani's office to use the phone and make a call back to Linda or to the family. Bevigniani's secretary, a girl called Annie, spoke good English and she would make the call for me and give me the phone.

I'd ring my brother Martin, who lived in a building at the top end of the farm and had a phone extension down to the farmhouse so he could put me through to mother.

I reassured mother and father that everything was going well, that I was eating well and being looked after. I didn't have to embellish my tales of life in Metz although I'm not sure father believed me when I told him how many hundreds of pounds I'd won racing my bike.

At the end of August I returned home to ride the Tour of Ireland. The opening stage went from Dublin to Kilkenny and passed within about 20 miles of my parents' farm so they came to the hotel after the stage to say hello. I thought it was going to be awkward telling them I was going straight back to France after the race but they seemed to have accepted it. I had a speech prepared about how the club's president was relying on me because we had some big races coming up but I didn't have to use it. A few people associated with the cycling club in Carrick had told them how well I was doing, so a lot of their initial worries had eased.

Before I left Metz, Bevigniani asked me if there were any other riders from Ireland who might fancy a place on the team for the following season. Pat McQuaid won the Tour of Ireland for the second year in a row and I suggested that he come out with me.

Bevigniani loved cycling, and Italian cycling in particular. He was brought up on the exploits of the great Fausto Coppi and he loved the history of the sport. I knew almost nothing about the history of the sport except what I had learned from the pages of cycling magazines. Living in France, I had begun to understand their obsession with the Tour de France. That July I watched the race on television for the first time and saw just how much the French amateur riders dreamed of taking part.

I still knew little about the other big races such as the Classics so I didn't appreciate the importance of the Giro di Lombardia – the Tour of Lombardy.

Bevigniani changed that. He had grown up in the Lombardy region and he used his contacts to get Velo Club Metz-Woippy an invitation to the amateur Tour of Lombardy. It was quite rare for foreign teams to take part in the race at that time.

The race was held in northern Italy, near Lake Como. The professional race was one of the most prestigious Classics and the amateur equivalent was seen as a place to spot some potential talent for the future. We travelled to Italy by car and stayed in a farmhouse belonging to a member of Bevigniani's family. We trained in the hills for a couple of days and ate pasta for dinner.

Since I'd moved to Metz, I'd become friendly with Romain Hilger, a rider from Luxembourg who spoke excellent English. He was in his mid-twenties but still believed it was not too late to turn professional. He was experienced, compared to many of the riders in the amateur ranks, and he knew who the riders to watch would be. In the days leading up to the race, he gave me a crash course in tactics and told me a bit about the top Italian, Dutch and Belgian riders who would be among the favourites to win.

I woke up on the morning of the race and pulled back the shutters to see proper Paddy weather. The rain was hammering down. On the way to the start, a lot of the roads were flooded.

Once we started the race, we went through some huge puddles. I looked down and the water was level with my bottom bracket and my feet went underwater as I pedalled.

The race was long for the amateurs – almost 200 kilometres and with lots of hills – but the weather seemed to galvanise my spirit. I felt good all day and when the attacks started, I managed to follow the best riders.

It was a day for the tough guys, a real war of attrition. Every time I looked behind, we'd lost another half dozen riders. Towards the end of the race, there were only 25 of us left at the front.

On the final hill, a Dutchman accelerated. Hilger had warned me to watch the Dutch so when a couple of Italians followed him I knew I had to go too. I later found out the Dutchman was called Henk Lubberding, who went on to have a fine professional career. It took a lot of effort to drag myself up to them so when I reached them, I tried to save a bit of energy for the sprint.

I won the race and when I crossed the line Bevigniani was the first to get to me. He was beside himself, going absolutely crazy. He was more excited than I was but it meant a lot more to him than it did to me. It was a big race but it was just another race. For Bevigniani to go home and win the Tour of Lombardy was huge.

I liked Bevigniani a lot, even though we couldn't talk much. My French was still very poor and he had almost no English. I felt at home in Metz and before I returned to Ireland for the winter I promised to return the following year.

There had been rumours that some of the professional teams

were interested in signing me, particularly after the Tour of
Lombardy, but I didn't feel ready. I was still only 20 and had only
been an amateur in France for half a season.

Bevigniani promised to look after me. He doubled my allowance and offered good bonuses if I won some of the bigger races.

My mind was made up. I'd return to Metz early in 1977 and
continue my education. And that was what I was going to do, until
a visitor came calling at the farm.

7. The Viscount

Monsieur de Gribaldy

I didn't know Jean de Gribaldy but I knew the name. Everyone in cycling knew the name. He was the Matt Busby of French cycling, with a reputation for spotting the best young riders and making them into champions.

Romain Hilger, my team-mate at Velo Club Metz-Woippy, had said that De Gribaldy had been asking about me. My victory in the amateur Tour of Lombardy had attracted the attention of a few professional teams but De Gribaldy was keen to get to me first.

When someone goes to the effort and expense of chartering a plane to take him from north-eastern France to Dublin, then asks a taxi to take him 100 miles into the Irish countryside and leaves the meter running while he conducts negotiations, you know he means business.

De Gribaldy was a respected and revered directeur sportif. One of the greatest. As a professional rider he was not a champion. His own racing career had been modest. He rode for the Peugeot team after the war as a domestique. That meant he spent most of his time working for others. It was as a team manager that he had earned his great reputation. He was known for spotting raw talent and nurturing it. He saw Joaquim Agostinho, a 27-year-old racing undiscovered in Portugal, and turned him into the rider who twice finished third in the Tour de France.

And De Gribaldy was known as a disciplinarian.

I knew that several teams were interested in signing me but I did not expect anyone to go to the lengths De Gribaldy went to.

I had spent the winter at home in Ireland, working on the farm, catching up with Linda and riding my bike ready for another season in Metz. I was happy to do another year as an amateur.

I did a bit of work for Martin, who had started a small agricultural business, renting machines to farmers and spreading muck on their land for them. I agreed to work a couple of days a week for him, mostly because I enjoyed driving the tractors.

One day in early December I was on my way back from collecting a muck-spreading tank from a farm on the other side of Carrick when I saw a taxi coming towards me.

I was taking up a lot of the road in my tractor but the taxi didn't pull over, instead it stopped in front of me. I thought they might be lost and needed directions.

Two men got out. One of them was wearing a pilot's uniform and the older man was wearing a suit that made him look like a gangster. They were from France. The pilot asked me, in English, if I was Sean Kelly, the cyclist. He then introduced me to Jean de Gribaldy and asked if we could all go back to the farm to talk.

Whatever must mother have thought when they had turned up at the farmyard earlier looking for me? She probably thought I'd done something terrible in France and that justice had turned up on the doorstep.

There were three visitors. De Gribaldy was wearing a pinstripe suit and perfectly polished shoes. His hair was always wavy and Brylcreemed and his glasses hung on a chain round his neck. The pilot had flown the plane from Dole airport, near De Gribaldy's home in Besançon. He was also the only one of the three who spoke English. The third man was a French rider called Noel Converset, who had been with me at the club in Metz.

And there was me, in muck-splattered jeans and Wellington boots.

De Gribaldy had an imposing presence and he said he was determined not to leave Ireland until I'd agreed to join his team.

That team was the Flandria squad, one of the biggest and best in Europe. Their most famous rider was Freddy Maertens, the Belgian who was world champion. They had two other top Belgian riders called Michel Pollentier and Marc Demeyer.

De Gribaldy explained that Flandria was expanding and splitting in two. The top Belgians would form a powerful, world-class group under the direction of another legendary manager, Guillaume Driessens, who was known as Lomme. De Gribaldy would be in charge of a fleet of young riders, most of them French. He wanted me to join the French half of the team, move to Besançon and learn the life of a professional.

I was impressed by De Gribaldy but I was reluctant. I had a nice arrangement in Metz, where I was learning without pressure, and I'd given Bevigniani my word I'd stay with him for another year.

De Gribaldy handed over to Converset to give me the hard sell. He began rabbiting on about the Tour de France and 'Freddy Maertens, champion du monde'. Converset's head was always full of dreams. I'd raced with him as an amateur and he was like a wild horse. You had to tie him up or he'd run off. But I didn't see life through starry eyes. I didn't think I was ready for that world.

De Gribaldy said that the Flandria set-up would be the perfect start to a professional career. There would be no pressure at first, I wouldn't be expected to win races and I would be spared the toughest races until I was ready. He said he wanted me to develop, not burn out.

I told him I wanted time to think about it so De Gribaldy got back in his taxi and went back to France without my signature on his contract.

A couple of days later, he telephoned and I stalled him again. Then he rang and offered more money. I wasn't haggling over money. I thought another year as an amateur would be better for me in the long run.

I knew I could win the biggest amateur races and I was unsure how big a jump it would be to the professional ranks. All I knew was that it would be harder and I'd have a completely different job. A lot of my time would be spent working for other riders.

Professional cycling was quite different back then. It was a much smaller world than it is now, so turning pro was a risk. There were only about 20 elite teams, of which 13 or 14 would get a place at the Tour de France. If I failed to make the grade with one of those teams, my career could be over within two years.

Very few teams took a chance on a rider who had failed to take his opportunity with one of the others. There weren't any second chances. So I preferred the idea of staying in Metz and becoming stronger so I was better equipped to turn professional.

I didn't interpret De Gribaldy's persistence as a show of faith in my abilities. In the end, it was a conversation during a Carrick Wheelers club ride just before Christmas that convinced me.

Someone asked me whether I was going to accept the offer from Flandria and I said that I was heading back to Metz.

'Why? This is the opportunity of your life. If you turn it down now, who's to say the chance will come your way again?'

So, the next time De Gribaldy called, I told him I would sign for his Flandria team but that I wanted time to break the news to Bevigniani first.

I was never confident on the telephone but the thought of making this call petrified me. I left it and left it but eventually I picked up the phone. I rang Annie, Bevigniani's secretary, and asked her to pass on the message. I could hear her telling Bevigniani and I could hear him telling Annie to persuade me to stay. I didn't like going back on my word at all but Bevigniani was gracious about it. I passed on my thanks to him and he wished me luck.

A few days later a contract from Flandria turned up in the post together with a list of instructions from De Gribaldy about how I was to spend the rest of the winter. I wasn't expecting a life of glamour but it dawned on me that working for De Gribaldy was going to be like joining the army.

8. Fast learner

Turning professional, 1977

I rode for Jean de Gribaldy for the best part of ten years and he was as intimidating the last time I saw him as he had been the first day we met. I can't think of any occasions when I openly contradicted him. His word was law and I never considered defying him.

As I got older and more experienced, I developed my opinions about things but even then I didn't go up against him head-to-head. There wasn't any point because he had an answer for everything. If you suggested that it might not be a good idea to ride Bordeaux-Paris, a 600-kilometre one-day race that took 18 hours, he'd dismiss you with a wave of his hand and say: 'It was okay for Jacques Anquetil.'

De Gribaldy believed in hard racing, lots of training and eating little. He kept his riders hungry, in a very real sense.

Although he was extremely disciplined he was not a harsh man. He didn't rant and rave, although he might thump his fist on the table if things had gone really badly. But he could get into a terrible mood that lasted hours. It wasn't a demonstrative rage. It was a quiet, controlled anger, which made it even more intimidating. You didn't want to see him get like that.

He was a hard taskmaster. He could tell if riders were cutting corners and he wouldn't tolerate it. But he wasn't a bully and he didn't have unrealistic expectations of his team. He didn't ask riders to do things unless he believed they were capable of them. Often, De Gribaldy's belief in me was greater than my own assessment of my abilities. He drove me on by demanding more.

If a rider made a mistake, he was lenient the first time and would take time to point out where he'd gone wrong. But he wasn't as forgiving the second time. He would accept losing as long as you'd tried your best but he hated shirkers and excuse-makers, and there are plenty of those in cycling. If he thought an excuse was coming, he'd cut you off mid-sentence.

There wasn't anything to be gained from complaining that we were tired, either. De Gribaldy didn't believe in tired. He thought you could maintain peak form for a long time before needing a break. He was old school. Racers raced to get into form, they raced when they were in good form and they kept racing until he said stop.

It is rare for anyone in cycling these days to have the level of authority De Gribaldy had. Nowadays everyone believes that their opinion is right. With De Gribaldy that was certainly not the case. He was always right and as long as riders did as they were told, they were fine.

But he wasn't a monster. The power didn't go to his head. He didn't tell people what to do just because he was the boss. De Gribaldy told his riders what to do because he thought it was what was best for them. He commanded respect because of the results his methods got.

De Gribaldy was cycling's equivalent of royalty. He was from a wealthy background, descended from Italian nobility, which is why he was nicknamed *Le Vicomte* – The Viscount – although his parents had been farmers, which is maybe why he took to me.

I MOVED TO BESANÇON to live in an apartment in the Place de la Revolution, next to De Gribaldy's shop where he sold bikes, mopeds and electrical appliances.

In January 1977, I travelled to Belgium for the Flandria-Velda team's official presentation – a gathering of sponsors, guests and journalists at a restaurant. Nobody paid any attention to me. It was all about Freddy Maertens, Michel Pollentier and Marc Demeyer – three of the biggest stars in Belgium. I realised that winning the amateur Tour of Lombardy meant nothing alongside Maertens in his world champion's rainbow jersey.

From Belgium we went to a little village called Lablachère in the Ardèche region of southern France. You wouldn't find it in the holiday brochures. It was a one-horse town, with no distractions. This was to be the base for our pre-season training camp.

We stayed at a little family-run hotel that De Gribaldy had been going to for years. I headed down to breakfast on the first morning and walked into the dining room where each little table was covered with a red and white checked paper tablecloth. There were bowls for our coffee, a small basket of bread rolls, some jam and a packet of cereal. I chose a seat and sat down. I noticed a greasy crescent-shaped mark had seeped into the tablecloth at each place. It turned out that the hotel owner had given everyone a large, buttery croissant but De Gribaldy had taken them all away before the riders came down.

According to De Gribaldy, pastry and bread were a cyclist's enemy. He taught me to discard the soft, doughy centre of a bread roll and to this day I tear that part out and leave it. His explanation was that the dough sat in the stomach for a long time and was difficult to digest.

Weight was one of his obsessions and in that respect he was years ahead of his time. He didn't need a rider to get on the scales; he could tell just by looking at them that they needed to lose a few pounds. At that time I was stocky and well built. Working on the farm and the building site meant I'd put on a good bit of muscle. I probably weighed close to 12 stone, which to De Gribaldy was grossly overweight.

The De Gribaldy diet was hard work but we were given no choice. After a long training ride we were ravenous but the evening meal was tiny. We were allowed a small bowl of soup, some salad leaves without any dressing, mayonnaise or even olive oil, followed by a tiny piece of chicken or beef and a little hillock of rice. There was rarely a dessert but we were sometimes allowed a little piece of cheese suitable for a mouse.

It was always Franche-Comté cheese, from De Gribaldy's home region. Wherever he went, he had a block of it with him. It's very similar to Gruyère and even now, when I taste it, the memories come back.

Every night I got up from the table with my stomach growling.

A couple of times I'd manage to save a roll from breakfast to fill a gap later in the day but usually the rations were so small there weren't any spare. One day during the training camp a few of the younger riders got together, went to the village shop and bought a packet of biscuits. There was Christian Muselet, Marcel Tinazzi and me and we were arguing about who would look after the biscuits because we were terrified of being caught with them.

The training was not as hard as I'd expected. Most of our rides were long and steady. These days the riders try to rip each other's legs off on the hills at the first training camp of the year to show how good they are. The new professionals are always keen to demonstrate that they belong but back then, there was a strict hierarchy to observe. There was no way anyone would dream of showing up Freddy Maertens in training. He was the star, our leader, and we were there to help him get fit for the season.

De Gribaldy didn't discuss many of his thoughts with the riders. He told us what to do and we got on with it. Anything he did share was on a need-to-know basis. He certainly didn't sit down to talk about my race programme for the season. I had no idea what was coming next.

It turned out that my first race as a professional was the Etoile de Bessèges, a five-day stage race held in early February on the south coast of France between Nîmes and Marseille, just down the road from Lablachère. I got stuck in, finishing tenth on the first day and taking third place overall behind two Belgians, Walter Planckaert and Serge Vandaele. Not a bad start.

From Bessèges we went to the Tour of the Mediterranean, where I won my first race as a professional – not that you'll find it listed in any of the record books. One of the stages finished in Marseille and I was in a great position as we came into the final kilometre. As we came to the line, I put my head down and gave it everything. It was very close between Jan Raas and me and I wasn't certain I'd won. Raas was one of the sport's rising stars. The Dutchman was already a renowned sprinter who would go on to win Classics and Tour de France stages, while I was an unknown from Ireland. The race jury gave the victory to Raas.

De Gribaldy was livid because he was certain I'd won. Raas

had put his arms up in a victory salute, which may have swayed the judges.

The organisers explained that there hadn't been a photo finish on the line and that the jury's decision was final. I didn't feel a sense of injustice that I'd been robbed because I wasn't certain I'd won. It wasn't until a few days later that De Gribaldy got his hands on a picture of the finish, taken by one of the press photographers working on the race. It was clear that my front wheel had hit the line ahead of that of Raas. De Gribaldy showed the picture to the head judge and although it wasn't going to change the result it made him feel better. The photo of that finish was pinned to the wall in the kitchen at his shop for years afterwards.

My education continued. I saw at close quarters that the sprinters could be reckless and ruthless and learned that it was a case of eat or be eaten. A couple of days after the sprint finish with Raas I was trying to move up in the final kilometre, hoping to win a stage of the Tour of the Med and leave the jury in no doubt. We were travelling at about 40 miles an hour when I felt someone grab my jersey. It was Charly Rouxel, a French rider, who held me back so that his team-mate could get in front of me. You could grab a good handful of those old, baggy woollen jerseys. If it had happened in an amateur race I'd probably have swung a fist at him but I was the new kid and I didn't feel like I could. After the stage my team-mates confronted him instead.

Straight after the Tour of the Mediterranean we headed to Nice to take an overnight ferry to Corsica. All the riders travelled together and before we boarded the ferry we had a big buffet meal. Quite a few of the guys regretted that because the crossing was hellishly rough. I was not a great traveller but I managed not to be sick. Some guys were really ill and got barely any sleep.

We got off the ferry the next morning feeling really green but had to go straight to the start of the race.

After a rough night on the sea the last thing we needed was the Tour of Corsica, because it was a hard race. The island is hilly and the roads were heavy and rough. Although I didn't win a stage in Corsica, I was riding well and was beginning to get into the rhythm of the professional races.

Following another seven-hour sea crossing from Ajaccio to Nice, five of us from the Flandria team crammed into one of the team's estate cars to drive to Lugano in Switzerland. We put the bikes on the roof, wedged our luggage in the boot and took turns to drive on unlit country roads through the Alps. There wasn't a motorway then. We drove through the night and after my stint at the wheel I tried to get some sleep under a ratty old duvet.

It was about two in the morning when we arrived in Lugano and it took a while to find our hotel because all we had was a piece of paper with the address on it. We had to hammer on the door until someone woke up and let us in. Then we grabbed a few hours' sleep before getting up at six to be ready for the start of the Grand Prix Lugano at eight. The Swiss love an early start.

The race was a handicap event open to amateurs as well as professionals and the field was split into groups according to ability. We set off at intervals, with the pros going last. There were only about 20 of us in the professional group so as soon as the flag dropped we sprinted away and got a very fast pace going, working together, taking turns at the front. Everyone had to do their share of the work and there was no hiding. Little by little, we caught all the riders who had set off before us but it had taken a hard chase.

On the last lap, I got into a move with five others and won the sprint comfortably. The 1977 Grand Prix Lugano was my first official victory as a professional. I wasn't getting carried away but De Gribaldy had been quietly impressed with how I'd settled in.

When I signed for Flandria, De Gribaldy had assured me that my introduction to the professional races would be gradual but he had obviously decided I was strong enough to cope with the step up because when I got back to Besançon, he told me that I had been selected to ride Paris-Nice, one of the most important stage races in France, with the Flandria 'A' team. I would be racing with Maertens, the world champion, Pollentier and Demeyer. As I was about to find out, it was like jumping from kindergarten to university.

LOMME DRIESSENS WAS THE man in charge of the Belgian wing of the Flandria team. He was every bit as intimidating as De

Gribaldy but in a different way. He wasn't as much of a mentor. He regarded his riders as the finished article. He had complete confidence in them to do their jobs and his team talks were simple.

'We've got the world champion and we're the best team in the world. Let's go and prove it.'

Riding for Freddy Maertens was daunting. Making a mistake that ruined my own chances was one thing but messing things up for Freddy was a lot worse.

Suddenly I was expected to know what to do but the truth was that I didn't really have a clue. Marc Demeyer was the captain of the team. He called the shots on the road and he could be a bully. At Paris-Nice he was on my case all day, every day.

Maertens won the prologue in Aulnay-sous-Bois, which meant we had to defend the leader's white jersey right from the start. We had to protect him all day and then prepare the sprint for him. Maertens won three sprints in a row but Demeyer still wasn't happy. He was built like a tank and could ride on the front all day, if necessary, and he expected everyone to be able to do the same.

I wanted to do the best I could but I didn't understand the tactics. I was just trying to avoid getting shouted at. The speed was a lot higher than I'd experienced in the early season races and I felt the weight of expectation that came with the Flandria jersey. The rest of the bunch was looking at us to control the race and set the tempo at the front.

Working for the world champion was special but the effort required was dizzying. I had to go back to the team car to collect bottles. On the climbs, I had to give Maertens or Pollentier a little shove as they went past, to help them save a bit of energy as they moved through the bunch.

One stage finished in Digne, where Eddy Merckx and Patrick Sercu beat Maertens in the sprint. Merckx was the greatest champion cycling had ever seen and Sercu was a terrific sprinter but Demeyer was really annoyed at the finish, saying we hadn't kept the speed high enough on the run-in. My job was to ride at the front when we were about five kilometres from the line and keep going as long as I could.

I swung off the front, exhausted, and the whole bunch flooded past me. I had to fight like crazy to stay with the peloton and I thought I'd done a good job, until Demeyer came up to me after the finish. He said that if I'd had the strength to stay with the bunch I could have done another kilometre on the front.

I didn't really understand the game. Demeyer expected me to sacrifice every last drop of energy for the team leader.

Maertens was a completely different character. Although he was the big star he didn't act like he was above everyone. He was gentler. While Demeyer shouted at me in Flemish and French, Freddy offered encouragement in English. When I helped him, he thanked me. At one point during the race he said: 'Keep going, you're doing well.' The way he treated me left a lasting impression because he didn't have to be nice.

Paris-Nice was on a different level to the events I'd started with. Although the race was only eight days long, they managed to squeeze in 12 stages. On four of the days, we raced a stage in the morning, took a break for lunch and a quick wipe down with a flannel and some eau de cologne, and then raced again in the afternoon, smelling like a cheap perfume factory.

We defended Freddy's lead to the end and he won the final time trial to make sure of overall victory. It had been extremely hard work but it felt very satisfying to justify De Gribaldy's faith in me. I was only 20 years old and had been a professional for six weeks but he had recommended me for Paris-Nice and I hadn't let him down.

I WENT BACK TO Besançon and life settled into a pattern. I'd get up in the morning and go training. We'd drop by De Gribaldy's shop to give him the keys to the apartment. That way he knew we weren't tempted to sneak back early. Sometimes I'd ride with Noel Converset, whose head was still full of fantasies of winning the Tour de France, although his dreams were slowly fading. He was already 26, which was quite late to be taking his first steps as a professional.

We'd train for two or three hours and then stop by the shop to have lunch with De Gribaldy. He'd get one of the shop staff to make us something, or he'd fix lunch himself. Again, this was so he could keep an eye on what we were doing. In the afternoon we'd go for another ride, usually at a very casual pace.

Unlike Converset, I was a realist. I wasn't looking too far ahead and I certainly wasn't getting carried away. Riding myself into the ground for Freddy Maertens had been hard work and even though I had done my job well, it didn't mean I'd made it.

But even I had to recognise that beating Eddy Merckx was quite an accomplishment for a first-year professional, even though by 1977 the Belgian was a declining force.

The Circuit de l'Indre was not a big race. It started in Château-roux in the middle of France and we had to cover a couple of laps of a big circuit before switching to a smaller circuit in the town.

Merckx was almost 33 years old and his career had suffered a steady descent but he still had an overwhelming presence. In his heyday, Merckx ate his rivals alive, which is why he was nicknamed The Cannibal. He'd won virtually everything there was to win, including the Tour de France five times. For almost a decade he stood head and shoulders above everyone else. Finishing second in a race won by Merckx was almost as good as winning.

I doubt he remembers the 1977 Circuit de l'Indre like I do. It wouldn't have been an important race for him. It was a windy day, which meant the bunch split up quite early on. The conditions encouraged some really aggressive racing but despite the attacks and the gaps opening everywhere, I didn't find it hard to stay the right side of every split.

We had about 40 kilometres to race and there were only 20 riders left at the front. Merckx was there, with a couple of team-mates from the Fiat team. On the last lap, I made sure I stayed at the front so I could see exactly what was going on. In the final kilometre, two Fiat riders came past me, with Merckx following right behind. Instinct took over. You didn't need to be a tactical genius to know this was the wheel I had to be on.

I jumped out of the line and latched onto Merckx. I remember thinking: 'For God's sake, don't knock him off.'

With 400 metres to go, the second of Merckx's team-mates swung off the front, leaving Merckx to take up the sprint. The Fiat team had left him with a lot to do but he was still strong. I stuck to his wheel until the last 80 metres when I pulled out of his slipstream, drew level with him and went past.

It was a strange feeling. It almost felt wrong. There was a split-second when I thought: 'Should I pass him?'

But then I saw the line and my heart took over. I went for it and I crossed the line first, ahead of Eddy Merckx.

I went to the podium and accepted the applause and the bouquet of flowers but I felt so awkward with Merckx standing beside me. I didn't dare turn to him. I don't think I even shook his hand, not because I was being rude. I certainly didn't talk to him. What would I have said? 'Bad luck, Eddy.'

So I just waved to the crowd and got off the stage without offending anyone.

Beating Merckx meant a lot to me but it didn't alert the world to my presence. It was just a small race in France and there was barely more than a paragraph in *L'Equipe*, the French sports newspaper.

My confidence was growing and quite quickly I got a lot bolder in the sprints. I learned the tricks and began to assert myself. If my rivals were happy to push and pull me around, I was happy to shove them back.

De Gribaldy told me not to fear the other riders. He told me I was as fast as them. I caught on quickly and I remember having to give Patrick Sercu a bit of a nudge in order to beat him to a stage win in the Tour of Romandy in Switzerland that spring. It doesn't take long to fit in.

I didn't ride any of the three grand tours during my first season as a professional but I heard all about the way Maertens dominated the Vuelta a España, winning 13 stages and the race overall, which was an extraordinary achievement. I went back to Ireland for the first couple of weeks of the Tour de France. I had very little idea of what was going on because the race wasn't on television at home. Only when I went back to Besançon did I catch some of it after I'd been out training.

After the Tour, the focus switched to the World Championships, which were to be held in San Cristóbal, Venezuela. We didn't have an Ireland team because I was the only professional rider in the country. Flandria paid for me to go to South America so I could help Maertens in the race.

Before we flew to Venezuela, we rode the Tour of Holland. It suited Maertens and Pollentier to push me into a leadership role while they kept their powder dry for the Worlds. By supporting me, they could get a good week's work done without being in the spotlight.

Having a full-strength Flandria team helping me was a great experience and the race turned into a showdown between us and the powerful Dutch squad, TI-Raleigh.

They won the team time trial and the next day Gerben Karstens, a TI-Raleigh rider, beat me in the sprint. Thanks to time bonuses I was well in contention for overall victory as we came towards the end of the race. Another TI-Raleigh rider, Bert Pronk, was leading by now but I was just behind him and my team-mates thought he might be vulnerable on the hills. The final stage was almost 250 kilometres long and turned into a real dogfight that went over one hill after another. I had the whole Flandria team – including the world champion – driving the pace but Pronk managed to hang on. I had to settle for second place.

In Venezuela, I rode better than any of the other Flandria men riding for the other nations, and finished 16th in a race that lasted over six and a half hours. Already I could tell how much stronger I was than I had been at the start of the season. My first year had exposed me to some of the toughest races and I had survived.

As I prepared to go back to Ireland for the winter, De Gribaldy issued me with a written list of instructions. They were very specific and governed every aspect of life. He told me how much I had to train, how much I could eat and drink and how much sex I could have.

The answers were: a lot, not too much, very little and only if you're lucky.

De Gribaldy also issued a list of foods that were forbidden. There were to be no bananas, no ice cream, fresh cream or chips. Chocolate was to be limited to one or two squares, beer to one small glass every so often. The idea was to keep training and start 1978 lighter than ever before.

The diet wasn't much of a problem. De Gribaldy's rules had been drummed into me all year and my stomach was used to being empty. I did treat myself to chocolate or chips but every time I did I felt guilty and could picture De Gribaldy frowning at me.

Alcohol wasn't a temptation. I wasn't a big drinker and there weren't any nightclubs in Carrick. There might have been a Christmas party but that was about it. De Gribaldy was probably used to handling the French guys who would go home at the end of the season and go totally crazy.

And sex? Well, in Catholic Ireland that wasn't much of a problem either.

De Gribaldy also sent me home with a cyclo-cross bike and told me to ride my road bike for a couple of hours in the morning and then head out into the fields and woods with the cross bike in the afternoons. He said it would improve my bike-handling skills, which I am sure it did, because at the start I fell off a lot and after a month or two I fell off a little bit less.

I was asked to go back to Besançon early. De Gribaldy had lined up a surprise for me – a fortnight of cyclo-cross racing in Switzerland. I was to live on a farm owned by some people he knew, train and then take part in some cyclo-cross races.

That was typical of De Gribaldy and it was precisely why riders didn't consider ignoring his instructions. I could easily have left the cyclo-cross bike in the shed and said, 'Oh yes, I rode it every day,' thinking he would never find out. But De Gribaldy always found out.

Riding in the woods near home was nowhere near adequate preparation for the cyclo-cross races in Switzerland. I got my head smashed in at every race.

The standard was so high. The Swiss had Albert Zweifel and Peter Frischknecht, the gold and silver medallists at the cyclo-cross World Championships for three years in a row. I was completely out of my depth.

De Gribaldy had lined up some decent start money but I felt a fraud accepting it. Well, almost.

I got dropped as soon as the gun went. These guys sprinted as if they were doing the Olympic 100-metre final. I realised that when I'd practiced running with the bike on my shoulder I'd been jogging along.

Within minutes I'd be in oxygen debt with my heart pumping out of my chest. More than once I threw up because of the effort. It was absolutely horrible but De Gribaldy had lined it up so there was no getting out of it.

EVERY MONTH THREW UP a new experience but one of the hardest was when I rode Paris-Roubaix for the first time.

I was at home in Besançon when I got a phone call on Friday morning telling me to get ready to travel north to Compiègne for the start of Paris-Roubaix on Sunday. One of the Flandria riders was sick, and I had to take his place. A mechanic was heading to De Gribaldy's shop to collect a load of reinforced wheels and he would then drive me up to Compiègne.

I had ridden the cobblestones in Belgium, at races like Ghent-Wevelgem, but nothing prepared me for what lay in store at Paris-Roubaix. I didn't even get a sneak preview of the *pavé* before the race because the rest of the team trained on the cobbles on the Friday, while I was travelling there.

My job was simple. I was told to stay with Freddy Maertens for as long as possible. The first section of cobblestones came after about 100 kilometres and as we got closer, the pace increased until it became a furious stampede. It was faster than some of the bunch sprints I'd done.

I was sprinting at full pelt and still riders were coming past me on both sides. And then we hit the cobbles. It sounds like an exaggeration but it was like going over the top. There were bodies everywhere. I couldn't believe that we were expected to race over roads like this.

The cobblestones in Belgium were like patio paving slabs in comparison. These were roads that time had forgotten. Only the local farmers used them and they were in very poor condition. The roads, if you can call them that, looked like someone had tipped a load of bricks into a muddy trench and left them there.

Every jarring thud hurt my elbows. I was convinced my wheels were going to buckle under me. Riders ran off the road and fell into the ditch. They went down in front of me with no warning.

Now I knew why no one had offered any words of advice before the start. There was nothing anyone could have said to make it easier.

I crashed three or four times on the first few sections of cobbles, without doing any serious damage to myself or the bike. But I was miles behind the front of the race and we'd barely started.

A group came past me and I managed to hang in with them for a while. I watched how they chose the best line and avoided the worst craters and slowly I picked up a few skills, but you couldn't say I was participating in the race – I was just riding towards Roubaix, falling further and further behind.

I had no idea how the riders at the front were managing to ride so strongly.

Eventually I decided enough was enough. I punctured and couldn't get a wheel for ages. There was not a team car to be seen so I finally got into the broomwagon, the vehicle that follows the last rider in the race and sweeps up the waste.

I sat in the back feeling pretty sorry for myself. There were still about a hundred kilometres to the finish, so I was in for a slow, humiliating journey.

In Roubaix, one of my team-mates asked me how I'd got on. I puffed out my cheeks. I said I never wanted to endure anything like it again.

His verdict was damning and to the point. 'You weren't going fast enough on the cobbles. You have to hit them quicker.'

9. Le Tour

1978

No race in the world comes close to matching the Tour de France. Until I rode it for the first time, I did not appreciate how hard it would be just to reach Paris. The stages are longer and faster than in other races and the battle for position is more intense. I started the Tour 14 times and finished 12. Over the course of my career the Tour grew beyond recognition, from a French national obsession to an event with global recognition.

When I first rode the Tour, there were eleven teams of ten riders, making a field of 110. By 1992, there were 198 riders. Riders from Australia and America had begun to take part, giving an international flavour. The Tour grew too big for the rural roads, so the character of the race changed.

In 1978, I was a bit of a novelty. I was only the second rider from Ireland to start the Tour de France. Shay Elliott, who won a stage and held the yellow jersey for four days in 1963, was the only one before me.

I had no idea I was in the frame for the Tour de France team until about a fortnight before the race began. In 1977, Maertens won the Vuelta a España and Pollentier won the Giro d'Italia so the plan for 1978 was to focus all our energy on the Tour. Flandria didn't even enter a team for the Vuelta or the Giro, so I had started to accept that my first taste of a grand tour might have to wait until the following year.

After all, with Pollentier going for the yellow jersey and Maertens aiming for green, there probably wouldn't be room for an inexperienced second-year professional.

I had guessed that three of the riders from the French side

of the Flandria team might go to the Tour and slowly it dawned on me that I might be one of them. De Gribaldy sent me to the Grand Prix du Midi Libre in May, then the Critérium du Dauphiné Libéré and the Tour de l'Aude. These were all hard, mountainous races that the riders used as preparation for the Tour.

On the final morning of the Tour de l'Aude, De Gribaldy grabbed my arm as I was about to head to the start line and said: 'We've decided that you will do the Tour.'

It was as simple as that.

Flandria had three leaders – Pollentier and Joaquim Agostinho for the overall and Maertens for the sprints. Marc Demeyer was the man with the whip. We had Herman Beysens, a Belgian who was always making jokes, and Albert Van Vlierberghe, who was 36 and counting down the days to retirement. Four riders from the French faction were chosen – René Bittinger, Christian Muselet, Marcel Tinazzi and me.

THE TOUR STARTED with a five-kilometre prologue time trial in Leiden in the Netherlands on a Thursday afternoon. It was raining all afternoon and the corners were treacherous. I finished 83rd out of 110. Hardly a glittering start to my Tour career. Jan Raas of the TI-Raleigh team won, but afterwards the team managers held a meeting and then asked the organisers to nullify the results because the weather had been so bad. TI-Raleigh was the only team not to agree. In the end, Raas kept his stage win but was not presented with the yellow jersey.

I may have been new to the Tour but the pressure was on the team for results. The journalists expected Freddy Maertens to win at least one stage but he kept getting beaten.

There were two stages on the second day of the race. In the morning we went from Leiden to St Willebrord and Raas sprung a surprise on us, attacking close to the end to get his hands on the yellow jersey. After lunch, we raced on to Brussels and Freddy was second again. This time he was beaten by Walter Planckaert.

As we came round the final corner with 500 metres to go, one of the motorbikes carrying a television cameraman got in the way. It was too close to the front of the bunch, which meant Freddy had to brake and then try to kick again, leaving him too much to do. The next day at St Amand-les-Eaux he was third, making it three top-three finishes in a row without a win.

Stage four was a team time trial from Evreux to Caen. It was 153 kilometres long, which meant almost four hours spent racing flat out on heavy, rolling roads. Some normal stages of the Tour these days are only around 150 kilometres but a team time trial of that length was torture, and I don't use the word lightly.

We started losing riders at around the halfway mark. With 50 kilometres to go we were down to six, knowing that the team's time would be taken as the fifth rider crossed the line. The whole stage was mental and physical agony. There wasn't a moment in the last hour when I didn't fantasise about sitting up and letting them ride away from me, but I knew I couldn't leave my team-mates in the lurch. If I dropped off, they would have one man fewer to share the pace-setting.

All the while, Demeyer was yelling at us to go faster but I had very little left to give. Towards the end I missed a few turns at the front of the line because my legs were completely empty.

The TI-Raleigh team won the stage. They were specialists at those long team time trials. We had gone as fast as we could but we were six minutes slower than them and finished fifth out of 11 teams. We got away lightly. The Spanish Kas squad finished almost 25 minutes down on the winners.

Afterwards, my arse was raw from sitting on the peak of the saddle and my shoulders ached from trying to hold an aerodynamic position. These were the days before special time trial bikes were developed to help the rider get into a low-profile position and cut through the wind. We were riding our regular road bikes. It was a really hard test and I would have accepted the pain if the stage hadn't been almost completely pointless.

The times for the stage did not count towards the overall standings. Instead, we earned a time bonus. Our team's reward for finishing fifth was 20 seconds. Twenty lousy seconds for almost four hours of suffering.

MAERTENS FINALLY WON his stage at Maze-Montgeoffroy

the next day and the pressure on us eased a lot. There were smiles around the dinner table in the evening and the next morning Freddy told us that he wanted to relax a little. He'd been in the hot seat for the opening week, trying to win a stage, and now he had one he could afford to sit back a bit. So we knew we wouldn't have to prepare the sprint for him. Instead, one of us could take a chance.

The sixth stage from Maze-Montgeoffrey to Poitiers covered 166 kilometres. It could have been a quiet day for everyone but someone always sees an opportunity to shake things up.

The TI-Raleigh squad had won the team time trial, which put Klaus-Peter Thaler in the yellow jersey, six seconds ahead of his team-mate Gerrie Knetemann. Joseph Bruyère of the C&A team was third, 46 seconds behind Thaler.

I had no idea of the internal conflicts that sometimes affected the Dutch teams and I only learned the story years later but there was a civil war going on at TI-Raleigh.

Thaler was a West German riding for a Dutch team. The Dutch and the Germans often don't see eye to eye. There's a lot of rivalry between them and when you add in the history of the war there can be quite an edge to that rivalry.

Apparently, Peter Post – the legendary and uncompromising manager of the TI-Raleigh squad – was not keen on having a German in the yellow jersey but knew that if TI-Raleigh won the team time trial, Thaler would take the race lead.

Knetemann told me years afterwards that he had tried to drop Thaler, his own team-mate, in the team time trial to Evreux by laying off the back of the line of riders by five or ten bike lengths and forcing the German to chase his way back on. It sounds crazy but I can believe it. They tried to take Thaler out the back door so that Knetemann would get the yellow jersey instead. The tactic didn't work because Thaler was riding strongly.

So, we came to the stage which finished in Poitiers and Knetemann had his eyes on taking the yellow jersey from Thaler – not that I knew anything about this little sub-plot at the time. I was just racing for myself.

With around 35 kilometres to go, the race suddenly burst into life. Bruyère, lying third overall, attacked and Knetemann reacted immediately. I saw this happening and, knowing that they were the riders placed second and third overall, sensed this was my chance. I went across to them, as did my team-mate René Bittinger and a Swedish rider, Sven-Ake Nilsson, who rode for the Miko-Mercier squad.

Once I'd caught Bruyère and Knetemann, I had a quick look round and saw we had a good gap. No one was in any mood to hang around. Knetemann had played a blinder. He was attacking his own team-mate, a team-mate wearing the yellow jersey, but could justify it by saying he was simply marking Bruyère, who was a significant danger man. And he knew that once we were away, TI-Raleigh would not chase, nor would Flandria or C&A, two of the other strongest squads. So we had a great chance of making the move stick.

Bittinger and I had a numerical advantage, so as we got closer to the finish we agreed to take turns to mark the other attacks. I was beginning to feel quite confident. Of the other riders, I thought Knetemann would be the strongest sprinter although he already had the yellow jersey in the bag and had done quite a lot of work to keep the break clear.

At the finish, I beat Knetemann quite comfortably. It was a great feeling. Winning always is. I thought: 'Feck, I've won a stage of the Tour de France. That's really something.'

Some professionals ride for years without winning a stage of the Tour. I'd been a Tour rider for less than a week and already had one.

But nothing changed dramatically for me after that. I wasn't suddenly the superstar of the Flandria team. It took a lot more than one stage win to climb up the hierarchy. The next day I was back to my duties, working for Maertens, who won in Bordeaux to make it three in a row for our team.

THERE'S NO TIME to get carried away at the Tour de France. The stages kept coming and a wake-up call was just around the corner. The first long individual time trial of the race was a 59-kilometre stage from St Emilion to Ste Foy-la-Grande. I finished more than seven minutes behind the winner – a Frenchman riding his first Tour, Bernard Hinault. Okay, so he was a couple of years older than me but his performance on his Tour debut put mine into sharp perspective. He'd ridden that stage almost four kilometres an hour faster than I had.

Then came the Pyrenees. Mercifully we only had one big Pyrenean stage but it meant a lot of suffering for me. I had ridden the Midi Libre and Dauphiné Libéré races just before the Tour and both of those events gave me a taster of the mountains but this was something completely new. We didn't skirt round the giants; we had to go right over them. And in the Tour, the riders at the front held nothing back. We hit them at full pace. I was still inexperienced at this sort of racing. I realised that I just had to block everything out and concentrate for an hour's climbing, stuff a newspaper down my jersey to keep the chill off my chest on the way down, throw myself into the descent and then do it all again on another big mountain pass.

THE TOUR WAS HARDER than anything I'd experienced before. As an amateur I'd ridden the Milk Race, which lasted a fortnight, but the length of the stages, the lack of time to recover and the heat all added up to a far more severe test. By the middle of the second week I was feeling very tired but I just took what came at me and hoped I'd hold together well enough in the Alps to have a chance of reaching Paris.

But I began to realise that the Tour's punishing schedule was unpopular with far more seasoned riders than me. Straight after the stage to St Lary-Soulan in the Pyrenees we were supposed to do another split-stage.

Split days were common in the Tour in those days. It meant we did a stage in the morning, took a break for lunch and then did another stage in the afternoon.

Racing like this was unpopular with the riders because it made for very long days. They'd much prefer to do one long stage than two shorter ones.

On July 12, we were supposed to race 140 kilometres from Tarbes to Valence d'Agen, then do another 96 kilometres on to

Toulouse in the afternoon. The reason the race organisers liked these stages was because they could double their money by charging two towns to host a finish instead of one.

There were plenty of complaints about other things but it was the split-stages that tipped the riders over the edge.

In those days, the riders were treated like second-class citizens. If the Tour was a circus, we were the lions and elephants who were supposed to perform the tricks. And Félix Lévitan, the man who ran the Tour de France, was the ringmaster. He was a severe man, a total dictator, and he wasn't afraid to crack the whip. The riders were scared of him; in fact, most of the team managers were frightened of him because they had raced under him.

Conditions for the riders were primitive. Sometimes we stayed in a hotel but often we were in a dormitory, with rows of little camp beds as if we were on a school trip. We were treated like children rather than professional athletes. After a tough stage in the mountains, no one wanted to be next to some big Belgian who snored, although I wasn't too bothered because I could sleep through anything.

The meals were provided by the organisers and we'd file into the canteen for a bit of meat, some pasta and green beans. Always green beans. The French served them with everything and by the second week I was sick of the sight of them.

We could put up with a lot. Six or seven-hour stages were the norm and we expected hard racing. But the split stages made everything a lot harder. Our day lasted 12 to 14 hours. We'd have to get up at six to have our usual pre-race meal of steak and pasta, then we'd do the first stage. The pace would always be high and we'd have a hectic finish because the chance to get a Tour stage win gets everyone on the point of their saddle.

Then we'd have time to get a quick wash down with a flannel, queue for lunch at the cafeteria for more green beans and then we'd have the opportunity to have a short nap. Rows of little camp beds would be lined up in a gymnasium or warehouse nearby. Then we'd put on a fresh set of kit, get back on the bike and race like stink for another three hours in the afternoon.

Lévitan had made the Tour a commercial success but the

conditions for the riders had not improved. Nor had the prize money on offer. No wonder our patience was being tested to breaking point.

There had been talk of a protest or a strike for a few days and it was the split stage on a baking hot day in the south of France that was the last straw. We rolled out of Tarbes in the morning and all the top riders, the champions and the experienced men, got together to discuss it. Lévitan was not happy that we were riding along at such a slow pace. He had his schedule to meet. We had to get the morning stage done on time or the afternoon one would start too late.

Lévitan, who travelled in the lead car, stood with his head through the sunroof and instructed the riders to race. After that there were some animated discussions.

The riders weren't in the mood to negotiate and word spread through the peloton that when we arrived in Valence d'Agen, where the morning stage was to finish, we were going to stage a go-slow protest before getting off our bikes to walk the last couple of hundred metres over the line.

We rolled into town and the crowd, who had no idea why we were not racing, booed and whistled. We slowed down to a halt, got off our bikes and walked. By now the atmosphere was very sour. Although the riders were united in their desire to make a point to Lévitan, it was an uneasy truce. I wouldn't have been surprised if someone had got back on their bike and tried to win the stage, even though they'd have been lynched afterwards.

At the front of the peloton was Bernard Hinault, the French champion, and already a spokesman for the peloton even though this was his first Tour. Also there were Maertens, Gerben Karstens and Jacques Esclassan, who were among the most respected riders. I was in the second row, next to the British rider Paul Sherwen. As we walked towards the line he said: 'If anyone goes for it, we go for it.'

Hinault marched forward like Napoleon. Lévitan and his assistant, Jacques Goddet, were livid but wanted to avoid an embarrassing showdown in public.

We spent an awkward hour-and-a-half in Valence d'Agen. As

far as the town's people were concerned, we'd ruined the spectacle. But the riders were unanimous and we felt we had to make a stand. Nothing changed immediately – in fact, split stages survived for another decade – but conditions did improve and the needs of riders were taken into consideration more.

The protest over, our point made, normal service resumed in the afternoon and we slipped out of Valence d'Agen then raced like lunatics to Toulouse.

THE THIRD WEEK of the Tour de France is when your body begins to shut down. The fatigue went so deep I had trouble sleeping. Even after a good nine hours, I'd wake up feeling barely rested. I was sick of eating the same food. Meat, pasta and always those bloody green beans. And every day took me to a new level of suffering. Through the Massif Central we went, with a time trial that finished at the top of Le Puy de Dôme, a dormant volcano.

I was scared of the Alps. I already knew the climbs were longer than those in the Pyrenees. Looking at the profile of stage 16 terrified me. It was 240 kilometres long and we had to go over mountain after mountain before we reached the big one, Alpe d'Huez.

I was sharing a room with Christian Muselet, who was suffering even more than me. I was just trying to survive and having Muselet with me helped. He'd point to a place on the map and say: 'We have to make it to here before we get dropped otherwise we won't make the time limit.'

The day to Alpe d'Huez was so hot and so long. I was in my own private world of pain, with no idea what was happening at the front of the race.

I fought my way to the top of Alpe d'Huez and someone told me my team-mate, Michel Pollentier, had won the stage and taken the yellow jersey. He also led the king of the mountains competition. Freddy already had the green jersey, so Flandria had all three of the Tour's big prizes. I was happy for the team but too tired to really take it all in. I was just chalking off the days until we got to Paris. Six more to go.

The atmosphere in the team should have been jubilant.

We were staying at the Hotel Le Castilan, a large chalet that overlooked the mountains. I went down to dinner, completely unaware of the controversy that was about to engulf our team.

The lobby of the hotel was full of journalists but that was not a surprise because the *maillot jaune* was among us.

Pollentier was not at dinner. Then someone told me that he had tried to fiddle the drug test after the stage. He had gone to the dope control with a bulb of clean urine under his arm, with a tube tucked under his jersey and running into his shorts. His plan was to squeeze the bulb of clean urine to fill up the sample jar.

The doctor observing the test was already suspicious because he'd caught a Spanish rider called Antoine Gutierrez trying to pull the same stunt moments earlier.

Pollentier was sent home and left Alpe d'Huez that night. After dinner, the rest of the riders met to discuss what had happened. Someone had suggested that the whole team was going to pull out but the sponsor wanted us to carry on because Freddy was still in the green jersey. I didn't want to go home because I wanted to make it to Paris but the riders didn't have a say at all. We just did as we were told.

The leader of the Tour de France being caught like that was a big scandal but the race didn't grind to a halt. I don't remember being asked my opinion by the journalists the next day. We weren't surrounded by cameramen when we left the hotel in the morning. The Tour went on without Pollentier. That was how it was back then. He'd been caught doing something he shouldn't and he had been sent home.

A few days later, I reached Paris in 34th place overall. I was an hour and ten minutes behind Bernard Hinault but finishing my first Tour felt like a major achievement. It had been hard – brutal at times – but I had never been close to giving up.

Because I had won a stage and made a bit of a name for myself, I was offered contracts to ride in some of the lucrative criterium races that are held all over France, Belgium and Holland after the Tour. I wasn't a star but I was becoming a somebody.

At one of those exhibition races in Belgium I saw Pollentier. Despite what he had done, I liked him. We had got on well and, like Freddy, he had always been kind and encouraging to me.

As we spoke, it didn't occur to me to ask Pollentier why he had done it. We didn't have that sort of relationship. And there was the hierarchy. He may have fallen from grace but he was still Pollentier and I was just Kelly.

Pollentier left Flandria to join another Belgian team, sponsored by a bicycle manufacturer from Namur called Splendor. At the end of the year, I followed him.

They offered me a contract, with a good pay rise, but the money wasn't the reason I chose to go. I could see how things would be at Flandria. Freddy Maertens was still the big sprinting star and I'd have to work for him most of the time. Pollentier was a different type of rider and he was offering me the chance to race for myself more often.

De Gribaldy thought moving to a Belgian team and living in Belgium would be a terrible idea. He had a downer on the Belgians because he thought they were disorganised and said they ate too many chips and drank too much beer.

He tried to get me to stay, saying that the progress I had made would be wasted if I left him.

And, for a while, it looked like he might be right.

10. Herman & Elise

My second family

I first met Herman and Elise Nys at the World Championships at Yvoir, Belgium, just south of Namur, in 1975. They were cycling fanatics who travelled round Europe watching races. It didn't matter where the World Championships were held, they would be there.

Herman had a soft spot for the Irish because he had done his military service in Northern Ireland. So, when he went to the 1964 World Championships at Sallanches in the French Alps, and noticed an Irish rider called Liam Horner was taking part, he knew he had to introduce himself.

He found that Horner had paid his own way to France and was sleeping in a tent at a nearby campsite because money was so tight. Impressed by Horner's determination, Herman found him a hotel and paid for a room, then said that if he were ever in Belgium the door to the Nys family home would always be open.

It was the beginning of a great friendship between Herman and Elise and generations of Irish cyclists. Over the years, they became like a second set of parents to me and they welcomed me into their home as if I was their own son.

After signing for the Splendor team, I left De Gribaldy's nest in Besançon and headed to Belgium. For a short while, I stayed with Robert Lauwers, the team manager, in a flat above a cafe. I lasted about a fortnight before I picked up the phone, called Herman and nervously asked if I could stay with them.

I didn't leave them for five years.

Their house was in a cul-de-sac in Vilvoorde, a suburb near Brussels. Herman and Elise were in their early fifties and their own son, Gustav, had grown up and moved out, so I took over his room. It was the perfect arrangement. As a professional rider, I was on the road so much I didn't need my own apartment. I didn't want to come home to an empty fridge and a pile of washing.

Herman understood cycling but he wasn't interested in trying to be my coach. He didn't interfere with my training or advise me about the races. He knew enough about cycling to have an opinion but he didn't tell me how it should all be done. Instead, he was very supportive and encouraging. But he was strict too. Herman was even more strict than my father.

He made sure everything was correct and above board. As I was a foreigner living in Belgium, he registered me with the town hall, sorted out life insurance and made sure my taxes were in order. There weren't many cyclists in Belgium who kept on top of their taxes in those days. There probably aren't now.

I didn't pay rent but I did give Herman and Elise money for my food. And I lived by their rules, which meant observing Herman's curfew. If I went out in the evening, which was rare anyway, he would ask me what time I got in.

'Twenty past eleven,' I'd say.

'No it wasn't, it was quarter to one.'

It was like living with a cross between my father and De Gribaldy, only with less freedom.

Herman worked as a book keeper at a chemical factory. He knew how finances worked and he believed in putting money in the bank and leaving it there to grow, which I did.

If there was a downside it was the fact that Elise was such a good cook. The kitchen always smelled wonderful and a lot of cakes came out of her oven. De Gribaldy would have had a fit if he'd seen the portion sizes but I thought I might offend her if I turned down her food or asked for a smaller serving. As a result, my appetite grew.

The Splendor team lived up to the chaotic picture of the Belgians that De Gribaldy liked to paint, particularly at the start. I couldn't fault Robert Lauwers for his enthusiasm. He was a very nice guy but he didn't know much about bike racing or how to organise things. Lauwers had tried to be a racer but didn't get any further than the amateur circuit in Belgium. For him, running a professional team was one way to keep his dream alive.

How he'd managed to convince anyone to sponsor his team, I don't know. Lauwers had got friendly with Michel Pollentier and told him he wanted to make him the star of a new team. Then, I heard, Lauwers drove up and down the Meuse valley visiting every company on every industrial estate, telling them he was building a team around Pollentier, until he found someone willing to sponsor the team.

That someone was Armand Marlair, the owner of Splendor, which made bikes and mopeds. Splendor had sponsored a small team in the mid-1970s, so Marlair didn't take much persuading.

My mistake was taking it for granted when Pollentier told me that Lauwers knew what he was doing.

De Gribaldy might not have kept the riders fully in the loop but his plans were always meticulously made. Right from the start at Splendor, I began to appreciate what I had accepted at Flandria as being the normal way of doing things. Splendor was run one day to the next. It was chaotic and everything was done just in the nick of time.

Leaving Besançon and moving to Belgium was a much bigger change than I had anticipated, too. I realised that it was harder to do good quality training in Belgium. The countryside around Besançon had been perfect for a professional cyclist. Everywhere I went there were hills. And hills are a cyclist's short-cut to getting fit. Every ride I did was a good work-out and if I looked like slacking off, De Gribaldy was there to kick me up the backside.

But in Belgium, I didn't have De Gribaldy telling me what to do. I had to devise my own training programme. Although I'd not written down how much and how often I'd trained the previous year, I thought I had a good idea of what needed to be done. Basically, I just copied the De Gribaldy plan – at least that's what I thought I was doing.

The countryside around Brussels is mostly flat and I didn't realise until after a few months that this posed a problem. I would get home after a five-hour ride thinking I had done a good day's work but it was nothing compared to riding around Besançon.

In Belgium, not only were the roads flat but there are traffic lights, pedestrian crossings and roundabouts everywhere. During a five-hour ride, about an hour was spent slowing down for a junction or sitting waiting for the lights to change.

I'd freewheel to a stop, then pull away again at a nice casual pace. I was training in a daze, well within my comfort zone, while convincing myself I was working hard.

Training properly has always been a real pain in the balls. And if it's not, then you're not pushing hard enough. Backing off a bit is so easy to do. Turning for home after an hour-and-a-half instead of after two hours is tempting as well. To get up in the morning and train hard every day requires mental stamina.

I didn't realise it but I wasn't training hard enough when I first moved to Belgium. Perhaps it was because I'd signed a nice contract and thought bike racing was going to get easier rather than harder. Whatever the reason, I was in for a bit of a shock.

Then one day I saw a group of Belgian amateurs out training. They came pelting past me, sprinting to get through the lights before they turned red. I watched them race away from me and the penny dropped. 'Holy shit. I've been on holiday here.'

It was already too late for me to salvage the early part of the season but I knew at that moment I'd wasted those first few months in Belgium.

There was an air of complacency at Splendor. Having joined a new team, I waiting for them to tell me that they were expecting results from me, but Lauwers was not on my case the way De Gribaldy would have been.

I am sure they were hoping I'd go head-to-head with Freddy Maertens and Jan Raas in the sprints at the Tour de France so what did it matter if I wasn't performing at my best in February and March? I won the Grand Prix de Cannes at the start of the season but that is the sort of race I could win even if I wasn't in top shape. Winning a race like that meant there was no panic from the boss but when we got to the bigger events in the spring, I knew I had slipped backwards.

Lauwers was too relaxed about things. 'Don't worry, the form will come later on.'

That was the last thing I needed to hear. No one asked how my training was going; they just trusted that I would deliver results when they needed them.

But the fact was, I hadn't done enough work and I was about to take a big fall. There was nothing driving me to do my best.

Lauwers seemed to make things up as he went along. Sometimes we didn't know when we were travelling or where we were staying until the last minute. Tactically he couldn't add much to the team because he hadn't raced at a high enough level. So really, his job was to drive the car.

The bikes were terrible, or rather the components were. We had many punctures because we were on cheap tyres. The brakes barely worked in the wet. More than once, I had to take my foot out of the toestraps and dig my heel into the road to get round a corner on a slippery descent.

We turned down a place in Paris-Roubaix, fearful that the cobbles would shake the bikes into shrapnel. It was ridiculous.

In the spring, I rode the Vuelta a España for the first time and immediately I felt an affinity for the race. It was a lot more low-key than the Tour de France but the Spaniards were passionate about cycling and the crowds in the towns could be huge. The race was held early during the season in those days so the weather was cooler than during the Tour, which suited me. But the sprints could be crazy.

I won the first stage in Seville, which suggested I might be on the verge of discovering some good form after a poor spring. The following day in Córdoba almost ended in disaster. It was a downhill finish, making it a very fast sprint. Around 250 metres from the line, a spectator climbed over the barrier into the road. A policeman tried to grab him but missed and suddenly there were two people in the road ahead of us.

A Belgian rider called Eddy Van Haerens ploughed straight into the policeman. I tried to bunnyhop Van Haerens' bike but got tangled up and went flying. I skidded until I'd taken all the skin off my arse and elbows. Then riders crashed into the back of us. It was a horrible pile-up and it made the next few days quite painful as my wounds wept through the bandages and at night the bedsheets stuck to me.

I won another stage in Benicassim a few days later but I still wasn't satisfied with how I was riding. The hills were particularly difficult as the lack of deep training caught up with me. The frustration boiled over at Zaragoza.

We were heading towards the line and I was in a good position, just behind Noel Dejonckheere, a Belgian who was a bucking-bronco style sprinter. He could be all over the place. He was a first-year professional who had made quite a splash by winning a number of races but really he should have been no match for me.

Dejonckheere was just ahead of me, quite close to the barriers. I was trying to draw level with him so he moved over, squeezing me towards the barriers. It wasn't a particularly dangerous move but it meant I couldn't get past him. Instinctively, I reached out and grabbed a fistful of his jersey, pulled him back and got past.

I crossed the line first but I knew an appeal was coming. Sure enough the head judge – a Belgian, but I'm sure that had nothing to do with it – relegated me to last place and gave the victory to Dejonckheere. I protested, saying that he had forced me into the barriers and I only grabbed his jersey to steady myself and prevent a fall. I didn't really believe that. I knew I was in the wrong but it was worth a try.

Sprinting could be a dangerous game at times. The gear levers were not integrated into the brake levers like they are now, so if I wanted to change gear during a sprint, I had to reach down between my knees to flick the lever on the down tube. I could be changing gear with one hand off the bars while someone else was swerving across in front of me.

Although the sprints were dangerous I didn't always wear a helmet. The helmets then were made of strips of leather that looked like a bunch of bananas on your head. Sometimes I wore a cloth cap – or *casquette* – to keep the sun off, but most of the time I didn't wear anything on my head.

When I think of some of the kamikaze moves we used to attempt, I wince a bit. But at the time I was never worried about crashing. Sometimes, back at the hotel in the evening, I'd replay a dangerous sprint in my mind and it would give me the shivers but the next day we'd all be doing it again, pulling the same crazy stunts. I never dwelled on the risks. My philosophy was that if I started to worry about the risks, I'd back off. And if I backed off, I wouldn't win.

The day after I'd grabbed hold of Dejonckheere's jersey in Zaragoza, we were giving it everything again in Pamplona. It was like the running of the bulls.

The lead judge wanted to keep a very keen eye on us this time so he made the official car drive very close to the front of the bunch in the final kilometre. That was a decision that had disastrous consequences, although it could have been a lot worse.

This time it was a clean sprint, which Dejonckheere won. I just didn't have the speed to go past him.

As we crossed the line, I looked up and saw that the lead car had stopped in the middle of the road just 30 or 40 metres ahead of us. I squeezed the brake levers hard, as if they were a pair of nutcrackers, but there was no time to stop.

I hit the back of the car and Pollentier, who had given me a lead-out for the sprint, went head first through the back window. We were very lucky it was not more serious. It seemed crazy that they could disqualify me for rough sprinting one day but risk our safety like that the next.

I'd won a couple of stages of the Vuelta and Pollentier went on to finish third overall but I didn't make it to the end of the race. In the final week I got a stomach bug, probably because I had broken the golden rule by drinking the water on the table at dinner.

My second Tour de France was a wash-out for me. Having won a stage on my debut, I was expecting to get at least another one but I was way behind where I needed to be to challenge the other top sprinters. The race started in Fleurance and headed straight for three days in the Pyrenees. I wasn't sprinting well but I was climbing even worse. I lost 20 minutes on the first stage and another seven the next day. I wasn't expecting to be to up there with the mountain goats but I was performing badly.

The team collapsed around me. Splendor riders were dropping like flies. Christian Dumont and Roger Vershaeve were outside the time limit at the end of stage two, which finished at Superbagnères. The next day we went over the Col de Peyresourde, Col d'Aspin and Col de Soulor but neither Ludo Loos nor Lievin Malfait made it to the finish.

Bernard Hinault was the favourite to win the Tour again but we hoped Pollentier might challenge. Having mountain stages so early in the race meant all but about five riders had any hope of winning, and we'd only been racing for three days. Pollentier was ninth overall but he was already three minutes behind.

After the mountains, the organisers showed their perverse sense of humour by scheduling an 86-kilometre team time trial from Captieux to Bordeaux. We had already lost four riders so we knew we were in for a hiding. Pollentier, Herman Beysens, Alain Desaever, Wim Wyngheer, Paul Jesson and I set off with heavy hearts and even heavier legs. Most of the other teams still had ten riders so we were at a huge disadvantage. We spent two hours at the absolute limit.

With only six men, my turn at the front came round so quickly that it was hard to get any recovery time. It was no surprise that we were thrashed. We were nine-and-a-half minutes slower than TI-Raleigh and finished 13th out of 15 teams. Only Fiat and Teka, who had lost five riders in the mountains, were worse.

The previous year, we had battered ourselves in the team time trial for a 20-second time bonus. Now the organisers had decided that our actual time for the stage would count towards the overall standings, meaning that Pollentier had lost another 9-33 and any chance of racing for the yellow jersey not because of his own failing but because of his team's weakness.

The Tour organisers were a sadistic bunch. Four days later we had another team time trial – this time 90 kilometres from Deauville to Le Havre. We did a bit better, finishing 10th out of 15, but we were still 6-32 off TI-Raleigh's pace.

It was difficult to accept that I was just making up the numbers in the Tour. I didn't expect to be one of the stars but I had hoped to challenge for a stage win. In the time trial at Brussels only seven riders in the entire field were slower than me. The sprints weren't much better. I was nowhere.

At Evian, I lost to Marc Demeyer, which was a bad result because although he was a big, strong rider, he was no sprinter.

The Alps cracked what was left of Splendor's spirit. They made us race up Alpe d'Huez two days in a row, which was great for the spectators and terrible for us. On the second day we went over a climb called La Morte, which I assumed was another of the organisers' little jokes.

One by one, the Splendor boys threw in the towel or were eliminated. Jesson finished outside the time limit, then Desaever, Beysens and Pollentier, all chance of a podium finish gone, pulled out. With six stages still to go, there were only two of us left. Wim Myngheer was my only companion.

As the riders went home, so too did our support staff so at the end there was just one mechanic, one *soigneur*, or masseur, and Lauwers to drive the car and give us the benefit of his advice.

I was having a bad time but Myngheer was suffering terribly. He was counting down the days to Paris like he was serving a prison sentence.

One of the only advantages of being down to two men was that we could have our own room, instead of having to share. Each morning Myngheer would come down to breakfast and sit opposite me in silence. We were just going through the motions, hoping Paris would come a bit sooner.

I still dreamed of winning a stage somehow but that was what it was – a dream. Deep down I knew I didn't have it but Lauwers was always optimistic. He had started the Tour telling us we were the best team in the world, that Pollentier was going to win the yellow jersey but we knew it wasn't true.

Now he was trying to rally me for one last effort. 'Sean, you can win the stage on the Champs-Élysées and finish this Tour in great style.'

But his words were as empty as my legs. I nodded but I didn't believe it any more than he did.

The stage to Paris slipped away too. My only chance of winning would have been if I had got into a little break but the first two riders overall, Hinault and Joop Zoetemelk, got away instead and they finished two minutes ahead of the bunch.

Hinault had been absolutely dominant. Zoetemelk was the only rider to get within 25 minutes of him overall. I was 38th, almost two hours behind Hinault. That wasn't what made it a bad Tour. It was the fact that I didn't come close to winning a stage.

Having a bad Tour de France made me question everything. I knew I couldn't drift through another winter and I had to cut back on second helpings of Elise's food.

Even though he was no longer my team manager, I could still hear De Gribaldy's voice, so I decided to listen.

Armand Marlair, presumably as disappointed as we were by how the Tour de France had turned out, realised that Lauwers was not the man to whip us into shape. He brought in Albert De Kimpe, another of the old school *directeurs sportifs* who riders respected before he even opened his mouth.

De Kimpe ran a tight ship and so things began to improve.

11. Breakthrough

1980

During the early years of my career, I was considered to be a specialist sprinter. I was brave, a little bit crazy, and fast. But the idea of challenging for the general classification in any of the three-week tours was a long way from my mind. I could climb reasonably well but feared the really big mountain ranges and always felt that the long, steep cols would catch me out.

I never set myself any long-term career goals. All I was focused on was becoming the best I could possibly be.

Apart from a couple of stage wins at the Vuelta a España, the 1979 season had been very disappointing. Falling short of my own expectations made me reassess everything. I wasn't scared of hard work but I had been too comfortable so I made sure I put a lot of miles in the bank. No corners were cut. If I failed to win races at least I would know I had put in the work.

Albert De Kimpe improved everything at Splendor. He made sure the bikes worked properly and he signed some good quality riders. Three Belgians joined the team – and Claude Criquielion, who was to become one of my best friends, Johan De Muynck and Guido Van Calster were a lot stronger than most of the riders we already had.

I felt a lot fitter at the start of the 1980 season but I couldn't convert that into wins straight away. I was second behind Pascal Simon at the Tour du Haut Var, a really tough one-day race in the south of France. I was third at Het Volk and the next day at Kuurne-Brussels-Kuurne, the two semi-Classics that open the Belgian season. The spring one-day races followed the same pattern – fourth at Milan-San Remo, second at the Grand Prix

Harelbeke and Brabantse Pijl, third at the Amstel Gold Race in Holland. Time after time I was finishing in the top places without actually managing to win. It can take a while to get into the habit of winning and it was getting frustrating.

I won a stage of the Three Days of De Panne and clinched the overall classification too, which gave me a great sense of relief. It was my first major victory for almost a year.

The press had noticed my consistency but had also said I lacked the ruthless streak necessary to become a champion. I never took too much notice of what the journalists said but perhaps they had a point. I was in danger of being a nearly man.

The Vuelta a España that spring rebuilt my confidence totally. I went into the race hoping to win a couple of stages before working for the team in the mountains. The Vuelta went far better than I had hoped. I won five stages, finished fourth overall and won the points competition. Three of my stage wins came in the final week, including the last one to Madrid.

Compared to the previous season, Splendor were riding brilliantly. We had four riders in the top ten – Criquielion was third, I was fourth, Van Calster was sixth and De Muynck was seventh – although we never looked likely to topple Faustino Ruperez, who won overall. Compared to the previous season, everything was going brilliantly.

One of the highlights of the Vuelta was the day Paul Jesson won the stage in Santander. I got on very well with Paul. He was from New Zealand and being so far from home was difficult for him at times, so to see him win a big race was great.

Just six weeks later, we all got a nasty reminder of how life can change at any moment. The prologue of the Dauphiné Libéré was held in Aix-les-Bains on a course that took us up and over a little hill. On the descent, Paul clipped a parked car, crashed and broke his leg just below the knee. It was a bad injury and we knew it was the end of his season but we had no idea things were going to take such a turn for the worse. A few days later he got an infection and the leg turned gangrenous.

They moved him from France to a hospital near Brussels and the next thing I heard, doctors had amputated his leg. That was a terrible shock. Herman, Elise and I went to visit him. I decided to go by the hospital at the end of my training ride, which was a mistake, because I felt very awkward sitting there in my cycling kit. I didn't know what to say. There was nothing I could say to make it better.

Crashes happen in cycling. Injuries are part of the life and for a while what had happened to Paul played on my mind, although I knew I couldn't let it change the way I raced a bike.

THE TOUR DE FRANCE was deep into the final week, with Paris just around the corner, and it looked like I was going to draw another blank. The stage win just wouldn't come. I was relegated from second place to last on stage nine in Nantes for cutting across Jan Raas in the sprint and that was the closest I had come. I battled through the Pyrenees and Alps knowing time was running out.

With four stages to go, I weighed up my chances. Only two were likely to end in a bunch sprint – the one at Fontenay-sous-Bois and the final one to the Champs-Élysées in Paris.

The sprints had not been working out too well for me, so I decided to take the initiative instead. Stage 19 from Voreppe to Saint-Etienne crossed over the Col de la Croix de Chaubouret before a descent into the city. It was the ideal place to get away from the bunch.

That makes it sound a lot simpler than it is. Getting into a break is never easy in the Tour de France because a lot of guys have the same idea. It comes down to timing and a bit of luck.

At the bottom of the climb, the riders started jumping about. They were attacking on both sides of the road but no one was able to get away. Then a Spaniard called Ismael Lejaretta accelerated and I immediately latched onto his back wheel. I thought a couple more might come with us but once we had the gap I realised it was just Lejaretta and me. The riders who had tried to respond were unable to stay with us because of the fierce pace Lejaretta was setting.

This was the ideal scenario for me. Lejaretta was an excellent climber but had no sprint finish to speak of. Neither of us were well-placed in the general classification, so we weren't going to worry the overall contenders. If I could stay with Lejaretta on the climb, I had a great chance to win the stage.

Staying with him was easier said than done. I was in real difficulty at times and had to dig very deep to hang on but once we got over the top the boot was on the other foot. I flew down the descent, taking big risks in the corners. I could hear him shouting: 'Kelly, *loco, loco*' – 'Kelly, crazy, crazy'.

The sprint was a formality. Lejaretta was never going to beat me. It had seemed like a long wait but I had finally got my second Tour stage win.

Suddenly the weight lifted from my shoulders and the pedals felt lighter. Two days later, I won the sprint at Fontenay-sous-Bois by about six lengths. It's amazing how a victory can relax a rider – you can bet that had I not won at Saint-Etienne I'd not have won at Fontenay. I nearly made it three out of four on the Champs-Élysées but I was edged into second place by Pol Verschuere of Belgium. Afterwards someone told me that had I not been relegated from second place in Nantes I'd have been just six points behind Rudy Pevenage in the race for the Tour's green jersey. I'd not really been aiming for the green jersey but this convinced me I could win it one day.

Things were back on track but I had no idea a kid from Dublin was about to come along and knock me off my perch.

12. A new rival

Kelly and Roche

One morning before the start of a stage of the 1981 Tirreno-Adriatico I was looking through a copy of *La Gazzetta Dello Sport*, the Italian sports paper, when I read that Stephen Roche, a 21-year-old first-year professional, had won Paris-Nice.

Alarm bells rang. I won't pretend it wasn't a blow to my pride.

I was 24 and had started my fifth season as a professional. I had won stages of the Tour de France and the Vuelta a España but I had never won an overall title as big as Paris-Nice. Stephen had been a professional for less than five minutes and he'd taken one of the biggest races in the world.

It was a kick up the backside. I knew Stephen and I liked him but make no mistake – I wanted to be the best rider from Ireland. By winning Paris-Nice, he had parked his tank on my lawn.

Stephen was a talented boy. He had made a good name for himself in Ireland by winning the Rás Tailteann in 1979, when he was still only 19. The Rás is a race for tough characters and Stephen had beaten them all. In 1980, he won the amateur edition of Paris-Roubaix, which was impressive but – like my win in the amateur Tour of Lombardy – didn't mean much once he got to the professional ranks.

A few weeks after Roche had turned pro, he beat Bernard Hinault at the Tour of Corsica, which was an impressive victory although not quite the same thing as keeping up with Hinault at the Tour de France.

But Stephen's victory at Paris-Nice sparked something in me. It wasn't jealousy, exactly, but it certainly gave me a feeling that I needed to push on. If Stephen Roche could win a race like that at the age of 21 then I should be able to.

People back in Ireland had been talking Stephen up. He'd been an outstanding junior and had enjoyed a very good year racing as an amateur in France but I didn't consider him a huge talent until he started to outdo me in the professional races.

We were very different characters. I was from the country, he was a city boy. I was quiet and reserved and he was much more talkative. He was confident, almost cocky. Over the years we became firm friends, and rivals.

There were days when we were at each other's throats on the road but, more often than not, we watched each other's backs, even though we rode for different teams. Put it this way, we very rarely raced against each other.

The exception was at Paris-Nice and Critérium International, two French stage races that suited us both. Some years we fought like cat and dog there. Once or twice we had a bit of a falling out.

ONE OF THE REASONS I had signed for Splendor in the first place was that I had been guaranteed top billing in the sprints. But at the start of 1981, Eddy Planckaert joined the team.

Eddy was the younger brother of Walter and Willy, two very successful riders, and it was soon clear he was just as talented. The problem for me was that De Kimpe could not seem to decide which one of us should be the protected sprinter.

In fact, Splendor was becoming a team with too many chiefs – or rather, too many riders who thought they were the chief.

This came to a head at Flèche Wallonne in April when three of us got into the winning break and messed it up big time. Back then, the race finished in the centre of Mons, rather than at the top of the steep Mur de Huy. I was the better sprinter out of Criquielion, Van Calster and me, so it should have been a simple tactic. The other two should have worked to set me up for the finish. Criquielion did some big turns on the front and chased down a few attacks but Van Calster was hovering around me, marking me as if I was a rival.

Van Calster was a good rider but when he first turned pro the Belgian press talked him up as the next Eddy Merckx, which is what the Belgian press did about anyone who showed a bit of talent. He probably saw this as his opportunity to win a big Classic and fulfill that promise.

When the sprint started, Van Calster rode for himself, I rode for myself and we lost the race to Daniel Willems. Van Calster was third and I was fourth. It never looks good when two riders from the same team finish high up in a sprint without actually winning so it was no surprise that De Kimpe was angry.

Although things were better, the management were still not firm enough with the riders. De Kimpe needed to lay down the law and make it clear what the consequences would be if people failed to follow orders. And perhaps we needed a guy like Marc Demeyer in the team -- someone to keep everyone in line out on the road.

After that I began to realise I needed to get out of that team and I let a few people know that I'd be interested in talking to De Gribaldy about going back to him.

Splendor's old problems never truly went away. The Tour de France was frustrating again. Freddy Maertens had barely won a race for three years but he beat me in Nice and from then on Splendor gave Eddy Planckaert the chance to go for the sprints instead of me.

I knew I had to be creative if I was going to win. The sprints were no longer my best chance of success. Stage 15 started in Besançon, my old home town, which perhaps gave me some inspiration. It was a long stage, which finished 231 kilometres away in Thonon-les-Bains, on the French side of Lake Geneva. Towards the end of the stage, we went over the Col de Cou, a second-category climb, that sent all the pure sprinters out of the back door. I was becoming a different type of rider, able to hang on over difficult terrain like this.

I knew that if I could keep up on the climb, I'd be able to beat all the climbers in a sprint. Criquielion did a great job, helping me stay in contact on the climb and then leading me out for the finish. I'd managed to win a stage of the Tour for the second year in a row even if I had shed my sprinter's skin.

The fact that I had become more versatile pleased me so I was surprised when I spoke to De Gribaldy and heard that he thought I was under-performing. He said I should be doing much more.

He said that if Roche could win Paris-Nice, so could I. He said that if I could finish second in the points competition at the Tour de France the green jersey should be mine. And he said that I should be finishing much higher up the overall standings.

The World Championships were held in Czechoslovakia and it was there that I met with De Gribaldy and decided to rejoin him.

He had built his own team, called Sem-France Loire, and he wanted me to lead it. Originally the plan had been for me to share the leadership with Joaquim Agostinho but there had been a change of plan because he had decided to go back to Portugal to look after his farm for a year.

There were some old friends at Sem – I knew René Bittinger and Marcel Tinazzi from Flandria. I took Ronny Onghena with me from Splendor because we had become good friends. We also had an American called Jock Boyer, who was an acquired taste because he could be a bit unusual. And the rest of the team were Frenchmen, including Alain and Guy Gallopin, who would become great friends of mine.

It was like going home. De Gribaldy hadn't changed at all. I was three years older, a little wiser, and a bit more successful than when we had last worked together but he treated me exactly the same as before. And he was about to drive me harder than ever.

13. Col d'Èze

The Race to the Sun

For seven years, one Sunday each March, a little hill overlooking Nice was my spiritual home: the Col d'Èze.

Paris-Nice was the first major stage race of the season. It usually started near the French capital with a prologue time trial and took a week to make its way south to the Riviera. On the way, we'd tackle some decent hills, either in the Massif Central or the Rhône Alps, before arriving in Nice. The weather could be cold and unpredictable in the north but generally it improved as we went on, which earned Paris-Nice its nickname. *La Course au Soleil.* The Race to the Sun.

The race had a tradition of finishing with a time trial on the Col d'Èze, which is a hill that climbs out of the back of Nice and heads upwards, overlooking the magnificent coastline.

I always considered Paris-Nice to be more demanding, more appealing and more prestigious than Tirreno-Adriatico, its rival event which takes place in Italy at the same time.

It was an important objective for all the French teams and De Gribaldy had a real bee in his bonnet about it at the start of the 1982 season. After the Tour de France, Paris-Nice in March and the Dauphiné Libéré in June were the most important races.

All winter, De Gribaldy had been on at me about Paris-Nice. He felt that the race was made for me. The terrain was perfect – the hills were tough but not as severe as the big mountains – and the racing was always aggressive.

Bizarrely for a race called Paris-Nice, the prologue was held in Luingne, a Belgian town just over the border from Lille. I was third behind Bert Oosterbosch of the Netherlands. Oosterbosch was a specialist at these short time trials. They weren't my strong point but when I was in good form I could produce a decent result. Finishing third was an encouraging sign.

The next day one of my team-mates, Jean-François Chaurin, went on a long solo break, spending more than 100 kilometres off the front. He won the stage by six minutes, enough of a lead to keep the leader's white jersey for a couple of days.

But Chaurin blew on the stage to Saint-Etienne, which was hit by terrible, snowy weather, and lost a lot of time. I felt really strong and won the stage ahead of the Australian Phil Anderson and Belgium's Roger De Vlaeminck to take the first of many white jerseys.

As we headed towards Nice, the race became a battle between a Frenchman called Gilbert Duclos-Lassalle and me. Duclos, as everyone called him, had won Paris-Nice in 1980, so he was the big favourite to win again. The French press were convinced that all he had to do was mark the Irishman and then pinch the white jersey in the Col d'Èze time trial at the end of the race.

On stage six to La Seyne-sur-Mer, I broke away with Duclos and my team-mate René Bittinger. René and I worked him over at the finish and I won the stage.

My overall lead over Duclos was just one second. I was not confident of actually beating Duclos on the Col d'Èze. I felt I needed more of a cushion, so on stage seven, I decided to go on the attack.

The stage went to Mandelieu, with the Col du Tanneron coming close to the finish. If you know the Tanneron, you'll know the descent is very technical and can catch out even the best bike-handlers. On that day, the weather was filthy. There was rain and a thick mist that made it hard to see far.

A French rider called Pierre Bazzo had been out in front most of the day and still had a big lead going up the Tanneron. I wasn't worried about Bazzo because he was a long way down overall. All the way up, Duclos and I watched each other. He must've been confident of getting the job done in the final time trial because he was happy to ride up the climb with me rather than try to take the white jersey.

My plan was to go to the front just as we went over the top and then hit the descent like a madman.

I wanted to put him on the defensive and force him to chase me down the descent. I thought that I could open a gap and then turn the screw by pushing it to the limit through the corners. The descent and flat run to the finish in Mandelieu was about 15 kilometres and I reckoned if I could gain 15 or 20 seconds that would tilt things in my favour on the Col d'Èze.

I did manage to open a good gap but the corners were very slippery in the wet and I pushed too hard through one of them and felt my back wheel slide away from under me.

While I was picking myself up, Duclos went by in a flash, meaning that I was now chasing him. Although he also crashed a bit further down the hill, he got up quickly and stayed ahead of me. I chased him as hard as I could but couldn't quite close the gap. At the finish, I crossed the line five seconds behind him.

That doesn't sound much but on a day when I had hoped to stretch my advantage over him, Duclos had actually turned a one-second deficit into a four-second lead.

Paris-Nice would be decided in the final time trial on the Sunday afternoon but before that we had a 60-kilometre stage from Mandelieu to the seafront in Nice, finishing on the Promenade des Anglais next to the beach.

With such an important time trial to come in the afternoon you might think I'd have taken it easy in the morning but that wasn't De Gribaldy's style. He wanted me to win that stage too.

Although it was only a short stage, it was very hard. The pace was fast from the gun and we went over the Col de Vence, which is a difficult climb. I stayed with the leaders and won the sprint. De Gribaldy was happy but not satisfied. Now he wanted me to finish the job.

Before the time trial there was time to go to our hotel for lunch. De Gribaldy supervised my meal, as he always did. I had a tiny piece of chicken and a couple of spoons of rice. He didn't like us to have salad for lunch because he thought it made you sleepy. Lunch was deliberately small because he didn't want me weighed down by a full belly on the climb.

I still felt hungry when I went to warm up on the climb but all

I was allowed was a bottle of warm tea with honey in it.

The time trial started quite late in the afternoon, so the wait seemed a long one. Cycling teams didn't have a bus or a camper van in those days, so we had to find a quiet alleyway to set up the rollers in order to warm up.

De Gribaldy found a little café near the start and we set up there, right next to a window that looked into the kitchen where I could see plates of omelette and frites being prepared.

I came off the rollers with about five minutes to go before I was due to start. There was no pep talk from De Gribaldy. The plan was simple. The Col d'Èze was just over nine kilometres long and I was going to go flat out from the bottom to the top.

'A bloc, tout de suite.'

Give it everything, straight away.

I sprinted down the start ramp, turned the corner and saw the road go upwards in front of me. I didn't want to get into a big gear too soon and make my legs feel heavy but I hadn't gone more than 50 metres when De Gribaldy leant out of the car window and shouted: *'Debout!'*

It meant he wanted me to get up out of the saddle, literally 'stand' on the balls of my feet and ride as hard as I could.

Our other team manager, Christian Rumeau, was driving the car, with De Gribaldy in the passenger seat so he could lean out of the window and shout instructions.

After sprinting for a hundred metres I sat down to settle into a rhythm. As soon as my backside touched the saddle, De Gribaldy yelled: *'Debout!'*

That carried on all the way up the climb. He only let me sit down for a few hundred metres before shouting again. He was driving me on, refusing me a moment's respite, until I was almost cross-eyed with the effort.

I could think of nothing but the pain. All the way up the climb I stared at a little patch of road just in front of me and followed De Gribaldy's instructions.

The Col d'Èze is the perfect climb for a time trial like that because it is a test of judgement. The road refuses to be bullied. The gradient changes constantly and when the slope eases the temptation is to back off and allow the legs to recover. With De Gribaldy yelling at me, that wasn't an option. I had to sit down, flick my gear lever up a couple of notches, get out of the saddle and power on.

At the first time check, I was well up on Duclos. As the race leader, he was the last to start and I knew he was a couple of minutes behind me on the hill.

By now, the adrenaline was keeping me going. De Gribaldy was listening to updates on the radio in the car. I was quite near to the finish when he leaned out of the window and shouted: 'We've got him. But keep going.'

My agony lasted 20 minutes and 50 seconds. It was the most intense experience I'd had up to that stage of my career. I'd never pushed myself that deep before but it had been worth it.

I won the time trial by 24 seconds but, more importantly, beat Duclos by 44 seconds.

Paris-Nice was mine but De Gribaldy was not one for wild celebrations. He was an extremely reserved man. He enjoyed winning but he never got carried away. I got a handshake and a pat on the back. All he said was: 'Now you know what it takes to win. You did the climb the way it needed to be done.'

FOR YEARS TO COME, Paris-Nice would be the big target for the early part of my season. I had started a run of consecutive victories that was to last seven years and once I got it rolling I became keener to ensure I kept it going.

Between Stephen and me, Ireland owned the Col d'Èze time trial. We won it every year from 1981 to 1989 but it's important to remember the final score was Kelly 5, Roche 4.

The 1983 Paris-Nice was again shaped by a treacherous descent of a wet Col de Tanneron. Having won the team time trial at Tain l'Hermitage, our Sem-France Loire squad dominated the race, taking the first three places overall. I took the white jersey at Mandelieu after distancing our nearest rival, Joop Zoetemelk, on the way down the Tanneron, then beat my team-mates Jean-Marie Grezet and Steven Rooks on the Col d'Èze.

In 1984, Roche and I had the first of our many battles.

Scotland's Robert Millar held the race lead after the team time trial at Saint-Etienne but the final few stages of the race were a straight showdown between the Irish. I had a good lead going into the Tanneron stage but Roche attacked on the climb and won by 23 seconds, cutting my advantage to just 11 seconds overall.

That was a nice lead to have before the time trial but Roche was a dangerous man to underestimate. I was reasonably confident my lead would be enough but I really wanted to beat him in the stage.

I was the last man to start the Col d'Èze climb and all the way up I knew I was losing time to Roche. Early on I was a couple of seconds down, then a couple more. With three kilometres to go I had lost ten seconds to Roche and Paris-Nice was in grave danger of slipping away. De Gribaldy was starting to get worried but I made my calculation. I had saved myself for the last three kilometres and I pulled back all of my deficit.

I won the stage ahead of Roche by one second. In a funny way it was actually more satisfying to beat him by a single second than it would have been to win by ten.

The following year, Roche beat me by one second on the Col d'Èze but I wasn't concerned because I had done enough to win the race overall, taking the white jersey from my team-mate Freddy Vichot on the final afternoon.

After a run of three wins, the expectation was that I would always turn up at Paris-Nice in good enough shape to keep the run going. But as my career progressed and I began to think about doing well at the Tour de France, I liked to start my season a little more slowly so I wasn't beginning to burn out by July.

The problem for me was that De Gribaldy expected me to be in top form early in the season. So I had to bluff him a little bit. As the years went on, I arrived at Paris-Nice a little bit below par and rode myself into shape as the week went on. Some years I think my reputation helped me win even though there were perhaps stronger riders.

I never raced in an anxious frame of mind but things just seemed to fall my way. I would watch the attacks go up the road before being captured by the bunch. I seemed to have a knack of getting in the breaks that stuck.

The 1986 victory was the most convincing of my seven-year reign. I won the prologue time trial and held the white jersey from start to finish. I finished in the top four of all ten stages, winning three of them, and my overall margin of victory over Switzerland's Urs Zimmermann was a minute and 50 seconds after the Col d'Èze time trial.

Although no one ever said anything to my face, I knew my run of wins was not universally popular with the other riders. I am sure the French wished I'd go off and ride Tirreno-Adriatico instead. I had even heard a suggestion that the organisers should pay me to stay away in 1987.

In fact, it took me a few years to realise that I should have been receiving appearance money for taking part in the race.

Paris-Nice was run by a charming woman called Josette Leulliot, who took over the race from her equally charming father, Jean, who died just before my first victory in 1982.

On morning in February 1986, I was in Cannes, waiting for the start of the day's Tour of the Mediterranean stage. Josette came up to me for a chat.

'Are you good for Paris-Nice this year?' she asked.

'Yes, of course,' I replied, thinking it was an odd question to ask someone who'd won four years in a row.

'It's the same fee as the last two years, I'm afraid,' she said, apologetically. 'We'd like to pay more but we've been having trouble getting new sponsors.'

I was surprised but I didn't want to let on that I hadn't been receiving her start money, so I just nodded and said: 'Okay.'

I had never seen a centime from the Paris-Nice organisers, so I assumed De Gribaldy had been pocketing it.

The teams would get start money, which would rise if they promised to bring the stars. It was clear Josette had been paying De Gribaldy to ensure my appearance. I couldn't confront De Gribaldy about it, and there was no way I could recover the money from the previous years, but I could make sure I got that year's fee, so after mulling it over for a few days I dropped it casually into conversation.

'By the way, I saw Josette the other day and she said she's going to pay me some appearance money this year.'

De Gribaldy didn't flinch. He just said: 'Okay, I'll make sure you get it when the cheque comes in.'

And so, a couple of months later, De Gribaldy forwarded on the fee I'd agreed with Josette.

De Gribaldy died in January 1987. He was killed suddenly in a car crash and the shock hit everyone in our team hard. By this time, we were sponsored by Kas, a Spanish soft drinks company, but it was still De Gribaldy's team.

Paris-Nice was my first major race without the man who had been by my side, on and off, for a decade. It was very strange not to have him yelling at me from the team car on the Col d'Èze.

That race was also when the rivalry between Roche and me threatened to boil over. Roche had endured a very poor year in 1986, having injured his knee in a crash while racing on the track in Paris the previous winter. At one stage it looked like his career might be in doubt but he began 1987 looking much more like his old self. By the time we got to Paris-Nice, he had already won quite a few races to remind his Italian Carrera team that he was still capable of performing at the top level.

My Kas team-mate Jean-Luc Vandenbroucke won the prologue time trial but Roche took the white jersey from him the next day when Carrera won the team time trial. We did quite well, finishing third, but losing ground to Roche so early in the race was a blow.

The fourth stage was a very difficult one. We had to ride 244 kilometres from Saint-Etienne to Chalet-Reynard, a little village midway up Mont Ventoux, the climb nicknamed The Giant of Provence. You can see it from miles away because it dominates the flat landscape surrounding it. The climb is very hard because the road barely changes direction. It just goes straight up the side of the mountain.

Because it was still early in the season, no one was in the mood to race flat-out so we rode at a pretty casual pace until we reached the bottom of the climb. It was already getting gloomy by that time. Once the road began to rise, the attacks started. We were trying to rip each other's legs off.

At times I felt good, but there were periods when I was just about hanging on. Inside the final 500 metres, I attacked and gave it everything I had. I won the stage but it was a huge effort to make to gain just five seconds over Roche, who still held the white jersey. We were in the saddle for seven-and-three-quarter hours that day. Ludicrous.

The next stage went from Miramas to Mont Faron, a short but steep climb that sits just above Toulon on the south coast of France. The hill would be another big battleground but Roche and I very nearly threw the race away that morning.

Jean-François Bernard attacked early and opened up a huge lead while Roche and I looked at each other. The rest of the bunch knew it was down to either Kas or Carrera to chase Bernard, but neither of us wanted to commit to a day's work on the front.

It was a case of 'No, after you,' until Bernard was out of sight. At the finish he still had more than three minutes over us.

Roche and I had a few words. I told him that as he was the race leader, it was up to his team to organise the chase. He said that by refusing to help I had lost Paris-Nice as well.

The next morning, Roche came alongside me in the neutralised zone and said: 'I'm going to attack. Are you going to chase?'

He wanted to recover some of the time he had lost to Bernard and keep his chances of winning Paris-Nice alive.

I agreed not to put any of my Kas riders on the front but said: 'You have to go alone, not in a group.'

It may sound strange, two of the favourites for the race talking like this, but we had this unspoken agreement not to deliberately harm each other's chances. I had no problem with Roche having a go on his own but if he went with other riders, who would help him build and maintain a bigger advantage, we'd have to chase.

Just 20 kilometres into the 208-kilometre sixth stage from Toulon to Saint-Tropez, Roche attacked alone and quickly gained three minutes.

Bernard's Toshiba team went to the front and began to chase, in an effort to defend his white jersey, but although they were working hard, the gap wasn't coming down. A few other teams eventually lent a hand. Roche had a big lead and I wondered what on earth I was doing but I stuck to my word and kept the Kas riders off the front.

By the time Roche had been caught, the Toshiba team was in bits and Bernard was left isolated and vulnerable. So, when we started the final climb and Bernard was dropped, he had no one to help him get back to the leaders.

Laurent Fignon won the stage, I was second and Roche was just behind me, meaning he took back the white jersey.

Fair play to Roche, he deserved the lead. He had been very bold. His attack had put Bernard under pressure and enabled him to regain the white jersey. With two days to go, it looked like my run of victories was coming to an end. Roche was 40 seconds ahead of me overall, which would be too much to take back even if I won all the time bonuses on offer in the sprints and beat him on the Col d'Èze.

Roche defended his lead with the minimum of fuss on the penultimate day and looked all set to win.

The final day followed the established format. There was a short but very tough road stage of 104 kilometres from Mandelieu to Nice in the morning, taking us over the Col de Vence, followed by the Col d'Èze in the afternoon.

Paris-Nice looked lost but I was determined to finish the race strongly by winning both stages. In the morning, I got the Kas riders together and we agreed to make the stage as hard as possible right from the start. If we were going to go down, we'd go down fighting.

We had a strong team, which included Acacio Da Silva, Iñaki Gastón, Freddy Vichot, Stephan Joho and the winner of the prologue, Jean-Luc Vandenbroucke.

The tactic was straightforward. As soon as we got out of Mandelieu, we would go to the front and set a searing pace.

The idea wasn't to drop Roche. He was too strong to be caught out by fierce riding. We were just trying to shake things up. If we could drop all the sprinters, I could win the stage, and give myself a chance of finishing second overall.

On the Col de Vence, Gastón rode at a very high tempo most

of the way up the climb before handing over to Vandenbroucke. I was suffering a lot but there was no way I could tell my own team-mates to slow down. I just had to hang in there until the top.

Roche was close by, pedalling smoothly.

As we approached the summit, the snow had been swept off the road and piled at the side and the surface had been gritted. The air was filled with big clouds of warm breath.

Then I heard a noise and knew immediately what it was.

Pssssssssss.

Someone had a flat tyre.

'*C'est Roche,*' said Vandenbroucke.

With that, he pushed harder on the pedals, upping the speed by about two kilometres an hour. I didn't look back.

We flew down the other side and suddenly plenty of others wanted to help drive the pace.

Roche had only one team-mate with him and by the time he had changed his wheel, his chances were gone.

At the finish, we made a mistake that could have been costly. Having done all the hard work, we failed to react quickly enough when Fignon attacked in the final kilometre. That meant I missed out on the time bonus but as the clock counted down to Roche's arrival, I knew I had done enough to win overall.

Bernard and Fignon were almost a minute behind me and Roche was at 1-27. There was no way they'd recover that on the Col d'Èze.

Driven by anger, I expect, Roche beat me by ten seconds in the time trial but it was nowhere near enough to take back the white jersey. He won the stage and I won overall so we had to go to the podium together, which was very awkward. There were some big sulks and a few fecks and I could understand his point of view because I wouldn't have been happy if I'd been in his position.

But what could we do? We'd set the pace from the start of the stage so there was no way we could wait for Roche. If we had waited, someone else would have attacked and then I'd have lost the race too.

The unwritten rule in bike racing is that you do not attack the race leader if he has a crash, a mechanical problem or a puncture.

But we didn't attack, exactly – we just carried on with a fast pace.

He was angry but that's bike racing. A puncture at the wrong moment can cost a big victory.

Stephen said a few things in the press afterwards, which was fair enough, but we soon got over it.

I WON PARIS-NICE for the seventh time in 1988 but I knew the run couldn't last for ever. I began to plan my exit strategy because I wanted to bow out undefeated.

Failing to win Paris-Nice would have made a big story. King Kelly loses his crown. I didn't want to see those headlines so I opted to vacate the throne and let others get on with it.

At the end of 1988 I agreed to join the Dutch PDM team, which meant that the decision was taken out of my hands. In those days, the top teams didn't take part in both Paris-Nice and Tirreno-Adriatico – they chose one over the other. PDM had already agreed to ride the Italian race.

So my seven-year run quietly came to an end although Roche kept the Irish flag flying by winning the time trial at Col d'Èze in 1989. I was racing at Tirreno-Adriatico when I saw the report in *La Gazzetta dello Sport*. This time, I allowed myself a little smile.

I'd vacated the throne but still Roche couldn't win overall because the Spaniard Miguel Indurain beat him.

14. Green & bronze

1982

If you look at the results, you might assume that winning my first green jersey at the Tour de France in 1982 was a formality. I finished with 429 points. Bernard Hinault, who won the Tour overall, was second, with 152 points. It was a huge margin of victory and most people probably assumed it was in the bag with eight or nine days still to go.

But to reach Paris in the green jersey meant I had to drag it over the Alps and suffer in the time trials. I had to cross the line on the Champs-Élysées to win. Nothing is certain until the end of the race so I was very nervous during the final week.

The green jersey had been De Gribaldy's next big target for me. I had begun to develop into more of an all-round rider rather than a specialist sprinter. In order to improve in the mountains, I had sacrificed a bit of my sprinting speed.

But De Gribaldy's calculations had been correct. I was still fast enough to finish in the first half-dozen on the flat stages but now I was able to get over the climbs and score points when all the other sprinters would be dropped.

In the first ten days of the 1982 Tour, I finished in the top ten seven times. That gives an idea of how consistent I was. By the time we reached the Pyrenees, I was already in a very strong position in the points competition.

The 12th stage from Fleurance to Pau was 249 kilometres – as long as the biggest Classics – and we had to go over the Soulor and the Aubisque. The mountains were misty that day but the racing on the Soulor was very fast and I fell back a bit. I had to chase hard on the descent and I managed to stay with the leaders over the Aubisque. The only man in the leading group of 18 that I was worried about was Phil Anderson, but the finish in Pau worked out perfectly for me. I had no idea then that it would be the last Tour de France stage win of my career.

I was lying fifth overall but I hadn't lost sight of the fact that the green jersey was my target rather than the yellow jersey. It was a good thing too, because the next stage caught me out.

Stage 13 was a combination of all the things that I feared. It was short, only 122 kilometres, which meant the fastest riders would race like lunatics over the climbs. The finish was at the top of a mountain, Pla d'Adet, and the weather was a lot warmer that day. My difficulty with the heat always seemed to be worsened when there was a jump in temperature overnight. I was in trouble on the first climb, the Col d'Aspin, and I lost almost seven minutes by the finish.

I took a bit of a pasting in the time trial that followed too, so my overall ambitions ended there.

But the mountains eliminated almost all of the sprinters from the green jersey competition, which meant I was certain to win, as long as I reached Paris. But I never allowed myself to take anything for granted. With Alpe d'Huez and a very hard stage to Morzine to come, I couldn't afford to.

My dream of winning in green on the Champs-Élysées came to nothing because I got blocked in and didn't manage to get my sprint started.

But it was a very successful Tour. I was 15th overall, 27 minutes behind Bernard Hinault, who was now the undisputed patron of cycling. This was his fourth Tour title in five years, putting him close to the great five-time winners who had gone before him, Jacques Anquetil and Eddy Merckx. Hinault was a tough, uncompromising figure. And he could be incredibly intimidating. He controlled the Tour completely. If a flat stage followed the mountains, he would want to have a fairly leisurely start to the day and we'd roll out and do the first 60 or 70 kilometres at a very easy pace. Hinault would ride at the front to make sure no one attacked. And if they did, he could dish out a frightening bollocking.

He'd catch whoever it was and say: 'If you'd been racing at the front in the mountains you'd be knackered like us. If you ever want to win a race, don't do that again.'

Hinault knew it was no picnic riding around at the back of the bunch in the mountains but he also knew they weren't racing with the same intensity as he was up at the front. He had the authority to lay down the law because of the way he won races.

People assume that we were close because we both came from a farming background. He was from rural Brittany and I suppose he had a similar upbringing but there was never a warm relationship between us. He was not the easiest man to talk to and if he was in a bad mood I got no more than a growl out of him. Even in his later years, by which time my stature had risen, I felt intimidated by him.

So we weren't close. When I went to the podium in Paris to get my green jersey, we shook hands and said 'congratulations' but that was about it. We'd been on the road for almost a month, so there wasn't much left to say.

WINNING THE GREEN JERSEY was a really big deal and it opened some doors for me. I was in demand for the criterium races that started once the Tour was over, running throughout August, and my appearance fee had risen a lot.

I raced almost every day that month – sometimes twice a day. The French Cycling Federation had a rule that their riders could not race twice in a day but if there were two events nearby, I'd race in the afternoon and again in the evening.

That made it a hard month, particularly coming straight from the Tour de France, but the money was so good it was well worth it. The criterium organisers all wanted the top stars at their races, so I was in demand and the green jersey meant my fee was doubled, or even trebled, from what I was used to.

A good fee in 1982 would be £500 – not bad for a two-hour race. (That's about £1,500 in today's money.)

Almost all these races were scripted by the organiser. He would decide which of the stars he wanted to win and he might suggest that a local rider also finished on the podium. The spectators wanted to be treated to a show, and that meant seeing the riders they'd watched on the television in July racing hard at the front, not sitting at the back of the bunch.

The racing was fast and aggressive. We had to sing for our supper and put on a good show. We couldn't just turn up, wave to the crowd and pick up our pay packet.

The schedule was gruelling though. There might be four or five days in Brittany and Normandy but then I'd have to drive back to Holland overnight, race there and then drive back to France. Sometimes I travelled with a mechanic or soigneur so that I could sleep instead of drive, but it was still exhausting.

And, of course, everyone wanted a green jersey. People assumed I had a suitcase full of them to give away but actually I only had three, which had to be washed by hand between races and left to dry on the parcel shelf in the car as we travelled to the next race.

The lifestyle was not ideal. De Gribaldy wasn't keen on me doing too much travelling because he knew I'd be eating at service stations and restaurants on the road.

In early September, the World Championships were held at Goodwood, in southern England. Stephen Roche and I were the Irish team and the day before the race we rode the course and talked about our tactics.

The course was not hugely selective. Although the hill would be tough enough at the end of the race to put the big sprinters at a disadvantage, it was unlikely a breakaway would succeed. Stephen and I agreed that we would follow the wheels and hope it came down to a sprint between a small group.

We knew the Italians would be very strong, and that their top rider Giuseppe Saronni was in exceptional form.

Everything came together in time for the last lap when Jock Boyer, the American who rode for my Sem-France Loire team, attacked. His team-mate, Greg LeMond, was one of the pre-race favourites so it was a surprise to see Boyer take a chance like that so late in the race. But it suited me perfectly because it meant the Italians, Dutch or Belgians would have to chase and that, in turn, would play into my hands.

I sat tight. It wasn't up to me to react, not least because Jock was a team-mate for 364 days of the year. The World Championships, which are contested by national squads rather than sponsored teams, is a one-off. Regardless of my own ambitions, I wouldn't have chased a team-mate.

And that is what made what happened next so remarkable. LeMond suddenly went to the front and started setting the pace. He was chasing his team-mate in the stars and stripes jersey.

To be fair, the fact they were wearing the same colours was no more than a coincidence. The USA wasn't a team in the same way Italy, France or Spain was a team. Jock was doing his thing and Greg was doing his. Even so, it wasn't the done thing.

I don't think Boyer would have won whatever happened because someone else would have chased eventually but it's still a talking point more than 30 years on.

As Boyer was caught, Saronni suddenly attacked with such force it was as if he'd been fired from a cannon. As soon as I saw him go, my head told me to react but my legs just weren't able to.

Saronni's timing had been perfect. LeMond hung on for second place and I managed to get up there to win the bronze medal. I was very happy with that. I didn't have the legs to do anything differently in the final kilometre, so it was a good result.

But winning the bronze medal confirmed what De Gribaldy had been telling me all year – that I was capable of winning the long, tough single-day races.

THE 1982 SEASON was a big leap forward. I'd won the green jersey at the Tour and a bronze medal at the World Championships. My decision to rejoin De Gribaldy had worked well.

When the season ended, I returned home and married Linda. I don't remember proposing and I wasn't the type to get down on one knee but I knew it was the right time to get married. I think I had been told it was now or never.

That autumn they named a square in Carrick-on-Suir after me. Sean Kelly Square. I realised that I had made my mark and that the people back home recognised and respected what I had done. As I said at the time, they don't usually do that for you until you're dead.

15. One day in yellow

The 1983 Tour de France

July 11, 1983 was my day in yellow. My only day in yellow. It was a painful day but I would not swap it for anything.

If someone offered me the chance to exchange my day in the yellow jersey at the Tour de France for a victory at the Tour of Flanders or even a world title, I would say no.

There are hundreds of professional cyclists who have never had the honour of leading the Tour so I was glad to have worn the *maillot jaune*, even if it was only for 24 hours.

But surrendering the jersey in the heat and poisonous fog of motorbike fumes was very hard to bear.

The Pyrenees were stiflingly hot that day. We had to go over the Col d'Aubisque, Col du Tourmalet, Col d'Aspin and the Col de Peyresourde, which are four of the biggest mountains passes in the region. The morning was very warm and I worried about it becoming unbearable as the day wore on because the combination of long climbs and suffocating heat was often my undoing.

I was in trouble as soon as we began to climb the Aubisque. One of the official race motorbikes was close by and I heard the radio spark into life, giving information to all the managers following the riders in the team cars.

'*Le maillot jaune est en difficulté.*'

When I lost contact with the leading riders, the motorbikes buzzed around me like flies. All the photographers had their lenses trained on me because they wanted to get their shot of the race lead slipping from my grasp. I understood that it was their job but I didn't want to make it easy for them.

I wanted to swat them away because the fumes from half a

dozen motorbikes were making the air thick and unpleasant. It was already difficult enough to breathe in the heat but as the bikes laboured against the gradient they spewed clouds of smoke into my face. The taste of petrol coated the inside of my mouth. It was horrible and it was irritating but I resisted the urge to wave my hand at them because that would give them a dramatic picture.

I began the day leading the Tour by a single second. I crossed the finishing line in Luchon ten minutes after the stage winner, all chance of winning the most open race in years completely gone.

I HAD WON THE green jersey and finished 15th overall in the 1982 Tour, so that winter De Gribaldy spent a lot of time trying to convince me that I should be much more ambitious. He told me I could win one of the spring Classics and then go to the Tour aiming to win the green jersey again and make the top ten. De Gribaldy was never too concerned about putting too much on my plate, except at dinner time.

The year began very well. I defended my title at Paris-Nice, then won the Critérium International, a two-day race in the south of France, before finishing fifth behind the world champion Giuseppe Saronni at Milan-San Remo, the first Monument of the new season. Everything was well on course for the rest of the spring Classics.

De Gribaldy's philosophy was to train hard in the winter, then race hard from the start of the season and keep racing. He didn't believe resting was all that important. Instead he feared that good form could evaporate if a rider stopped racing, even if only for a week. So the schedule of racing was always full.

Before the Tour of Flanders, the first of the Belgian Classics, we went to the Tour du Midi-Pyrenees, a race that wasn't all that important but De Gribaldy preferred me to be there than at home. He would say: 'Why train when you can race?' And if I was in a race, he wanted me to go for the victory. There was rarely a chance to just coast in with the bunch.

One day at the Tour du Midi-Pyrenees, there was a crash in the bunch as we were preparing for the finish of the stage. I went down pretty hard and as soon as I tried to get up off the floor I knew my collarbone was broken.

They took me to Pau for an x-ray, which confirmed that and also revealed I had fractured my scaphoid, the bone between the wrist and the thumb.

I knew a broken collarbone would keep me off the bike for a while but I wanted to get back to Belgium so I could see a specialist who would help me back into action as soon as possible.

So the next morning, I was awake at six, waiting for the team's *soigneur* to arrive on the ward so he could sneak me out of the hospital. He gave me a tracksuit to wear because I'd been brought in wearing my race kit and all I had was a pair of the hospital's pyjamas. We waited until the coast was clear, walked past the desk and out. I got on a flight to Lille where Herman, Elise and Linda picked me up and took me to see the sports injury specialist at the Pellenberg clinic near Leuven.

I'd hoped that a doctor more used to dealing with sports people might have better news but he didn't. I was told to stay off the bike for six weeks, which meant I would miss the entire Classics campaign. Worse than that, I feared it would ruin my preparations for the Tour de France.

I was terrible at being a patient. I'd been told to stay off the bike but I only managed a couple of weeks. I rigged my bike up to the static trainer in Herman's garage and put a box next to it so I could get on and off more easily. I turned the handlebars upright so I didn't have to bend over as much, which would put more weight on my healing collarbone and hand.

It was a mind-numbingly boring way to train, staring at the garage walls, but it meant I could do two or three hours a day until my collarbone was strong enough to get back out on the road.

My return to action was at a small race in France in early June. I'd been out of action less than two months and although it was only a low key event, I was happy to win a stage.

After that came the Tour of Switzerland, which was a much tougher challenge. Ten days long and with some huge mountains to cover, it was the fourth-hardest stage race of the year after the three grand tours.

Most people thought a race of that difficulty would be beyond my reach but after an enforced rest, I felt fit, strong and, more importantly, fresh.

The Tour of Switzerland was always a race I enjoyed. The weather in June was usually good and the scenery was spectacular, although I didn't often get caught up in admiring it. The hotels were much better than we were used to in France, Italy and Spain and the prize money was always very generous. Combine that with a strong Swiss Franc and the fact we were always paid promptly and it was a very nice race.

After winning the time trial in Geneva, I was in a very strong position overall and on the longest, toughest mountain stage, my team put the leader, Roberto Visentini, in trouble. The Italian was dropped on one of the climbs, which meant I took the yellow jersey. From then on, it was relatively straightforward to defend the lead until the finish.

Winning a race like the Tour of Switzerland soon before the Tour de France meant that a lot of journalists added me to the growing list of contenders. De Gribaldy began singing the tune that I could win the Tour.

I was not so sure. The previous year, I had been 15th, which was a good result, although I was almost an hour behind the winner. In a race like the Tour, an hour is a lot of time to make up. I usually suffered at least one bad day in a three-week race, and my weakness was when three tough mountain stages came one after another. I could usually cope with the first two but I often felt vulnerable on the third.

It's very easy for a journalist to add a rider's name to the list of contenders but the Tour de France is the ultimate test of a rider's all-round ability. The stages are longer, the pace is faster and the pressure is so much greater than at any other event.

DE GRIBALDY'S CONFIDENCE in me grew when we found out, a few days before the start of the Tour, that Bernard Hinault would not be riding. The Frenchman had won the race at the first attempt in 1978 and defended his title in 1979. In 1980, he led in the Pyrenees until a knee injury forced him to pull out. Then he returned to win back-to-back Tours in 1981 and 1982. Hinault was only 28 and he had four titles to his name. He had been the favourite to equal Jacques Anquetil and Eddy Merckx as five-time winners until his troublesome knee flared up again.

With Hinault absent, the Tour was up for grabs and everyone knew it. The Dutch rider Joop Zoetemelk and Belgian Lucien Van Impe were the only two former Tour champions in the field, and they were both 36 years old, so the likelihood was we'd have a new winner. Another couple of Dutch riders, Johan Van der Velde and Peter Winnen, were worth watching for because they were both very good in the mountains. So too was Beat Breu of Switzerland, although he was not so strong in the time trials. The French thought Jean-René Bernaudeau was in with a chance. No one mentioned Laurent Fignon, who was only 22 and would be riding the Tour for the first time.

My victory in the Tour of Switzerland meant I was added to the list and although I was not as confident in my abilities as De Gribaldy seemed to be, I felt that if the newspapers were including Phil Anderson as a possible Tour winner then I deserved to be on the list too. The Australian was a good rider but he wasn't someone I feared. He was just as likely to suffer a bad day in the mountains as I was but I was better at the time trials.

The Tour was wide open but my priority was still the green jersey. I knew it would make the race very difficult because I would have to chase points from the first day while the other contenders would be able to sit in the bunch and wait for the crucial mountain stages. Sprinting two or three times a day was very draining.

One of my biggest rivals for the green jersey was Eric Vanderaerden, a Belgian guy with a blond perm who was to become my nemesis. We had some crazy battles in the sprints and there was real animosity between us. I didn't deliberately make enemies, and I doubt he did either, but we rubbed each other up the wrong way. He could be as reckless as I was and, like me, he knew every trick in the book. He was an aggressive sprinter who rarely backed down. We'd try to squeeze each other towards the barriers and, if we thought we could get away with it, we'd pull each other's jerseys. Every now and then we threw punches at each other too. We just didn't get on but I suppose when you've got two cowboys trying to pull the same stunt, a bar room brawl is inevitable.

At the Grand Prix de Fourmies one year, we were practically wrestling each other in the sprint. It was only a small French race but neither of us wanted the other to win. Because of our antics, neither of us won, but after the finish we carried things on. I shoved him square in the chest, which made him really mad. He tried to give me a kick in the privates but as he swung his foot the sole of his standing foot slipped and he flew backwards and landed on his rear. It was a good thing too, because it was a good, firm kick. If he'd connected I'd not have been able to sit in the saddle for a week.

In the 1983 Tour, Vanderaerden won the prologue time trial in Fontenay-sous-Bois, taking the yellow jersey, but I was close enough to know that if I won a couple of intermediate sprints I might be able to take it from him. The intermediate sprints were really important for me. There were points on offer towards the green jersey competition as well as bonus seconds, which were deducted from the overall time.

But going for every sprint was a risky strategy.

The opening road stage went from Nogent-sur-Marne to Créteil. I chased every time bonus on offer at the intermediate sprints and managed to lift myself to second place overall, still 21 seconds behind Vanderaerden. The effort of going for those bonuses meant I was nowhere when it came to the sprint for the stage win. It was like taking one step forward and a couple back.

In the team time trial the next day, we lost more than two minutes so I tumbled way down the overall standings again.

Over the next few days, I continued to chase the time bonuses to scramble back up again. It took me a couple of days to get back into the top ten and another day on, I was up to seventh.

While I had been climbing the overall standings, the lead had passed from Vanderaerden to Jean-Louis Gauthier then on to Kim Andersen, a Danish rider who had broken away on stage three over the cobbles near Roubaix.

Stage six was a time trial from Chateaubriand to Nantes. I finished sixth and made up enough time over 58.5 kilometres to move up to third overall, 57 seconds behind Andersen, with the Aussie, Phil Anderson, in between us.

With three days to go until the Pyrenees, where my chances of taking the yellow jersey might disappear for good, I was within striking distance. I just had to keep chipping away.

By the time we started stage nine, from Bordeaux to Pau, I was up to second overall. Still 25 seconds separated Andersen and me. Some of the pre-race favourites were already two, three or four minutes behind me, so I was already very well placed with the mountain stages approaching.

But my immediate attention was on trying to take that yellow jersey from Andersen. As I closed the gap, he had begun to contest the intermediate sprints to limit the damage I could do to him. Although he was not a great sprinter, few riders targeted those intermediate sprints, so my gains over him were minimal.

Bordeaux was not long behind us when we came to the first intermediate sprint. I won it but Andersen marked me and took third place.

Then Philippe Chevalier, a French rider who was a long way down overall, broke away and was clear on his own for the rest of the stage. Towards the end, Gerald Veldscholten of the Netherlands got away from the bunch to take second place.

That meant there was only one time bonus, for third place, up for grabs. As we approached Pau, I did the calculations and knew that if I won the sprint for third, I would take the yellow jersey from Andersen by one second.

The sprint for the line was ferocious. Because I was so desperate to win it, I went from quite a long way out and the Belgian Etienne de Wilde came back at me very fast. I had to dig really deep to get that third place but as soon as I came to a halt after the line, someone confirmed what I already knew. I had taken the *maillot jaune*. It was a very special moment.

It had taken me a week to chisel away at Andersen's lead before finally I took it, just in the nick of time, with the mountains to come. Herman and Elise had been following the race for a few days and that evening, being good Catholics, they took the bouquet of flowers I'd been given on the podium to the grotto at nearby Lourdes and said a little prayer.

It didn't do me a lot of good.

TEN DAYS INTO THE TOUR and with 13 to go, I was in a very good position. There was only one stage in the Pyrenees, so although my lead was only one second over Andersen, who was not a good climber, I was minutes clear of most of the danger men. The climbers would be sure to attack but if I could just survive that brutal stage from Pau to Luchon I would have a few days to recover before the Alps.

But my day in yellow also happened to be one of my worst days on the bike. I asked my legs to help me but they said nothing in reply.

It was a very demoralising experience. I knew the yellow jersey had gone very early in the stage. The leaders quickly gained several minutes on me and after the second climb I was just limiting my losses, trying to prevent a disaster becoming a catastrophe.

Although I was in the yellow jersey and all eyes were on me, it was a very lonely day.

When I arrived in Bagnères-de-Luchon, ten minutes behind the stage winner, Robert Millar of Scotland, I just about had time to wipe my face before heading to the podium. I had lost the yellow jersey but I was still in green.

Pascal Simon, a French rider, was now the race leader. When I got back to the team car, I wrung as much of the sweat out of my yellow jersey as I could and folded it up, with my race numbers still pinned to the pockets on the back, before placing it in my kit bag.

IT WAS DISAPPOINTING to lose the yellow jersey, and particularly to have such a bad day in the mountains, but my Tour was far from finished. I was still fourth overall. Pascal Simon was six minutes ahead of me but he was not a proven Tour contender so there was no way of telling how he'd shape up in the Alps.

A place on the podium was still well within my reach and I had the green jersey to defend.

But the race was about to enter a strange phase. The *maillot jaune* can do funny things to a rider. Simon's first day in yellow was to prove almost as disastrous as mine.

The next stage went from Bagnères-de-Luchon to Fleurance, on really difficult roads. They were rolling and heavy because the sun melted the surface and made them sticky.

My team-mate, Joaquim Agostinho, got away in a break. Like me, he'd had a bad day in the Pyrenees and wanted to make up some time. Agostinho was a dangerous rider to allow off the leash so Gilbert Duclos-Lassalle, one of Simon's team-mates in the Peugeot squad, went with him.

Agostinho was almost 40 years old but he was still a good climber on his day and in such an open Tour, Peugeot wanted him to stay out of contention rather than become a potential threat to Simon in the Alps.

So although they had Duclos in the break, the Peugeot riders went to the front of the bunch and began to chase to bring Agostinho back.

Jock Boyer, another of my team-mates, decided to go up to the front of the bunch to disrupt Peugeot's rhythm.

This is another of those complicated areas of bike racing etiquette. You're not supposed to interrupt the chasing riders. If one team wants to set the tempo, the others are supposed to let them get on with it. But there's also nothing to stop a rider from getting into the pace line and rolling through to the front at a casual speed to try to knock the edge off the chase effort a bit, and that is what Boyer did.

Usually a word or two is enough to make a rider back off but Boyer didn't back off and the Peugeot boys didn't take kindly to him being a nuisance.

There was a bit of a discussion between Boyer and Simon and suddenly there was a crash. Did Boyer cause the crash? I don't know because I didn't get a good view of the incident. I just saw the yellow jersey on the floor and then heard the commotion that followed. Boyer was not the most popular guy in the bunch but he wasn't the most hated either. However, there was a lot of talk about it afterwards and the general opinion seemed to be that Boyer had been in the wrong.

Later on, we found out that Simon had fractured his shoulder blade. The talk around the dinner table was that Simon's race would surely be over, so it was a surprise that he started the next day. He was determined to carry on because he had the yellow jersey. He could get on the bike, just about, and pedal, so he decided to press on for as long as he could. Perhaps he thought he might recover.

With five stages to go before we reached the Alps, three of which were hilly and another was a time trial on the volcano at Le Puy de Dôme, the race entered a very unusual period. Everyone was treading on eggshells.

One of cycling's unwritten rules is that you must not attack the *maillot jaune* after a crash or a mechanical problem. Technically, Simon was fair game but because he was injured, no one wanted to be the bad guy who exploited his weakness by attacking. The code of honour in the peloton is complex and although there were plenty of people who wanted to win the race, no one wanted to be the one to put Simon out of the back of the bunch.

Because he had shown great courage by continuing in the race, Simon was now a hero.

The overall race was neutralised for a few days as Simon gritted his teeth and battled on with his broken shoulder.

With the Alps looming, everyone knew the end was coming for him. Simon's lead over Laurent Fignon was down to 40 seconds and I was back up to third place, 1-21 behind Simon, having spent a week winning bonus sprints and following a very strong time trial on Le Puy de Dôme.

Simon finally pulled out of the race on the road to Alpe d'Huez, during the 17th stage, with just five days to go to Paris.

At the point that Simon climbed off his bike, I was second in the Tour, just 41 seconds behind Fignon and well in contention if I could do well on Alpe d'Huez. Unfortunately, the Alpe was too much for me, as it often was, and I lost three minutes to Fignon, who was now the surprise of the Tour.

I finished seventh overall in Paris, 12 minutes behind the new star of French cycling, Laurent Fignon, but close enough to think that I might be able to push for the podium in the near future.

And I won the green jersey again, by another big margin.

The only disappointment was that victory on the Champs-Élysées slipped away again. Of all the sprints to misjudge, it had to be the one in Paris. Coming round the final corner I was in a perfect position, on the wheel of Eugène Urbany, who had been a team-mate of mine at Splendor. I thought he was a good guy to follow but once we'd got round the corner into the final straight he stopped his effort and I had to slow down, change my line and then try to go again.

By then Gilbert Glaus had come from behind me at a very fast pace and the gap had opened too much by the time I had a chance to react. I was second and victory in Paris was never so close again.

AFTER THE PRESENTATION ceremony on the podium I went to a hotel in the Porte St Cloud district of Paris for a meeting. We didn't have the big post-race celebrations the riders have these days. Instead I had a shower and a bite to eat and met with Daniel Dousset, a Frenchman who was one of the managers on the criterium circuit, to discuss my contracts for the coming month.

After the meeting I headed back to my car, which was parked around the corner, ready to drive back home to Belgium. I noticed one of the windows had been smashed and my bag was gone.

My heart jumped because my yellow jersey – my only *maillot jaune* – was in one of the bags that was taken.

The police found my bag and some of my stuff strewn in a nearby street but my jersey had gone.

A little while later, I contacted the Tour de France organisers and they sent me a replacement jersey with the logos of my team sponsors, Sem and France Loire, pressed onto the front. It's framed at home now but it is not the same.

I am not usually a sentimental person. During my career I barely spent a moment thinking about my jersey and trophy collection. I was very fortunate to have Herman to curate it for me as I kept adding to it. He looked after everything and when I retired we put the lot in a van and took it back to Ireland.

When I was competing I was so occupied with the effort of training, racing and travelling that the trophies seemed less important. I know I am fortunate because there are a lot of riders who don't have a trophy collection to speak of.

It wasn't until later, when I stopped and had time to think, that I got a pang of disappointment. I had left that yellow jersey exactly as I'd worn it. Deliberately so. The number 99 was still pinned on the back. It had dried out but it still contained the sweat I'd shed that difficult day in the Pyrenees.

I wondered for a while whether someone would realise that it was a genuine yellow jersey worn in the Tour de France, recognise what it meant to me and return it in the post to me one day.

But it has never turned up and so it must be considered gone forever.

Whoever took it, and whoever has it now, probably thinks they have a very nice souvenir. But I can assure them it can never mean as much to them as it means to me.

16. Joining the club

The 1983 Tour of Lombardy

Like any community, the peloton has a hierarchy. There are the stars to win the races and there are the *domestiques* – the helpers – to fetch the water bottles.

To become one of the stars, you have to win a big race and that is far from an easy thing to do.

De Gribaldy had been on at me for months, telling me that it was high time I won a major Classic to prove myself capable of becoming one of the top riders.

But cracking into the small group of stars who were always among the favourites for the major one-day races was easier said than done. At the time, the Classics were controlled by people like Jan Raas of the Netherlands, Roger De Vlaeminck of Belgium, a couple of Italians, Francesco Moser and Giuseppe Saronni, and one or two others. They were the riders who won the biggest races each season and they wanted it to stay that way.

They didn't want any upstarts coming along to upset the order of things, so they liked to gang up to maintain the status quo.

Cycling has always been the same. The top riders want to stay at the top for as long as possible. There are only a small number of big races to go round, so they'd rather ensure those honours were shared among a small group of elite riders, otherwise there would be less to go round.

That's not to say that the riders sat down and divided up the races between them because it's not that straightforward. But in a Classic, the top riders would prefer it if a rider from the club won rather than have to admit a new member.

It was a bit of a catch-22 situation. You couldn't be a big rider unless you won a Monument. And you couldn't win a Monument unless you were a big rider. So, it took something special to earn membership of the club.

Later in my career, I did much the same thing myself, although it wasn't really a conscious thought. It was just an instinctive thing. For example, although Claude Criquielion and I rode for different teams, we would sometimes work together in the Classics. If he felt he didn't have the legs to win, he'd give me a hand instead, knowing I'd return the favour another day. It wasn't a financial arrangement; we just looked out for each other when we could.

I WAS NOT A young whippersnapper, I was 27 years old and about to enter the peak years of my career. De Gribaldy would argue that it was long overdue, but I was finally admitted to the club on Saturday, October 15, 1983 and by the narrowest of margins.

How fitting that my first Monument victory would be the Tour of Lombardy. I'd won the amateur version of the race six years earlier. It is known as the Race of the Falling Leaves because it has an autumnal feel. The course is hard, covering 250 kilometres and taking the riders over some difficult climbs in the Lombardy region of northern Italy.

And because it was the last major race of the season, there was often a sense of desperation in the air. Riders who had endured a poor season could salvage some success at the last moment. In those days, everybody rode the Tour of Lombardy – no one went on holiday early. Having missed the spring Classics with a broken collarbone, I was particularly motivated.

The race was very aggressive, particularly in the latter stages. Pedro Muñoz, a Spanish rider, was out in front and built a nice advantage on the San Fermo della Battaglia climb, which came about nine kilometres from the finish in Como.

My Sem team-mates, Jean-Marie Grezet and Eric Caritoux, worked really well on the climb to close the gap down a bit. The effort meant that they were dropped from our group as we got towards the summit, which left me without any team-mates for support.

As we tackled the descent towards Como, there were only 18

of us left. My only ally was Stephen Roche and he began to take up the chase to bring Muñoz back. He knew the race was going to end in a sprint and that he had very little chance of winning it, so he decided to give me a hand. His Peugeot team manager, Roland Berland, was unhappy because he thought Roche shouldn't have worked, but the tactic suited Peugeot's other rider in the break, Phil Anderson, just as much as it did me.

We came into the finishing straight and the sprint opened up. It was very, very close. There was barely a wheel's length between four of us – Greg LeMond, Adri Van der Poel, Hennie Kuiper and me.

I kept my head down, closed my eyes and threw my bike forwards the final half metre – a bit like a 100-metre sprinter dipping his chest to hit the tape first. I wasn't certain I had it – not at all – because we hit the line in the blink of an eye. I didn't know for sure until we saw the photo finish.

I sensed that LeMond was coming back at me as we hit the line. At the end of a long, difficult race like that, when the conditions had been wet and everyone was tired, Greg could be very strong in the sprint.

Then someone confirmed that I'd won it.

De Gribaldy was as happy as I'd ever seen him. He did like it when his riders proved him right.

I was now a fully-fledged member of the club but there was no time to celebrate because we had to get in the car and drive north to Switzerland for the Critérium des As – the Race for the Aces – a motor-paced exhibition race which was held in Geneva the following day. Entry was by invitation only and the organisers liked the biggest names in cycling to take part.

The race was only 100 kilometres and the course was flat but because each cyclist was paced by a motorcycle called a Derny, which is a bit like a scooter, the speed could easily hit 60 kilometres an hour. Coming a day after the Tour of Lombardy it could be very hard on the legs. The adjustment from racing up the steep hills in Italy to powering a big gear on the flat was difficult to make.

And, like most critérium races, the organiser liked to have a say in who won, to ensure the crowd were treated to a show.

As Greg LeMond had recently won the world title, the race organiser decided the American should win the Critérium des As.

The problem in a motorpaced race was that the riders on the Derny bikes had as much say in the outcome as the cyclists because they had their hands on the accelerator.

With two laps of the Geneva circuit to go, my Derny driver took off. I looked round and saw we had a big gap. LeMond was nowhere to be seen. I knew this wasn't what the organiser wanted so I yelled to my Derny driver to slow down.

I didn't want to annoy the organiser or put my appearance fee at risk. Eventually, LeMond and a French rider, Pascal Poisson, caught us and we managed to ensure that LeMond won the race so everyone went home happy.

I'd just won the Tour of Lombardy. I'd joined the club. But in professional cycling, it rarely pays to forget your place in the order of things. The hierarchy has to be observed.

17. The King
April 1984

There's a myth that grew as my career went on. Some people said that if it was raining on the morning of a race, I would draw back the curtains and rub my hands together in glee. The perception was that I relished the bad weather, enjoyed it even, but that was certainly not the case. No one likes to be cold and wet – it was just that my body coped with the conditions better than a lot of others. I was as miserable as everyone else – it's just that I was able to keep pushing hard.

There were times when the bad weather was too much, though. On a couple of memorable occasions, the weather caused my body to shut down. One time was a downpour during the 1985 Tour of Flanders when the temperature dropped dramatically. With 40 kilometres to go I was still in the leading group but I was cooked. Hennie Kuiper was away and Phil Anderson went after him. I was in the chasing group with Eric Vanderaerden. As usual, we were watching each other like hawks. He can't have realised that I was finished, that my race was over.

Vanderaerden also didn't realise that my only interest left in the race was to make sure he didn't win, so I was doing my best to bluff him, hoping I could take him to the grave with me.

Eventually he realised I was running on empty, so he set off in pursuit and rode across the gap to Kuiper and Anderson. By now, I was really suffering. The cold and wet had got to my bones. As we neared Geraardsbergen, the last town before the finish, my legs deserted me. They were cold, rigid and blue.

I needed to pee but I thought I'd wait until I got to the bottom of the Muur, the famous climb that goes up through the town and then up again to the little chapel at the top of the hill.

As I reached the bottom of the climb, I relaxed and let the warm pee run down my legs so it would warm my muscles a bit. Without doing that, I don't think I'd have got over the Muur.

It was grim but not as grim as reaching the finish to discover that Vanderaerden had caught Kuiper and Anderson and had won the race. I finished 14th, which was nowhere, but I at least made it to the finish.

Rarely did I drop out of a race close to the end because the conditions were too extreme, although there was one exception. The 1980 edition of Liège-Bastogne-Liège was held in a blizzard.

The weather in the Ardennes was so bad, only 21 riders made it to the finish inside the time limit. Bernard Hinault won, finishing almost ten minutes clear of the next man. It was a battle for survival from the moment we reached Bastogne and headed back to Liège via a succession of steep hills.

I was way down, struggling along, unable to feel my hands. I could barely squeeze the brakes because my fingers were so cold. Ice had clogged up my brakes anyway. My face was numbing. The snow stung the skin.

I was 15 kilometres from the finish – with less than half an hour left to ride – but I was dreaming of getting off my bike and getting warm. I didn't want to ride another metre.

I knew Herman and Linda were out on the course somewhere. Because it was so close to the finish, Herman parked his car at the side of the road but hidden behind a hedge so I wouldn't see it. Then they stood back a bit, out of view.

They knew that if I spotted them, I'd be off my bike and in the back of the car in a moment. He was right.

I saw the nose of the car, then spotted them and I pulled over and called it a day there. Herman tried to convince me to go on, because I was so close to Liège, but I refused. There was nothing to gain from riding another 15 kilometres in the snow. I wasn't going to get a result worth shouting about and I might have done more harm than good by pushing on.

Generally speaking, I could cope with the harsh weather. And being able to tolerate it when others began to fade increased my chances of winning some of the toughest races. I could tell myself that if I was suffering, others were bound to be hurting even more.

DE GRIBALDY HAD long been telling me I could be a man for the Classics but it wasn't until I won the Tour of Lombardy at the end of the 1983 season that I really believed it.

I felt a lot more confident at the start of 1984. I won Paris-Nice for the third time in a row, and Critérium International for the second but my focus was on the big Classics in April – the Tour of Flanders, Paris-Roubaix and Liège-Bastogne-Liège, in particular.

I felt so strong at the Tour of Flanders – probably too strong, because the Belgians worked me over. The Tour of Flanders is their biggest race and they were never wild about a foreigner winning it. But because I felt so good, I showed too much of my hand and they took advantage.

We came to the Muur in Geraardsbergen in quite a big group. The climb is towards the end of the race and it's the place to find out who has got it and who hasn't. Any riders who have been hanging on a bit will be dropped immediately.

I put the pressure on a bit, split the group up, and the Belgians followed me, like I was the Pied Piper.

Among them were Jean-Luc Vandenbroucke of the La Redoute team, Jean-Philippe Vandenbrande and Rudy Matthijs of Splendor and Ludo De Keulenaer and Johan Lammerts of Panasonic. Lammerts was a Dutchman, which is more or less the same as being Belgian in the Tour of Flanders.

Although I was outnumbered two-to-one by both Splendor and Panasonic, I wasn't too concerned because I felt so good.

I was sure one decent attack would whittle the group down further. If anyone came with me, I was confident I could deal with them in the sprint.

The other riders were reluctant to work with me so I did a lot of work on the front. I wanted to keep this group of half a dozen clear, rather than let any of those who had been dropped get back on and then have the chance to jump us.

I was happy enough to work because I thought they were no

match for me in the sprint.

But as we got closer to the finish, they started attacking me, one by one, and left me to close the gap each time. One would go and the others would all sit behind me, waiting for me to respond. So, I would close the gap and then another would attack and I'd have to do it all again.

The Belgians were clubbing together because I was the big favourite. They gave me a good, old-fashioned working over.

Although I was getting tired I was still able to respond to the attacks, but I was getting fed up with their tactics so I decided to call their bluff. When Johan Lammerts – a Dutchman, and the only other foreigner – attacked, I freewheeled and pretended I didn't have any strength left. I just let him go.

It was the mistake of my life because the Belgians let him go as well. They all sat up, we looked at each other and by then Lammerts had gone. I consoled myself with the fact that at least it hadn't been one of the Belgians who had ridden away.

Lammerts crossed the line alone and I won the sprint for second, just to prove a point.

At the finish, De Gribaldy was not happy. He was singing his usual tune about the Belgians and Dutch being untrustworthy. He thought I should have raced the race instead of getting sucked into their games. Instead of letting Lammerts go, I should have been up out of the saddle chasing him, no matter how tired I felt. It was not the time to play around. Throughout my career, the Tour of Flanders was the one that got away. It was the only one of the five Monuments I never won. In retrospect, the 1984 race was my best chance.

DE GRIBALDY USED to keep us very busy, so instead of staying in Belgium to race at Ghent-Wevelgem on the Wednesday between the Tour of Flanders and Paris-Roubaix, we flew to northern Spain to ride the five-day Tour of the Basque Country instead.

All the other teams would stay in Belgium, do short recovery rides on Monday and Tuesday, then race at Ghent-Wevelgem, which is another Classic though not quite on the same level as the Monuments, and then head over the border to train on the cobbles for a couple of days before Paris-Roubaix.

Not me. After the Tour of Flanders, I had a shower at the hotel and then went to a little airfield at Wevelgem to get on a plane that had been chartered to fly us to Bilbao. We arrived late in the evening, had a bite to eat, went straight to bed and got up in the morning for the first stage, which I won.

I'd ridden a Classic on the Sunday, and won the first stage of the Tour of the Basque Country on the Monday. I won another two stages, which gave me the overall title too. After the final stage on Friday afternoon, we flew back to Paris, drove to Compiègne, where Paris-Roubaix starts, and spent Saturday trying to rest.

It was a crazy schedule, really, but De Gribaldy saw no problem. He thought the best way to prepare for one big race was by riding another big race.

PARIS-ROUBAIX IS A horrible race to ride but a beautiful one to win. My technique on the broken, battered cobblestones had improved a lot since the first time I'd ridden it in 1978. But it was still a race that made me nervous. I felt I had a good chance of winning, although I could never be sure whether Lady Luck planned to give me a helping hand or flick me into the gutter.

I was one of the pre-race favourites but that doesn't mean much at Paris-Roubaix because the favourites can crash or have a puncture just like anybody else.

It rained all day on Saturday and although it wasn't raining on the morning of the race, the sky looked grey and uninviting. I definitely didn't look out of my window and smile to myself because I knew we were in for a hard day. But I did know that the wet cobbles would increase my chances because a lot of riders wouldn't fancy it in these conditions.

Even on a dry day, only around 25 riders have any hope of winning Paris-Roubaix. The distance, the speed and the cobbles mean it takes a special rider to win.

In the wet, we can reduce the number of candidates to around a dozen. And, of them, a couple will crash or puncture at the wrong moment and another couple will have a day when they don't feel strong enough.

So, as I rolled out of Compiègne, leaving behind its grand buildings, heading for the old First World War battlefields, I knew I had to be careful and patient for the first half of the race.

Paris-Roubaix is a hard enough race without me being the architect of my own downfall by taking crazy risks. I needed to ride near enough to the front to avoid the crashes and chaos, without sapping my energy by being on the front, in the wind. Even if everything went my way, I still had to be prepared to push myself to my maximum.

Tactically speaking, it was not a subtle race. There is nothing particularly complicated about Paris-Roubaix. It is a test of strength and courage. The distance – more than 260 kilometres – is no more daunting than any of the other Monuments, but there are 55 kilometres of terrible cobblestones that are very draining to ride over.

Knowing the punishment that lies ahead, it can be tempting to sit tight for too long. I didn't want to wait until the race had run away from me before making my move.

The first section of cobbles – *pavé* – comes after about 100 kilometres. Two riders from the La Redoute team – Alain Bondue and Gregor Braun – had broken away before that sector and already had a nice advantage.

Because they were team-mates I knew they would work very well together to ensure that the strongest of the two would be able to survive as long as possible. There was a chance they'd be able to collaborate well enough to stay clear all the way to the finish. Their sponsor, the La Redoute clothing company, had its headquarters in Roubaix too, which would have added extra motivation.

By this stage in my career, I was relatively comfortable on the cobbles. I had come to understand them. I respected them and I could read them. Even in the wet, I felt in control. The technique sounds quite straightforward. I had to relax a little so that I wasn't trying to fight the bike's natural inclination to follow the line of least resistance. Instead of trying to 'steer' the bike, I let the bike find its way a little. That sounds counter-intuitive but it works.

The temptation to flinch every time my front wheel took a heavy hit from a pothole, or when my back wheel slid in the mud, was still great but I had learned to go with the flow.

Because of the previous day's rain, the mud and standing water made the cobbles treacherous. I avoided the puddles, as far as I could, because it was hard to tell how deep the water was or what lay beneath. Occasionally there was no choice but to ride through the water and hope for the best.

A lot of riders didn't have the stomach for this sort of thing, so as we headed north towards Roubaix, in the suburbs of Lille, the group around me got smaller and smaller.

I was feeling good, so I started to get itchy feet. Bondue and Braun were still well ahead of us and on the cobbles it is hard for a group to organise a chase because we tend to ride single-file over the *pavé* sections. It's impossible to get a relay going until we're back on the smooth roads. That gives the riders in the break a little advantage.

I wanted to go off in pursuit of Bondue and Braun and see which of the riders in my group were capable of coming with me. With around 80 kilometres remaining, I dropped back to the team car and told De Gribaldy I was going to attack. He told me to wait, saying that it was still far too early.

A little bit later I talked to him again. He still refused to let me go but he practically had to put a rope around my neck and tether me like a horse.

With 45 kilometres to go, I could wait no longer. We came to a section of cobbles at Orchies and I accelerated away from the others. The gap to Bondue and Braun was still 1-45.

Once I'd got across the Orchies section of *pavé* I looked back and saw someone was coming across to me. It was Rudy Rogiers, a Belgian riding for my old Splendor team. I slowed down a bit so he could catch me.

This was the ideal situation for me because Rogiers would be a useful ally as we chased the two La Redoute riders but he was no sprinter, so was little threat to me if it was me against him at the finish.

Bondue and Braun were obviously going pretty well because it took quite a lot of effort for Rogiers and me to get across to them. Riding on those roads can be very difficult mentally, as well as physically. The roads are flat and dead so I had to work for every metre. There's no downhill so there's hardly any opportunity to freewheel and give the legs some respite.

I was riding more strongly on the cobbles than Rogiers so I led over every section. Rogiers did what he could on the smooth roads but I knew I was going a lot better than him, which began to make me nervous. The way things were panning out, this race was now mine to lose.

We caught the two La Redoute riders on the cobblestones just after Wannehain, with around 20 kilometres to go.

As soon as we caught them, I went straight to the front and carried on driving the pace. That meant Braun was dropped immediately but Bondue hung in there for a while and I towed my two passengers towards the velodrome at Roubaix.

In the back of my mind lurked the warning from the Tour of Flanders the previous week. I didn't want to fall for the sucker punch again even though I was certain that the final few sections of *pavé* would suck the remaining fight from Bondue and Rogiers.

Finally we lost Bondue. He slipped and fell on the cobbles at Camphin-en-Pévèle, which is a really horrific sector. The fall was probably a result of fatigue.

When it was just Rogiers and me, De Gribaldy came alongside us in the car. His instructions were simple. 'Whatever you do, don't mess up the sprint.

I knew Rogiers was tired. I knew that 100 times out of 100, I should beat him in the sprint, but I still had butterflies.

Linda was following the race with the photographer, John Pierce, and when they parked up at the velodrome, she stayed in the car with her knitting because she couldn't bear to watch, even though John told her the victory was in the bag.

I was worried that something might happen to the bike after the punishment it had taken on the cobbles. Or I could get a flat tyre just before arriving in the velodrome and have to sprint round the concrete track on the rim.

Just before we swung into the velodrome and pulled onto the track I slowed down to put Rogiers on the front, to make him lead out the sprint. I'd towed him most of the way to the finish, so his part of the unspoken deal was to lead out.

I took a few deep breaths to calm myself down. I looked down to check I was in the correct gear for the sprint and to ensure there wasn't any mud that was likely to jam my chain or derailleur during the finale.

Arriving in the Roubaix velodrome after 260 kilometres, more than 50 of which are on the hellish cobbles, is one of the experiences that makes the hairs on my neck stand up. The crowd roared as we entered the velodrome and came onto the track but then they fell very quiet, anticipating the finish.

Rogiers began the sprint and I went past him quite easily. That final lap and a bit of the track looked easy but what had gone before was not. I had been fortunate. I was covered in mud and my whole body ached, but I had not suffered a puncture or crash all day. The gods of Paris-Roubaix had smiled on me.

That evening I lay on the bed in my room at Herman and Elise's house. The cobblestone trophy they give the winner of Paris-Roubaix was downstairs on the kitchen table. My bike was left, unwashed, against the wall in the garage. It was covered in grey-brown mud from the fields.

I don't think I'd ever felt so tired after a race. I'm not sure I ever did again. My palms buzzed as if I had pins and needles. Every muscle ached. My undercarriage was raw.

I went for a pee and the burning sensation made me wince. The hours spent sitting on the peak of the saddle, clattering over the cobbles, had left their mark. I was dehydrated but I didn't want to drink anything because I didn't want that pain again.

The following morning I hauled myself out of bed. It took enormous willpower to force myself to go for a short spin on my training bike. I knew I had to turn the pedals for an hour or so to help me recover from the effort because my next race was only two days away.

On Wednesday I started Flèche Wallonne but the plan was always to stop after 100 kilometres. By Friday I began to feel a bit more like myself but I didn't consider myself a contender for Liège-Bastogne-Liège at the weekend.

I wasn't sure how well I'd recovered and I was concerned

about the number of steep climbs in the second half of the Liège-Bastogne-Liège course. Paris-Roubaix is the most extreme one-day race but Liège-Bastogne-Liège is probably the hardest.

Going from one to the other in the space of a week was a very difficult adjustment to make. The switch from racing on the flat roads of northern France to the steep hills of the Ardennes was like night and day.

Paris-Roubaix is all about pushing a big gear for hours, which requires a lot of brute force and pure power. In contrast the steep hills in the Belgian Ardennes meant the rhythm was constantly changing. Climbing those hills, coping with the intensity of riding in a small gear, was a big shock.

Only two men had won Paris-Roubaix and Liège-Bastogne-Liège in the same year: Rik Van Looy in 1961 and Eddy Merckx in 1973. Both were legends of the sport who had won all the Monuments. No one gave the Irishman any hope of following them so I felt very relaxed. I'd won a lot of races already so there was no pressure on me. My strategy was basic: hang on as long as possible, follow the wheels and see if I could make the final selection of riders when the time came.

In those days the race finished in the centre of Liège, on the Boulevard de la Sauvenière. It wasn't the uphill finish we have today. All day, I rode without fear. And because I had nothing to lose, I found I could hurt myself to stay with the leaders. At times I had to dig very deep on the climbs but as riders kept getting dropped I knew my chances were rising.

Laurent Fignon of Renault and Phil Anderson of Panasonic attacked with 40 kilometres to go. I was in a group of seven, just behind the two leaders. Marc Madiot and Greg LeMond were Fignon's team-mates, so they weren't going to chase. Steven Rooks was with Panasonic, so he didn't need to work either. That left Claude Criquielion, Acacio Da Silva, Joop Zoetemelk and me.

Criquielion did a lot of work to bring back Anderson and Fignon and we could see them ahead of us for a long time on the run-in to Liège. But we didn't catch them until a kilometre to go.

Criquielion tried a late attack, Madiot countered, and I closed the gap easily. LeMond worried me most because he could sprint.

Anderson had a fast finish too but he was likely to be tired having been in the break with Fignon.

With 300 metres to go, I found myself on the front. That was not the ideal place to be, so I decided to just go for it. I began my sprint and gave it everything. I was so strong no one could come past me.

The spring of 1984 was the peak of my career. I won two of the Monuments and was runner-up in two others.

The newspapers nicknamed me King Kelly.

As nicknames go it was quite a nice one to have.

18. Pipped on the Champs-Élysées

The 1984 Tour de France

In 1984, I came within a few metres of winning the green jersey for a third successive year. On the final morning of the Tour, I put the jersey on. Later that day, Frank Hoste of Belgium grabbed it from me on the Champs-Élysées.

After such a long, difficult battle with Hoste, it was a bitter pill to swallow. I'd had to work so hard to get the jersey in the first place and thought I had it all sewn up. He had other ideas.

The opening few days of the Tour did not go well. Hoste won the first sprint finish in St Denis. I knew Hoste was a fast sprinter but at that point I did not know he would become my big rival.

My chances of overall success were damaged too. My Skil team lost a lot of ground in the team time trial to Valenciennes. We could manage only ninth place and conceded 1-22 to Laurent Fignon's Renault team. That was a lot of time to give up to the defending champion.

If the morning had been a disappointment, the afternoon was a disaster. We had a stage from Valenciennes to Béthune. It was only 83 kilometres but after the effort of the team time trial everyone was nervous about how their legs would feel. To make matters worse, it rained all afternoon and as we got closer to the finish there were crashes and punctures. With around 20 kilometres to go, we went through a little village, turning left and right and breathing in as the road narrowed. The road was wet and the brakes don't work as well in the rain so when the bunch came to a halt in front of me, I didn't have time to stop.

I skidded, went into the back of someone and hit the floor. I wasn't hurt but I'd managed to wipe out the spokes in my front wheel. The rest of the bunch streamed by me, then came the team cars, roaring past like they were in a grand prix. Only one of my team-mates, Freddy Vichot, stopped for me.

I got a replacement wheel from the team car but by the time Freddy and I got going, we were well off the back of the bunch and behind the line of vehicles that makes it easier to regain contact with the riders.

The pace was really on at the front of the bunch. Even if we'd been in between the team cars it would have been a difficult chase but at least we'd have been able to get a little bit of shelter from the cars and make our way forwards gradually.

But being so far back and with only 20 kilometres to go, we had no chance of catching them. We needed the whole team back there with us.

I was angry that only Freddy stopped for me. If I could have chosen one guy to wait with me it would have been him because he never held back. If there was work to be done, he'd do it. Some of the others tended to look the other way so they could pretend they hadn't seen me. Having done a hard team time trial in the morning perhaps they didn't fancy doing another one, or maybe they were dreaming of getting in a break a few days down the line and didn't want to make any effort, but it was their job to wait for the team leader.

Freddy and I finished 1-34 behind the bunch, capping a bad day. In less than 140 kilometres of racing, I'd lost almost three minutes. When I got to the team car, I slammed the doors a bit so everyone knew I was annoyed. I was not happy at all but I wasn't someone who would start shouting at people as soon as I crossed the line. Back at the hotel we had a bit of a discussion and I told them that it was their job to wait for me and help me back to the bunch. They said they hadn't seen me. I had to give them the benefit of the doubt because I'd been wearing a plain rain jacket over my Skil jersey. The riders didn't have radio contact with each other in those days so word spread pretty slowly. There was no point wasting energy being angry about it. I knew that wouldn't change anything.

It wasn't just the time I lost that disappointed me but also the fact I'd slipped behind Hoste, Eric Vanderaerden and Adri Van der Poel in the race for the green jersey.

A few days later at Alençon, Hoste won again and I was second over the line. It wasn't until I got back to the hotel that I found out I'd been relegated to last place in the bunch for irregular sprinting. The race jury said I'd impeded Gilbert Glaus by squeezing him into the barriers that lined the finishing straight. As far as I was concerned, I had held my line and it was the barriers that moved inwards, narrowing the road.

We tried to lodge a protest with the race jury but it was pointless. They are right and the riders are wrong. They say: 'We'll look at it again,' but, in my experience, they never change their minds.

It wasn't until later in the race that I realised the significance of losing those points in Alençon. Although the number of points on offer during the following day's time trial from Alençon to Le Mans was not as generous as for the flat stages, I knew it was a chance to make up ground on Hoste. I rode extremely well over the 67-kilometre course, finishing second to Laurent Fignon by only 16 seconds but ahead of both Bernard Hinault and Stephen Roche. It was, arguably, the best time trial I ever did in the Tour.

As we reached the Pyrenees, I had an advantage over Hoste because I knew I could score points where he could not. Robert Millar won stage 11 at Guzet Neige and by the end of the day I was up to eighth overall.

Just as I rode to my strengths, so Hoste did to his. He started going for the intermediate sprints, which meant I had to go for them too. I knew I was taking on a lot, fighting on two fronts like this but I didn't feel I had any other option if I wanted to win the green jersey. I'm not saying Hoste had an easy ride during the mountain stages, because it's never easy for the big sprinters to haul themselves up and over every col, but he could preserve a little bit of energy whereas I was racing hard to protect my overall position.

Stage 15 to Grenoble was a hilly day and I knew that Hoste would be out of the points. Freddy Vichot attacked on the descent into town and I managed to take fourth place. After finishing seventh in the mountain time trial to La Ruchère I was a little bit closer to Hoste. It was slow going but I was gradually reeling him in.

After the rest day came the Alpe d'Huez stage and again it was to be my undoing. Jean de Gribaldy's obsession with diet meant that on the day of the 22-kilometre time trial and the rest day I'd eaten lightly.

The stage was quite short, only 151 kilometres long. The racing was very aggressive on the early climbs, and it was a scorching hot day. Basically, it was a combination of all my weaknesses. Fignon was so strong and he wanted to make sure everyone – especially Bernard Hinault – knew it, so he attacked whenever he had the chance. Luis Herrera, the little Colombian climber, was another who could accelerate and make life a misery for me.

I spent the whole day way outside my comfort zone. The heat and the pace being set by the climbers meant I had to ease back a little bit and ride at my own rhythm. Before we reached Alpe d'Huez, we did the Côte de Laffrey, which is a horrible climb because there isn't a descent after it. Instead there's a false flat which means there is no chance to recover before reaching Bourg d'Oisans and the bottom of the Alpe.

I lost nine minutes to Herrera, who won the stage, but if I'd tried to stay with them earlier in the stage the damage would have been much greater.

The final week of that Tour was brutal. After the rest day we'd had a mountain time trial and then four difficult mountain stages in a row. What followed was ridiculous. Stage 21 was from Crans-Montana to Villefranche-en-Beaujolais – 320 kilometres, or almost 200 miles.

I was awake before six so I could eat breakfast, and the stage was underway at eight o'clock. We crossed the finish line in Villefranche at 5.30 in the afternoon after almost nine-and-a-half hours in the saddle. It was savage.

I'd managed to score points in the Alps, so the race for the green jersey was now between just Hoste and me. With only a time trial and the final stage to Paris to go, I considered myself a narrow favourite but was prepared for the contest to go all the way to the Champs-Élysées.

At the halfway mark of the epic stage to Villefranche, the organisers had put a 'bumper' intermediate sprint. Perhaps it was to make sure we were all still awake. There were almost as many points on offer there as at the finish line.

I won that sprint and, for a few hours, I was leading the competition on the road. But Hoste was far from beaten. He won the stage late that afternoon, and I was only third, so he kept hold of the jersey.

The penultimate stage was a time trial. I was second, behind Fignon, but the points I gained gave me the green jersey at last. With just the final stage to Paris left to ride, I had managed to peel the green jersey off Hoste's shoulders.

I studied the results that night and knew that I had to finish no more than one place behind Hoste on the Champs-Élysées to keep the green jersey.

On the final morning of the Tour, the whole peloton travelled north by train for the final stage. I saw Hoste on the train and we had a brief conversation. We agreed not to contest the intermediate sprints early in the stage. It suited me not to have to race for those points because it would mean I'd be fresher at the finish.

As it turned out, a break was already up the road when we got to the intermediate sprint so there weren't any points for us to fight for, so it came down to the final sprint on the Champs-Élysées. My tactic was very simple. I had to stick to Hoste's back wheel and not let him out of my sights. Coming into the final kilometre, I had him exactly where I wanted him but as we came round the final bend, I got blocked and he got away from me a bit.

I was still confident I could get back to him but he started his sprint and I still had to get past a number of riders. I was boxed in, too close to the barriers, so I had to give Phil Anderson a bit of a shove in order to get through.

I was probably the fastest rider over the last couple of hundred metres but I had started my sprint from too far back. Vanderaerden won the stage, Hoste was third and I was close behind him. Unfortunately, Bernard Hinault, who was over on the other side of the road to us, got in between and bumped me down to fifth.

That was enough to give Hoste the green jersey by just four points. I was incredibly frustrated and De Gribaldy was angry, reminding me: 'You have to keep your eye on the Belgians.'

When it came down to such a narrow margin it was tempting to look back and see where I could have scored more points. What if I'd not crashed on the road to Béthune? What if I'd settled for third or fourth place instead of squeezing past Glaus at Alençon, giving the jury the opportunity to relegate me?

But the result is the result. Frank Hoste's name is in the record books and that's that.

Although I was disappointed not to clinch the green jersey because no one had ever won it three times in a row before, I was satisfied with how the Tour had gone.

I was fifth overall and my career as a rider for the general classification was still progressing in the right direction. Fignon had been unbeatable in the mountains and the time trials and he deserved to win but when I looked at the results I began to feel that I was ready to challenge for a place on the podium.

I was 16 minutes behind Fignon – almost half of which I lost in one day at Alpe d'Huez – but the podium was only five minutes away. I'd lost almost three minutes with one disastrous day early in the race and had probably paid the price in the mountains for having to race against Hoste in the intermediate sprints.

I could see areas where I could improve and, if I altered my priorities so that I didn't have to chase the green jersey, I might give myself a better chance overall. The problem for me was that De Gribaldy didn't want to put all his eggs in one basket. He liked me to go for the green jersey and then see what I could do overall. He wasn't about to let me sit back in the first week like many of the other overall contenders.

So although people were beginning to talk about me as a future Tour winner, I still had my doubts. I was vulnerable in the high mountains, especially when it was very hot. If a journalist asked me whether I felt I could win the Tour, there was only one answer I could give. 'Yes.'

But I knew that absolutely everything would have to go my way if I was going to actually pull it off.

19. Number one
1985

By the end of 1984, I was officially the number one rider in the world. The UCI, the world governing body, had introduced a computerised ranking system in the spring and my victories at Paris-Nice, the Tour of the Basque Country, Paris-Roubaix and Liège-Bastogne-Liège meant I was the first world number one and I was still top of the list at the end of the season.

I also won the Super Prestige Pernod, which was a season-long competition designed to crown the most consistent rider of the year. Points were on offer at all the biggest one-day events and stage races.

As I was the undisputed number one rider in the world, De Gribaldy came up with the idea that I should ride all three grand tours in 1985. Back then, the Vuelta a España was held in the spring, so it would mean riding the Spanish race in April, grabbing three days of rest before the Giro d'Italia started and then trying to recover enough to ride the Tour de France three weeks after that. It was a crazy schedule of nine weeks of racing in just over three months.

But I knew better than to challenge De Gribaldy over it. I was the world number one but he was still the boss. He didn't consult me about my programme of races. He set the agenda and I was expected to follow it.

Our Skil team had a new co-sponsor – Kas, the soft drinks company from Vitoria in the Basque Country, northern Spain, which was run by a cycling fanatic, Louis Knorr.

Kas had sponsored a team in the 1960s and 1970s but had been out of the sport for a few years. I wouldn't be surprised if, during negotiations, De Gribaldy had said to Knorr: 'Kelly is going to do all three big tours next year,' to seal the deal.

When De Gribaldy put the plan to me, I just said, 'Okay,' and waited for the idea to quietly go away. There was no point arguing with him because he didn't like being contradicted. If I had said I didn't want to do it, he would have dug his heels in. My tactic was to agree by not disagreeing and then slowly plot my escape route.

I'd done that before. One year, De Gribaldy was determined that I would ride Bordeaux-Paris, a ridiculous 600-kilometre race that started in the middle of the night and took almost 18 hours. Part of the way the cyclists were paced by motorbikes, not that it made the race any easier.

In its day, Bordeaux-Paris was one of the most prestigious events but it was well past its sell-by date. De Gribaldy felt my name should be on the roll of honour and he was convinced I would win it. I thought it was a stupid idea to do that race just six weeks before the Tour de France. I knew it would take three weeks to recover fully and my preparation for the Tour would be compromised.

'Nonsense,' said De Gribaldy. 'After three days, you'll be fine. Jacques Anquetil could win Bordeaux-Paris and then go to the Tour de France.'

If I tried to come up with any reason not to do something, De Gribaldy would have an argument up his sleeve that trumped it. I couldn't win.

So I had to bide my time. The only way to get out of anything was if I was injured. A week after the spring Classics, about three weeks before Bordeaux-Paris, I said I had tendonitis in my ankle. Quietly, the idea was dropped and I got my way.

I hoped the same thing would happen again. De Gribaldy had already told the press that I'd be doing the Vuelta, the Giro and the Tour, which got plenty of publicity for our team's sponsors.

But when I was asked about it, I was deliberately vague.

I knew it was a bad idea. The Vuelta would go okay and I'd probably get through the Giro, even if there were only three days to recover, but there was no way I'd be competitive at the Tour with six weeks of stage racing under my belt. I knew I'd run out of gas, so I had to get out of either the Vuelta or the Giro by hook or by crook.

A journalist asked me about the plan and I said that I would probably pull out of the Vuelta after two weeks so I could be fresh for the Giro.

Knorr was not happy about the idea of me pulling out of the Vuelta, which was his home race and priority. He wanted me to do all of the Vuelta.

The discussions went on for a little while but, in the end, De Gribaldy came to me and said that the Giro was off the menu. I was to do the Vuelta and then the Tour. This time, I was more than happy to agree with him.

THERE WAS NO WAY the spring Classics campaign could match up to the previous year. How could it? I was consistent and put up a strong defence of my two titles. I was third at Paris-Roubaix, which was won by Marc Madiot, and fourth at Liège-Bastogne-Liège, which was won by Moreno Argentin.

After the Classics I went to the Vuelta a España for the first time since I'd finished fourth in 1980.

I wasn't our team leader for the general classification. I was there to aim for stage wins and the points competition and support my team-mate Eric Caritoux, who was the defending Vuelta champion.

Caritoux rode well, but as the race entered its final week we knew he wasn't going to repeat the previous year's victory. He eventually finished sixth. I had won three stages, held a firm grip on the points competition and would reach Madrid in ninth place overall. As preparation for the Tour de France, the race had been perfect for me.

The 1985 edition of the Vuelta a España is best known, to British fans at least, as the race when Robert Millar got ambushed by the Spaniards on the penultimate day.

Millar was one of the best climbers around. He was small, light and lively in the mountains and he had a knack of varying his pace, which made it very difficult to stay with him.

We had done all the difficult mountains and Millar was in the yellow jersey and set to become the first British rider to win one of the three major tours, even though his lead over the second-placed rider, Francisco 'Pacho' Rodriguez of Colombia, was very narrow, at only ten seconds.

The final stage to Madrid would be a formality so Millar only had stage 18 from Alcalá de Henares to Segovia to survive. It was a 200-kilometre stage over some really lumpy territory but Millar's Peugeot team really should have had it all under control.

I always liked Millar, although he could be very awkward at times. He had left Glasgow and headed to France to try to make it as a professional and, against all the odds, he'd succeeded.

He wasn't an outgoing guy. I wasn't exactly talkative but some days I'd roll alongside Robert in the bunch, say hello and get nothing more than a grunt. I'd know better than to try to engage with him, so I'd move on and talk to someone else.

When he was on form, he had a very dry sense of humour which appealed to me, although not everyone got it. He could give the impression that he was surly and unfriendly but despite that, he wasn't unpopular in the bunch. People respected him as an individual and when he was being Millar people just said: 'Well, that's Millar.'

The thing was, because he had made it by himself, he gave the impression that he didn't need anyone else. That day, it turned out he needed a few friends who were prepared to help dig him out of a hole.

Stage 18 was pretty unremarkable for a long time but a break went away quite late on and no one seemed to know who was in it or what was going on.

Remember, these were the days long before radio technology. We couldn't talk into the microphone and ask the *directeur sportif* back in the team car what was going on. We got our information from a guy on the back of a motorbike who wrote the time gaps and the numbers of the riders in the break on a chalkboard.

Quite often, the time gaps weren't very accurate. The guy on the motorbike would drive up to the break, pull over at the side of the road, start his watch and then wait for the bunch.

When the bunch arrived, he'd write the time gap on the board, show it to the bunch and then drive up to the break to show them. In the time it took to do all that, the race situation could change a lot.

And, let's be diplomatic about this, the chalkboard could show whatever the guy on the motorbike wanted it to show.

Eventually we were told there were two Spanish riders away – Jose Recio of the Kelme team, who was no threat to Millar overall, and Pedro Delgado of the Seat squad, who definitely was.

Delgado was three minutes down overall, which sounds like a lot but he was too close to be allowed away on such a lumpy, unpredictable stage.

For quite a while the guy with the chalkboard told us that the gap was about a minute or a minute-and-a-half so there wasn't any reason for Millar to panic.

But then, all of a sudden and with less than 30 kilometres to go, the chalkboard said Recio and Delgado were seven min-utes ahead and the picture looked very different. Millar and his Peugeot team had a battle on their hands.

The two Spaniards must have been riding like stink up ahead while we were being given the impression things were okay. I think the Spaniards pulled a fast one on Millar.

Millar was isolated. He only had a couple of team-mates with him, one of whom was the British rider Sean Yates. He desperately needed more help but the French guys in the Peugeot team had done a bit of a disappearing act. I have no idea what happened to the rest of the Peugeot riders but that was the way the French teams could be when the going got tough.

Obviously, the Spaniards in our group sat on their hands. Like the Belgians, they preferred a home win. It suited them to let Delgado go up the road and take Millar's yellow jersey. They'd rather that than some guy from Scotland who didn't smile much winning their national tour.

Millar didn't have many options. With two Spaniards giving it everything up ahead, and at least four minutes to recover in under 30 kilometres, it was going to take a massive effort. Millar came to me and asked if I'd help, so I went to the front with a couple of team-mates – Caritoux and Dominique Garde – and we started to ride. A couple of guys from the Panasonic team joined in but that was it. The Spaniards sat behind us and enjoyed the ride.

The gap was too big and even though we gave it everything, could we be sure the information on the chalkboard was accurate? It seemed to stay at six minutes for quite a while.

By the finish, we had brought Delgado's lead down to three-and-a-half minutes. It was good going but it was not enough. There was only so much we could do in that time.

When he crossed the line, Millar had lost the yellow jersey to Delgado by 36 seconds. To have closed that gap, we needed another six or seven kilometres and a few more guys prepared to work with us.

It was a stitch-up really. Millar had no chance. I watched the television pictures that night and noticed that Recio and Delgado had a load of motorbikes swarming round them, filming for TV and taking photos, no doubt, but also giving them a nice slipstream to follow. In our group we had fresh air and open road in front of us.

Spain was the wild west. The cowboys looked after each other and didn't like someone from out of town coming in.

I was sorry for Millar and had been happy to help because he was like me – a stranger on foreign soil trying to do his best. For us, we were playing away from home every week so it made sense that we joined forces every now and then. But we'd left it too late that day because we didn't realise how serious the situation was.

THE 1985 TOUR DE FRANCE was the best of my career. I finished fourth overall, 6-26 behind Bernard Hinault. That was the closest I ever got to winning the Tour. I also took the green jersey for the third time, equalling the record held by Jan Janssen, Eddy Merckx and Freddy Maertens.

I was pleased with my progress. Hinault was still better than me in the mountains and the time trials but I was continuing to improve. Each year I was edging closer to the podium and although I thought overall victory might never be within my reach, I thought I could finish in the top three.

It was so easy to look at the results after the Tour and add up where I had lost time to the winner and believe that I could avoid those losses the following year.

In 1985, I lost 45 seconds in the prologue time trial in Plumelec. My Skil team was 2-52 slower than Hinault's La Vie Claire squad in the team time trial from Vitré to Fougères, and I lost another 2-52 to him in the individual time trial at Strasbourg.

I was 3-20 adrift at Morzine in the Alps and lost 35 seconds and 49 seconds in the two time trials at Villard-de-Lans and Lac de Vassivière. Add all that up and it accounts for more than 11 minutes of time lost to Hinault. If I could eliminate half those losses, I'd be within touching distance – or at least I'd be able to avoid the energy-sapping chase for bonus seconds in the intermediate sprints.

On paper, my worst day in the mountains – the one to Morzine – was far less damaging than my worst day in previous years. That meant my climbing was getting better.

The problem was, I'd conceded more ground in the time trials than I did in 1984.

For me, the Tour de France was like spinning plates. I could do everything well enough in isolation – I just couldn't get everything going at once. To win the Tour, the bad days had to be better than everyone else's bad days.

In retrospect, those intermediate sprints were too much. I knew I needed the points for the green jersey and the bonus seconds to compensate for any ground I lost in the mountains or time trials, but the effort of sprinting two or three times a day for a fortnight caught up with me in the end. Perhaps it was counter-productive.

There were areas where we could have improved. We gave up almost three minutes to Hinault and Greg LeMond in the team time trial. They finished first and second overall and the time they gained there was a big advantage over their rivals.

De Gribaldy was ahead of his time in a lot of respects but we never trained specifically for the team time trial, even though it was crucial to my chances in the Tour.

We could have worked on our technique the week before the Tour as other teams had started to do but we didn't. We just got on our bikes and expected to ride 73 kilometres as a well-drilled unit. It's very easy to lose a lot of time if the formation is a bit ragged and that's what happened.

Although I could look back and see where I had lost ground in the 1985 Tour de France, while I was in the thick of the race I was fighting hard on two fronts.

I got off to a really good start in the points competition but it was now three years since my last Tour de France stage win and I just couldn't get myself a victory.

I was third at Lanester and second at Vitré where the Belgian rider Rudy Matthijs won back-to-back stages. At Reims, Eric Vanderaerden and I were up to our old tricks, pulling each other's jerseys in the finishing straight. It was a really rocky sprint and we were so obsessed with each other we let Francis Castaing win it. Vanderaerden and I were both disqualified and relegated to last and second last in the bunch but Castaing would never have won that if we'd concentrated on sprinting instead of wrestling.

I was well in contention for the yellow jersey before the first long individual time trial, which went from Sarrebourg to Strasbourg. Thanks to the time bonus sprints, I was fifth overall, right in the thick of things. LeMond was only four seconds ahead of me and Hinault only two ahead.

But the time trial brought me back down to earth.

In the mid-Eighties, bicycle technology was advancing very rapidly. There was a lot of new equipment and everyone wanted to experiment if they thought there was an advantage to be gained.

When I first started, we rode the Tour's time trial stages on our regular racing bikes, perhaps with a few modifications to save some weight. We might have some more aerodynamic brake levers and cut back the handlebar tape. Some riders got their mechanics to drill holes in the brake levers to make them lighter and we'd ride the lightest tyres.

But by 1985, the design of time trial bikes was evolving. There were bikes with big sloping top tubes so the rider could get very low over the front, giving them a more aerodynamic shape. We used upturned handlebars that looked like a bull's horns, and disc wheels were starting to come in. Some riders used aerodynamic helmets too but they looked like pudding bowls and were uncomfortable in the hot weather.

A few guys had ditched the old toeclips and straps for the new clipless pedals. Everyone uses them now but at the time they were revolutionary. I wasn't a stick-in-the-mud but I couldn't see the point of ditching my pedals because they worked perfectly well. I found them comfortable whereas some of the guys who used the early clipless pedals complained of knee problems.

I resisted that change for about eight years and I was one of the last guys to give in. When I joined the Festina team in 1992, Shimano tried to get me to use their clipless pedals. I stuck to my guns. At the end of that first season, Festina's management told me I had no choice. Their contract with Shimano meant we all had to use the clipless pedals, and that winter I used a set on my mountain bike so I could adjust to them.

In the time trial at the 1985 Tour, we had some disc wheels, which were state-of-the-art at the time. The carbon-fibre wheels were solid so they didn't create as much drag but they were also lightweight.

The stage was 75 kilometres long and I was setting off just two minutes ahead of Hinault. Knowing he would be chasing me was terrifying and motivational at the same time because he was so strong in the time trials.

I set off and tried to get into a good rhythm but after about 15 kilometres I had the shock of my life. There was a huge bang and I was surrounded by a cloud of white fluffy stuff. It was a miracle I didn't swerve off the road into a ditch.

I had no idea what had happened. For a split-second I wondered if some madman had fired at me with an air rifle. Or had I run over a chicken and the white stuff was its feathers?

Then I realised my back wheel had collapsed under me and I was scraping along the ground on what was left of it. The disc wheel had exploded and the white polystyrene from inside had burst everywhere. I have no idea why it happened. Perhaps it was a faulty wheel, or maybe the heat had caused the polystyrene to expand. Either way, I'd had a lucky escape.

I had to ride the remaining 60 kilometres on my standard

road bike, which was a big disadvantage, especially with Hinault bearing down on me.

It wasn't long before Hinault caught and passed me. The rest of the stage was a battle to keep him in sight. I'd already lost more than two minutes and I didn't want him to gain even more on me.

Hinault was on fire that day. Stephen Roche was second on the stage, and even he lost 2-20. Some of the flyweight climbers lost six or seven minutes.

From then on, I knew I couldn't win that Tour. Hinault was too good and his team-mate LeMond was just as strong, if not stronger. But I felt I could make it onto the podium as long as I didn't suffer a bad day in the mountains.

That Tour is remembered for the crash at St-Etienne which left Hinault angry and with two black eyes. Phil Anderson got the blame for that one. I was in the group just behind and I saw a crowd around the yellow jersey as Hinault was picking himself up off the floor. Hinault said Anderson caused him to crash and I must admit, I found I had to give Anderson a fair bit of room in the sprints because when he got out of the saddle, he'd come flying back towards me like he'd opened a parachute. Hinault was in a really sore mood for a few days after that. He was nicknamed The Badger and now he looked like one too.

Coming out of the Alps and heading towards the Pyrenees, Stephen Roche was 27 seconds ahead of me. I felt, with the final time trial at Lac de Vassivière to come, I could overtake him but on the short stage to the top of the Col d'Aubisque he opened a bit of a gap on me.

It was only 52 kilometres from Luz-Saint-Sauveur, over the Col du Soulor and then to the summit of the Aubisque. When Roche attacked, I didn't want to chase him straight away because he had a chance to gain time on LeMond and Hinault and possibly win the Tour. I was hoping someone else would take up the chase but in the end I went clear of the rest. Roche won the stage and I was second.

The time trial around the lake at Vassivière in the Limousin region didn't quite work out as I hoped. I beat Roche, but only by five seconds, so he became the first Irishman to finish on the podium at the Tour and I was fourth, with another green jersey to go with it.

I was 29 years old and I knew if I was ever going to win the Tour it would have to be in 1986 or 1987. Time was running out.

AT THE END of the season, I was in the hunt for the Super Prestige Pernod title again but needed good results in each of the final two Classics – Créteil-Chaville and the Tour of Lombardy – to overhaul the leader, Phil Anderson.

Anderson rode for the Dutch Panasonic team, which was run by Peter Post. Panasonic's bitter rivals were another Dutch team, Kwantum, run by Jan Raas. I used their rivalry to my advantage.

Créteil-Chaville is the race we call Paris-Tours now. At that time, it was run the other way round from the town of Créteil to Chaville in the Parisian suburbs. Just as the race was hotting up, Anderson had a problem with his bike and I got into a break with several Kwantum riders. I had a word with Adri Van der Poel, one of the Kwantum boys, and agreed that if one of their riders got away, I wouldn't chase. It would go in my favour if Anderson failed to score points. In return, Kwantum wouldn't work against me at the Tour of Lombardy. They didn't need much persuading because they saw it as a way of stopping Panasonic from winning the Super Prestige and getting one over on Post.

Kwantum's Ludo Peeters got away on the last hill and that was that. I finished third, scoring enough points to catch Anderson, who was way back, and then I won the Tour of Lombardy to clinch the Super Prestige title and end the season on a high note.

20. The farmer's son & the city boy

The Nissan Classic

On September 25, 1985, the first stage of the inaugural Nissan Classic started at Trinity College in Dublin. Thanks to Stephen Roche and me, cycling was booming in Ireland and the time was right for a national tour that was open to professionals. There was the Rás Tailteann, of course, but that was an amateur event. The criterium races that had been held in Dublin had drawn huge crowds but we didn't really know what to expect from the Nissan Classic. Would people turn out to watch a stage race on a weekday, we wondered?

We need not have worried. The crowds were huge. I never expected to see so many people and it was quite overwhelming.

The first Nissan Classic started in Dublin and worked its way round the country, arriving back in the capital five days later. Wherever we went, we were treated like heroes. Whether it was Wexford, Cork or Galway we were offered enough free drinks to keep us drunk until Christmas.

Although it was a nice homecoming, and it was getting towards the end of the season, I knew the racing would be deadly serious.

For Roche and me, this was our World Championships. I was going to do everything I could to win the race, and I was sure he would too. Actually, let's be straight about it: I wanted to bury Roche that week.

The race was nicely balanced. There was a time trial from Carrick-on-Suir to Clonmel on the third day which was on my home roads, although I thought it might actually suit Roche more.

I didn't want to take any chances, so I went for every time

bonus sprint I could in an effort to gain a bit of an advantage.

The rivalry between Kelly and Roche captured the imagination. The crowds came out, the television and newspaper reporters were interested and cycling was top of the agenda in Ireland. That was something I never expected to see and it made me realise that people back at home had taken notice of what we had achieved in Europe.

One unusual aspect of the Nissan Classic was that although it was a professional race, there was a handful of amateur teams too, so there was a big difference in ability between the strongest riders and the weaker ones. The terrain in Ireland could be very difficult, with lots of steep hills, and if the wind blew the bunch could easily have been cut to ribbons and scattered across three counties. With more than 100 miles to race, there was a danger half the field could be put out of the back in the first half an hour if we went full on. No one wanted the riders to drift home in ones and twos because it wouldn't make anyone look good, so there was an unspoken agreement that we would keep things together for the first 50 miles or so.

Around halfway through the first stage, which went from Dublin to Wexford, one of the Dutch riders, Teun Van Vliet, started setting a strong pace at the front of the bunch. We knew then, the agreement was over.

A few attacks started to go clear but they were brought back. Everyone was getting a bit impatient. The front of the bunch was like a coiled spring and I could see things were going to kick off.

I was at the front, paying attention. I was determined to get in the break that stuck. If Roche was in it, fair enough, but if he missed it, I was going to give it everything.

With about 25 miles to go, the race blew to pieces. It was a free-for-all. About ten of us got clear and never looked back.

As soon as I knew Roche wasn't with us, I put my head down and went for it like it was the last lap of the World Championships. Adri Van der Poel was in the group and he rode like hell too. Van Vliet, who had started the action, was with us, along with a couple of Danes and a couple of English riders, one of whom was Paul Sherwen, a team-mate of Roche's.

By the time we reached Wexford, Roche was out of the picture as far as the overall classification was concerned. There were a few laps of a circuit in the town and the crowds were enormous. Every school playground we passed was full of cheering children. Near the finish line the people were three or four deep. The crowds were bigger than at the Tour de France.

At the finish, I beat Van der Poel in the sprint to become the first rider to wear the yellow jersey in the Nissan Classic. Roche's group came in ten minutes later.

If the crowds in Wexford had been big, the turn-out in my home town Carrick-on-Suir was even bigger. Racing on the roads where I had ridden as a youngster was so much fun. We did a few laps of a circuit that took us over Seskin Hill. Leo Van Vliet, who was away with Eric Van Lancker, won the stage, then Van der Poel pipped me in the bunch sprint.

Because of the time bonuses, we were level on time. The next morning we had a 13-mile time trial from Sean Kelly Square in Carrick to Clonmel. There had been a bit of discussion about who should have the yellow jersey because we were tied on time and were also level on points. Normally, the race leader sets off last in a time trial, so there was a bit of uncertainty about the order.

In the end, the officials decided I should set off last, one minute behind Van der Poel, although I decided not to wear the yellow jersey.

What followed was one of the best performances of my career. I caught Van der Poel for one minute, then I passed Van Vliet, who had set off two minutes before me.

I won the stage and my average speed was almost 50 kilometres an hour. Roche was second, but 49 seconds slower, which is a big gap in a 13-mile race. Afterwards he joked that I must have taken a short-cut but he knew there was no short-cut from Carrick to Clonmel, unless I'd taken a speedboat up the river.

In the afternoon, Roche attacked on St Patrick's Hill in Cork to win the stage. He won again the following day in Limerick. Well, we had to let him have a couple of stages.

On a couple of stages we had a bit of criticism from the race officials for riding the early part of the day at such a casual pace.

Pat McQuaid, who was in charge of the race, came up to me and said: 'Will you get someone to start riding? We're behind schedule.' I replied: 'You realise there's a headwind and we've got 80 miles to go?"

The stages were much too long considering the lack of strength in depth of the field and the fact it was late in the season. We always raced the last hour or so at a very high pace and put on a show for the crowds in the towns but to race all day at that intensity would have been madness. If we had, only about half the riders would have made it back to Dublin.

I WON THE 1985 Nissan Classic but the rematch with Roche would have to wait because he missed the following year's race with an injury.

But I had far from an easy ride. The Canadian Steve Bauer pushed me all week and took it right down to the wire. He was a tough competitor and a very decent sprinter.

Bauer won the second stage, which went to Limerick, to take the yellow jersey. I kept chipping away at him by winning time bonuses in the sprints but if I gained six seconds, he'd take four, which made it very hard to overtake him.

The third day was very hard. In the morning, we did a stage that looped into the countryside round Kilarney, going over the Gap of Dunloe and Moll's Gap, two nasty climbs. I punctured on the rough roads and my team-mate Jörg Müller had to give me his wheel so I wasn't left behind.

The afternoon stage finished in Cork, with four climbs of St Patrick's Hill, which is a very steep road. Just as we turned onto the bottom of the hill the first time, my chain jammed. I just about got my foot out but I toppled over in the road. Meanwhile, Acacio Da Silva, my team-mate, fell in the opposite direction. Between us we caused as much chaos as we could, blocking the road accidentally-on-purpose so only about five riders got through.

I had to take Alfred Ackermann's bike because my chain was completely stuck and he was the only one of my team-mates who used toe-clips and straps – everyone else was using clipless pedals. I chased back and won the bunch sprint to draw level with Bauer on time. That gave me the yellow jersey because I was narrowly ahead of him on points.

The stage to Clonmel was on my turf. We had to do several laps of a circuit round Carrick that went over Seskin Hill, so I decided to put my local knowledge to good use.

I attacked on the descent of the Ragwell climb. The edges of the road were gravelly and I was going much too fast but I thought I could gain time on Bauer, who did not know the roads. In my eagerness to gain time, I pushed my luck too much and fell on one of the corners. Bauer overtook me and managed to finish second on the stage, while I was only fourth, so he was back ahead of me overall with one day to go.

The Nissan Classic came down to the sprints during the final stage to Dublin. One second at a time, I chiselled away at his advantage. At the first intermediate sprint, I was second, just ahead of Bauer, to cut his lead to a couple of seconds. At the next sprint the result was the same, so Bauer's lead was just a single second.

Everything hinged on the final sprint. Teun Van Vliet attacked and went clear on the last lap around Parnell Square.

Then Vanderaerden went – typical that he'd see an opportunity to make life harder for me – which meant the time bonus for third place was the only one still up for grabs.

It was a straight fight between Bauer and me and I just about got it, taking the three-second bonus that gave me the Nissan Classic title for the second year in a row.

ROCHE WAS BACK IN 1987 and it was a glorious homecoming for him because he had won the Giro d'Italia, the Tour de France and the World Championships that season. Eddy Merckx is the only other rider to have done that in the same year.

Roche, Martin Earley, Paul Kimmage and I were cheered and clapped on the back wherever we went that week. I imagine it was what it was like to be a member of the Beatles in the Sixties.

While Roche enjoyed his lap of honour in the rainbow jersey, I wanted to win the race for a third time, which I did thanks largely to a strong ride by my Kas boys in the team time trial.

The West German rider Rolf Gölz won in 1988 and the

following year my home race was dominated by my nemesis, Eric Vanderaerden. That was a bad, bad Nissan. I was not in great shape because I'd had a difficult end to the year but I always gave everything I had on home soil. It was very hard to keep going right to the end of the season, particularly when the weather could be so bad in late September and early October, but the crowd always gave me a lift.

I had no answer to Vanderaerden that year. He was on fire and it was unbearable to see him win my race.

We had a time trial from Kilkenny to Carlow. Vanderaerden was already in the yellow jersey and I was second overall, still in with a shout if I had a good day. Vanderaerden was on the road behind me in the time trial and with about seven miles to go I could hear a motorbike behind me. I knew it would be the motorcycle outrider looking after Vanderaerden.

He drew level with me, which was a really bad moment, and then pushed on past. I thought about grabbing his jersey and pulling him back, just for old times' sake.

Vanderaerden kept winning the sprints and was always smiling. I had to grin and bear it. That's not a week I spend a lot of time thinking about.

In 1990, my PDM team-mate Erik Breukink won after a very good performance in the time trial, so most of my time was spent helping him to defend his leader's jersey. But the following autumn, after a disastrous Tour de France, I was extremely motivated to win the Nissan again.

The toughest day was stage four from Limerick to Cork, with several finishing circuits on St Patrick's Hill. The weather was horrible, with a cold wind and rain all day. At kilometre zero, the Belgian rider Etienne De Wilde attacked, which sparked a day of full-on racing and constant attacking. The wind was blowing a gale and whenever we changed direction so it was coming at us from the side, the whole bunch would be in one long line, with everyone pushed right over into the gutter.

My team-mate, John Talen, was going for the sprints jersey. There was an intermediate sprint at Tipperary, after about 15 miles of the stage, and we came into the town at such a rate I thought we'd never make it round the first corner. We did a lap of the town, then the hot-spot sprint, and as we left the town there was a steep hill which split the bunch into pieces. The racing was savage.

Johan Museeuw of the Lotto team was leading overall and his team went backwards. They couldn't cope with so much attacking so he was left without any support.

Museeuw's team-mates spent about 15 miles chasing and as soon as they regained contact with the leading group, my team-mate Raúl Alcalá attacked, which meant the Lotto boys had to go straight to the front and carry on riding hard.

I knew the roads so well that I knew this effort would catch up with the Lotto riders later in the day.

With 25 miles to go, Sean Yates, the British rider representing the Motorola team, attacked. The weather was perfect for Yates and I knew he wouldn't hold back so I chased after him.

Yates was so strong. When it was his turn at the front, he was riding so strongly I was finding it hard to recover from my own effort. We were gaining a lot of time over Museeuw and the rest, so I knew I was going to take the yellow jersey.

Once we reached Cork, I set the pace on St Patrick's Hill and Yates came past me over the top and led down the fast, steep descent, sweeping round the wide corners at a speed that made me fear we would not get down in one piece. Each lap, he seemed to push it even harder. I followed and hoped for the best.

At the finish Yates won the stage and I had done enough to set up a fourth overall victory. Winning at home was always sweet.

21. An unwanted holiday in July

1986

I was about to start my tenth season as a professional. Louis Knorr's Kas company had taken over as the main sponsor of our team and there were to be a few changes, although Jean de Gribaldy still called the shots. Christian Rumeau was his number two and Kas appointed a Spanish *directeur sportif* called Faustino Ruperez. We also had a new general manager, Ramon Mendiburu, with whom I got on very well.

Most of the French riders from the Skil-Sem team stayed with us, although we lost Eric Caritoux, who joined the Fagor squad. About half a dozen Spanish guys came in, including Iñaki Gastón, who turned out to be an excellent *domestique*. We also signed Jean-Luc Vandenbroucke, a Belgian from La Redoute, who was another very willing worker.

De Gribaldy probably wanted to continue as he was, with a mostly French team and a French sponsor. But the team was getting more costly for him. I was the number one rider in the world and was looking for a bigger contract.

A few teams had approached me towards the end of 1985 and I dropped that into conversations with De Gribaldy in the hope that I could get a better deal.

De Gribaldy was not quite as hands-on as he had been. He left Rumeau to run the French races and Ruperez did the Spanish ones. My role stayed more or less the same. I was the leader for the Classics, the Vuelta and the Tour de France. There was no one in the team you could call a co-leader.

After winning Paris-Nice for the fifth year in a row, I won Milan-San Remo for the first time. Mario Beccia and Greg

LeMond attacked on the Poggio and no one wanted to chase. Eric Vanderaerden was glued to my back wheel, following me wherever I went. I wanted to set off after Beccia and LeMond but I definitely didn't want Vanderaerden coming with me because he would be a big threat in the sprint, so I fiddled with my gears and pretended they had slipped, to force him to come past me. Then I attacked him and rode across the gap. I took a few moments to recover once I'd caught them, then went to the front to make sure no one else came up from behind. I won the sprint from LeMond quite comfortably.

A couple of weeks later came the Tour of Flanders. Having won Milan-San Remo, I was the big favourite and everyone was watching me. I also felt very good. At the end of the race, I was in a group with Adri Van der Poel of the Kwantum team, Steve Bauer and Jean-Philippe Vandenbrande.

I was weighing things up in my mind. I had a chance to win the Tour of Flanders but for Kas and Louis Knorr, Paris-Roubaix the following Sunday was a much more important race. At that time, the Tour of Flanders was not shown live on television in Spain and Knorr used to joke that there was no market for soft drinks in Belgium, where they drink beer with their breakfast.

I had a chance to win the Tour of Flanders but I also thought the opportunity to win it would come round again another year. My form was so good, and it wasn't suddenly going to disappear in a week's time, so I thought I should do what I could to give myself a chance to win Paris-Roubaix. I came to an agreement with Van der Poel, who wanted to win the Tour of Flanders.

I did some big turns on the front to ensure that Bauer and Vandenbrande didn't manage to get away from us and Van der Poel followed, doing only the occasional turn, saving his legs for the sprint. Yes, I let the Tour of Flanders slip through my fingers but I'd traded it for a bit of co-operation at Paris-Roubaix.

I knew that to win Paris-Roubaix I had to be in absolutely top form whereas the Tour of Flanders was a race where I could bluff a little bit if I wasn't the strongest guy because it's more tactical. Tactics don't come into it as much at Paris-Roubaix because the race is about strength and survival.

As we always did, we squeezed the Tour of the Basque Country in between the two Classics, flying out the evening after the Tour of Flanders and returning the day before Paris-Roubaix. I won in Spain and flew to France feeling very confident.

On the Sunday, I called in the favour, to make sure of victory.

Four of us got clear on the cobbles at Camphin-en-Pévèle. There was me, Van der Poel and two Belgians, Rudy Dhaenens and Ferdi Van den Haute.

That year the race didn't conclude in the famous velodrome. Instead the finishing straight was outside the La Redoute clothing factory on the outskirts of Roubaix. That made it a slightly more conventional sprint finish, with less cagey tactical play. We had the full width of the road to play with.

As we got into the final kilometre I was very nervous, even though I knew I could rely on Van der Poel to give me a hand.

In the final 400 metres, Van den Haute jumped and I shouted to Van der Poel, who was on the front, to chase him, which he did. That gave me the perfect lead-out for the sprint and I came past them to win the race.

I'm often asked whether it felt different that year, finishing in the street rather than the velodrome, but Paris-Roubaix is Paris-Roubaix. I'd won the race, so we could have finished in a car park for all I cared.

BECAUSE OUR MAIN sponsor was now a Spanish company, the Vuelta a España became an even more important objective than it had been before. I won two stages and climbed really well in the mountains, particularly the Sierra Nevada, to get myself onto the podium. I also won the points competition again.

I was five minutes behind the winner, Alvaro Pino, and four behind runner-up Robert Millar, without having targeted the race specifically. I didn't feel like I had pushed myself to the limit, so I thought I could be on the podium at the Tour de France later in the summer.

My final preparation race before the Tour de France was the Tour of Switzerland. I stayed out of the fight for the overall classification, preferring to save myself for the Tour.

On the final stage to Oerliken we went over a difficult climb that was about seven kilometres long. I lost contact with the leaders on the way up and a group of about 20 went away. I wasn't too concerned because I thought I could rejoin them on the descent.

I found myself in the convoy of team cars behind the break and I hit the descent pretty fast. I was overtaking the cars on the straights and braking late into the corners. It's always pretty risky descending in among the team cars like that.

Suddenly there was a corner that was a lot tighter than I had expected. I had to brake hard and hope for the best. There was a little stone wall on the side of the road and I remember the top of it had pieces of stone, pointing upwards, that had been stuck into the top of the wall. They call it a cock and hen in the building trade and you definitely don't want to land on one.

I lost the back wheel a bit as I tried to get round the corner. I managed to keep it upright but as I went round I had to release the brake, otherwise my tyres would have skidded and I'd definitely have gone down. My only hope was to let go of the brakes and try to throw it round the bend. I didn't quite make it.

I hit the wall and flew over and down about 30 feet, falling through the tree branches. I can still picture myself falling through the trees. I burned the skin on the palms of my hands trying to grab onto the branches to break my fall. The bike got caught in the tree and I kept falling until I reached the bottom.

Eventually I came to a halt and, finding I could still move, was confident nothing had broken. I managed to crawl up on all fours. It took me ages and as I climbed up I could hear the team cars going past. I was worried the race was going to carry on and not notice I had gone. I assumed my bike was out of view from the road so how would anyone know I had plummeted over the edge?

When I got to the top, I realised there was no way I could reach my bike. It was wedged firmly in a tree.

Fortunately, I had got back up to the road before the entire race convoy had passed and I flagged down the broomwagon, the last vehicle in the long, long line that sweeps up the tired and fallen riders.

My worst injury was a nasty deep cut in my leg. It had opened up quite badly so I had to go to hospital to have it stitched up. With only two weeks to go to the Tour, I knew I wasn't going to recover in time. The wound was too·deep, there was the risk of infection if it opened up again, and it was sore.

Having ridden eight Tours in a row it was very hard to stay at home. I never jumped up and down in excitement before the Tour because I knew that it always meant a lot of suffering. Even a successful Tour is a painful experience.

But to miss the chance to win a stage or wear one of the jerseys was a huge disappointment. For the first time, I realised just what the race meant to me. Sitting at home in July was more painful than suffering in the mountains. The biggest show on earth would go on without me, of course, but to be fit – apart from the cut in my leg – and not be there was horrible.

I spent July training on my own in Belgium. I couldn't bring myself to watch much of the Tour on television although I caught the last hour or so of the big mountain stages. I noted how well Urs Zimmermann, the Swiss rider, did. He finished third behind Greg LeMond and Bernard Hinault. I don't mean any disrespect to Zimmermann, because he was a very good climber, but to see a rider like him on the podium made me wonder how well I might have done.

AFTER I RECOVERED from the injury, I tried to make the most of the end of the season. I won a string of smaller races – stages at the Tour of Aragon in Spain and Paris-Bourges in France, as well as the Tour of Catalonia overall. I was fifth in the World Championships at Colorado Springs, won by Moreno Argentin.

And finally, I managed to win the Grand Prix des Nations time trial, which had been an obsession for De Gribaldy.

There was not a time trial at the World Championships in those days, so the Grand Prix des Nations was seen as the unofficial title race. De Gribaldy thought it was the ultimate test of a bike rider.

The distance was daunting – 89 kilometres – and the course brutal – up and down all the way. At that time, the race was held in Cannes and dipped up into the hills behind the French Riviera.

Fausto Coppi had won the Grand Prix des Nations, Jacques Anquetil won it six times in a row and nine times in total. Eddy Merckx won it and Bernard Hinault had five titles to his name.

Anyone who was anyone had conquered the Grand Prix des Nations and De Gribaldy was always on at me, saying I needed to win there too.

I knew he wouldn't let me skip the event until I won it, so in 1986 I was keener than ever to give it everything I had. The distance was frightening enough, but the fact that we had to cover two laps of such a difficult course made it mental torture as much as physical agony.

The first lap was horrible because I knew I had the second one still to come, and the second lap was pure hell. It was one of the least enjoyable things I've ever done on a bike. I started well but I was quite a long way down on a couple of Frenchmen, Martial Gayant and Laurent Fignon, after the first lap.

I clawed my way back into contention and by the final check-point, after 75 kilometres, I was up to second place but still 39 seconds behind Fignon. That was a lot of time to make up but I gave it absolutely everything.

De Gribaldy was in the team car behind me, listening to the time checks over the radio, and as I went over the last little climb he shouted to me that I was only three seconds down on Fignon.

I took so many risks on the way down. On the run-in to the finish I pushed so hard. All I was thinking was: 'If I win this, I never have to do it again.'

As it turned out, I did ride the Grand Prix des Nations again but never with the same murderous intensity. Once was enough.

Coming towards the end of the season, I was still the world number one, having held that ranking for three unbroken seasons and I was closing in on the Super Prestige Pernod prize for the third year in a row. All I needed was a good result in the Tour of Lombardy, which turned out to be a very strange race.

22. Trading races

The 1986 Tour of Lombardy

A group of us were a long way clear of the rest and knew that the Tour of Lombardy was ours to fight over. There was me and my team-mate Acacio Da Silva. Phil Anderson of Panasonic, Flavio Giupponi and Gianbattista Baronchelli of Del Tongo and Leo Schoenenberger of a small Italian team, Dromedario.

It had been a tough day because the start of the race was very fast. We'd been part of a larger group that got clear on one of the climbs and then split up when we went over another hill until there were just six of us left. The rest of the bunch had given up any hope of catching us because we were about eight minutes clear with 40 kilometres to race.

Acacio and I were in a strong position but Del Tongo also had two riders in the break so my concern was that we'd cancel each other out and Anderson would get an easy ride to the finish. I was determined that didn't happen because Anderson would be a threat in the sprint. Acacio was doing a lot of work to make it a hard race for the others while I could follow the wheels and save a bit of energy for the finish. I felt confident that I was on course to win the Tour of Lombardy for the third time in four years.

Del Tongo were desperate to win. Baronchelli dropped back alongside his team car to talk to his *directeur sportif* and there were some discussions between our team and his. Then I had a long chat with De Gribaldy. I wanted to win the race but it was clear that Del Tongo were prepared to pay for some co-operation. The talks went on for about ten or 15 kilometres.

Then events took a peculiar turn. I was at the back of the line of riders and suddenly the race organiser's car bumped into me and I went down. The race organiser was a man called Vincenzo Torriani, who was nicknamed The Bull. He ran the Giro d'Italia, Milan-San Remo and Tour of Lombardy and ruled Italian cycling in much the same way Félix Lévitan ran the Tour de France.

I got up, chased back to the group and eye-balled Torriani. He looked straight ahead as if nothing had happened. Perhaps it had been a mistake.

I said to De Gribaldy that either Acacio or I could win the race but considering I'd been bumped off my bike I was starting to think we might have a situation on our hands.

We suspected Baronchelli, who was 33, needed a good result to get another contract with Del Tongo for the following year. We knew Torriani would prefer an Italian winner – there had been only one home win at the Tour of Lombardy in seven years.

I would have liked to win the Tour of Lombardy – and I felt that Da Silva and I were strong enough to get the job done – but the price kept going up and in the end De Gribaldy made the call. The deal was that if Baronchelli made a move, we would leave it to Anderson or Schoenenberger to react.

In the streets of Milan, with two or three kilometres to go, Baronchelli attacked. I looked at Anderson. He didn't respond and nor did I. We both knew that if he wasn't going to chase, Baronchelli would ride away to the finish and win the race.

And that is exactly what happened.

A week later, Da Silva collected the cash and we shared it among the team.

That Tour of Lombardy was a very unusual situation because it was the end of the season and Baronchelli wouldn't have been in a position to repay a favour until the following spring.

So De Gribaldy got the best result he could for the team in the circumstances. But you'd be mistaken to think the result of the race was fixed. It wasn't. The latter part of any big bike race, when everyone is tired or desperate, is like a game of poker. Everyone does whatever they can to make the best of the hand they have.

23. Farewell Jean
1987

Jean de Gribaldy lived his life on the road so I suppose it was inevitable he would die on the road.

Whether we were in Belgium or Brittany or right down in the Pyrenees, if the mood took him, De Gribaldy would clap his hands together and announce: 'Right, I'm going back to Besançon.'

Often he'd get up from the dinner table at 10 o'clock and drive through the night because he wanted to get home to look after his shop the next day.

In those days, there wasn't the network of motorways in France that we have now, so he'd cut across country on unlit roads, overtaking slower cars, pushing the speed limit.

He always drove fast. I am not normally a nervous passenger and I can drive quickly myself but there were times when De Gribaldy had me on the edge of my seat.

The time after I'd won the Tour of Lombardy in 1983 sticks in my mind. We had to leave Como straight away and drive across the mountains to Geneva in time for the Critérium des As the following afternoon. It was a five-hour drive and it was already gloomy and spitting with rain as we set out.

De Gribaldy never shared the driving and he rarely stopped, unless he needed fuel.

We went at quite a rate, overtaking other cars all the way. We hit the twisty mountain roads and he'd take the racing line through the corners, trusting that he'd see the headlights of any oncoming cars in plenty of time to pull over to his side of the road.

I could usually sleep wherever I was, especially after a hard race, but I didn't dare nod off. And I couldn't question De

Gribaldy about anything, not even his driving, even though I really wanted to ask him to slow down a bit.

Coming down the mountain in Switzerland I could hear the tyres squealing as we went round the corners. The rubber was just about clinging to the roads. I feared a patch of oil or grit might send us spinning over the wall and into a dark ravine. It was pitch black and the headlights only showed us the small patch of road ahead.

I was gripping the edge of my seat so I decided to say, very timidly: '*C'est glissant, non?*' meaning 'Is it not slippery?'

He turned to me, taking his eyes off the road and one hand off the steering wheel, and batted away my concern.

'Ah, the roads in Switzerland are so clean and well-maintained, they're never slippery.'

AT THE START OF January 1987, the Kas team had a training camp in Combloux, not far from Sallanches in the French Alps. We were there to do a bit of cross-country skiing, which was the way a lot of teams got their riders tuned up for the season in those days. Things were always pretty relaxed on those skiing trips and everyone was happy to be there before the harder pre-season training started.

We were just arriving back at the hotel for lunch when Christian Rumeau intercepted me in the lobby and took me away from the other guys.

He didn't waste time saying what he had to say.

'Jean is dead.'

The words hit me like a punch in the stomach.

It was very upsetting. I had spent a lot of time with him. For the best part of a decade he had been my guide in professional cycling, my mentor. Like Herman Nys, he was almost another father to me. He'd been with me during all of my greatest successes and many of my most painful disappointments.

Even when he got up and headed back to Besançon all of a sudden, his presence stayed with me. It was as if he was always watching me.

I thought back to my early years with him when he drummed

into me how important it was to keep the weight off over the winter. Every time I was tempted to have a square of chocolate I thought of De Gribaldy and knew I'd be disappointing him.

At times it was like being in the army. The routine and the regime was tough but he wanted his boys to do the best they possibly could.

When I first met him, I knew next to nothing about cycling – only what I had picked up racing for Ireland and in those few short months in Metz. He had taught me everything about how to train and race. Although he ruled by a sort of fear, it wasn't his way to shout or bully people. The fear was of letting him down.

And although he was old school and very traditional, he was ahead of his time in a lot of ways too. He was obsessive about diet at a time when riders still got up to eat a huge steak before a race. In the days when riders trained for five or six hours every day, De Gribaldy encouraged me to vary the intensity of my training.

Often I'd go out twice a day for shorter rides but train at a faster pace. It took a few years but soon everyone was doing that.

And now, all of a sudden, at the age of 64, he was gone.

They said his car was found not too far from Besançon and the suggestion was that he had fallen asleep at the wheel and had run off the road.

We stayed in Combloux until the funeral and the atmosphere was very sad. Then we went up to Besançon to pay our respects. That was a very tough day.

At first I wondered how the team would carry on without him. It was Jean de Gribaldy's team. Although things had slowly evolved since Kas got involved, he still set the tone for everything we did.

His death left such a big gap but because he had run things so well, we just carried on. We knew what we had to do.

Ramon Mendiburu took over as the general manager of the team and Rumeau and Ruperez took on more responsibility and we carried on. Mendiburu was the perfect character to fill the void left by De Gribaldy because he was a similar character. He was well organised and the riders respected him. He had their attention when he spoke without needing to shout. Authority like that doesn't come easily to everyone.

But I missed De Gribaldy a lot. There were many moments when I found myself thinking about him and wondering what he would have said about a certain situation.

One of the first significant times I thought about him was during Paris-Nice later that spring, when Stephen Roche punctured and we carried on with our fast pace to sew up the race. De Gribaldy would have approved of that. After the race we didn't have a big celebration but in our own way each of us was remembering De Gribaldy. That one was for him.

Occasionally we'd help ourselves to a dessert after dinner and someone would say: 'If Jean could see us now,' and we'd angle the knife to cut a slightly smaller portion than we really wanted.

IT WAS DIFFICULT without De Gribaldy but the season had to go on and as the races came thick and fast it was just a case of getting stuck in. After the way he'd lost Paris-Nice, Roche was out for revenge at Critérium International at the end of March and we had a big showdown. On the second day of the two-day race there were a couple of stages – a short, hilly stage from Antibes to Cassouls in the morning and a time trial in the afternoon. Although it was only 89 kilometres, the morning stage was sure to be fast, intense racing. And, as fate would have it, we had to go over the Col de Vence, which is where Roche had punctured during Paris-Nice a few weeks earlier.

Roche and I got away on our own and things really began to heat up. We were sharing the pace-setting fairly evenly but as I came off the front and prepared to settle in behind him, he attacked me. Roche knew I preferred a fast, even pace on the climbs rather than sudden accelerations.

I closed the gap down and as I got level with him I said: 'If you do that again, I won't work with you.'

He said: 'Okay.'

We carried on working together again and after a kilometre or so, he did the same thing again. He waited for me to come off the front after my stint and then he jumped me.

I was getting annoyed by now. I was on the limit but he was taking the mickey out of me riding like this. I had to work really hard to catch him but when I did I gave him a lot of abuse.

We carried on like this all the way up the climb. I knew he was doing it on purpose to get me back for what happened at Paris-Nice. It was perfect tactics by Roche – making me ride in a way he knew I found uncomfortable.

You might wonder why I bothered working with him but I was the world number one and that meant riding in a certain way. I didn't want him accusing me of sitting on his wheel and taking a free ride to the finish. I wanted to do my share. After the descent, I outsprinted him to win the stage and later that day I took the time trial to win Critérium International.

It was quite funny, really, two Irishmen trying to get under each other's skin like that. I couldn't resist reminding him that the score that spring was 2-0 to the farmer's son.

I was not on top of my game at the Classics that April but I had a bigger priority that spring. Before he died, De Gribaldy had told me it was time to win the Vuelta a España. I was ready to give it everything I had. And I very nearly pulled it off.

24. The pain in Spain
The 1987 Vuelta a España

The first time I noticed the sharp little pain was during the 15th stage from La Coruña to Vigo. It was a small but intense discomfort at first but throughout the latter part of the stage I was shifting in the saddle a lot more than normal. It's not unusual to get little sores and pains when you're two weeks into one of the big tours but this felt different. I delved into my shorts thinking maybe a piece of grit had got stuck in there but all I could feel was a small, hard lump under the skin.

When I got to our hotel I shut myself in the bathroom to investigate. There was a boil on my perineum. It was only small but when I pressed it, the pain was severe. I called for the doctor and he said it was a cyst, caused by an ingrowing hair.

The Vuelta a España was within my grasp. With a week to go until we reached Madrid, I was lying second overall, just 39 seconds behind Luis Herrera, the Colombian climber.

There was a time trial at Valladolid to come and I knew I could make up enough time on Herrera to win the Vuelta. He flew up the mountains like a little bird but he was no match for my power in a flat time trial. The equation was simple. If I could ride strongly in Valladolid I should gain enough of a lead over Herrera and the German, Raimund Dietzen, who was lurking just behind me, to defend the yellow jersey through the remaining mountain stages and on to Madrid. It would be close and Herrera would be sure to put me under pressure on the climbs but I was riding very well. Everything was under control.

Or it was until the cyst reared its ugly head.

The Vuelta was hugely important to our team. Louis Knorr of

Kas wanted to win it even more than the Tour.

We had a strong team and we started very well. My team-mate Jean-Luc Vandenbroucke won the prologue time trial in Benidorm to take the first yellow jersey of the race. I was second and another Kas rider, Alfred Ackermann, was fourth.

The following day, I won the stage in Albacete to take the Vuelta's yellow jersey for the first time in my career.

After that, Roberto Pagnin, an Italian rider, and I played pass the parcel with the yellow jersey for a few days. He took it from me then I got it back after winning the time trial in Valencia.

On the stage that finished in the velodrome in Barcelona, Pagnin attacked and took the jersey back by a few seconds. But with the mountains ahead of us, and all the strong climbers already behind me, I was in a very good position.

THERE WERE TIMES during the race when I felt I could hear De Gribaldy's voice. It was as if he was still with me.

There's a lot of time to think during a grand tour and if you are not careful, you can drive yourself crazy assessing your form, weighing up your rivals and looking ahead. The questions went round and round in my head. Do I feel okay? Will I be able to follow the best riders in the mountains? What about the time trial? Have I got enough time on this guy? Am I too far behind that guy? Unless you are able to control those thoughts, they can become destructive. Thinking the same thoughts over and over again is not necessarily positive.

De Gribaldy's big strength was keeping me focused on the job in hand and helping me push those questions and doubts to the side. He was never one for giving out a lot of praise but he was sparing in his criticism too. He knew that winning a grand tour would take a lot of energy and that the race could be lost in the mind before the legs even started to weaken. At the end of a hard stage, when I was very tired and tempted to think back over what had happened that day, he had a way of getting me to move on. He would say: 'You rode very well today but it's done. Let's rest and do the same again tomorrow.'

Faustino Ruperez was very good but he wasn't De Gribaldy

so during the race, I would say to myself: 'What would Jean say?'

THE FIRST MAJOR TEST of the Vuelta was the mountain stage to Andorra. The climbers gained time on me but I felt pretty good on the climbs. Some of the men I was concerned about who finished ahead of me were Vicente Belda, Herrera, Laudelino Cubino, Pedro Delgado and Angel Arroyo but I knew that I had to ride my own race rather than get caught in a fight with the climbers in the mountains. That would be a short-cut to disaster.

They were all more explosive than me on the steep gradients so trying to match their accelerations was a dangerous game. I might be able to follow them for a while but if they kept attacking, I might blow eventually and lose a lot more time than if I stuck to my own rhythm and tried to limit my losses.

At Andorra, the climbers clawed back some of the time I'd gained in the first week but I was still in the yellow jersey and my lead over Julien Gorospe, who was second, was still just over a minute.

The same group of riders put me under more pressure the next day on the very difficult climb to Cerler, which is the ski resort just above Benasque, the last town before the French border. Bagnères-de-Luchon, where I lost the *maillot jaune* in the 1983 Tour, is on the other side.

Cubino won the stage, ahead of Herrera and Belda, but it was Dietzen, a West German riding for the Teka team, who took the yellow jersey. He had been 1-16 behind me overall at the start of the stage but at the end of the day he led me by two seconds. In grand tour terms, two seconds is nothing. That night, I assessed the damage and was happy. I had lost two minutes to Cubino and Herrera but it could have been worse. They were both excellent climbers and I figured they would be disappointed not to put more time into me. Trailing Dietzen by a couple of seconds was ideal because it spared me and my team the burden of the yellow jersey and meant Dietzen would have to cope with that pressure while his team-mates would tire themselves out defending the lead.

The climbers had relatively few opportunities to distance me but they would have expected me to crumble on the 11th stage to Lagos de Covadonga in the Asturias. The climb is a really hard one. After 12 kilometres the road arrives at a pair of lakes that sit between the rocks.

It's a spectacular view and although the climb was a new one for the Vuelta, having first been used in 1983, it had already gained a reputation. The gradient was very uneven, which made it especially tough for me. The riders who'd won there – Marino Lejaretta, Dietzen, Pedro Delgado and Robert Millar – were all fine climbers.

I knew I had my work cut out to stay within striking distance.

Herrera turned the screw that day. He was so small and light that he could fly away from the rest of us. He also rode at a really erratic rhythm. One minute he was motoring, then he seemed to falter and all of a sudden he'd dart away again. His was a horrible wheel to have to follow. There was never a chance to get into a steady rhythm.

So I ignored Herrera, as much as I could. There was nothing I could do to influence him. I couldn't climb the mountain at his pace and rhythm and I couldn't slow him down so I focused on getting to the top as quickly as I could.

He won the stage and gained almost a minute-and-a-half on me but I actually rode really well and finished third on the stage, ahead of all the other overall contenders. It was the best result I could realistically have hoped for.

Herrera had taken the yellow jersey but I was still second. I was 39 seconds behind him but with all four of the summit finishes now behind us, and 11 flat or lumpy stages to go, including the time trial at Valladolid, I was in a great position.

The Vuelta wasn't in the bag – far from it – but I could afford to feel more confident about how the second half of the race would pan out than Herrera would. In fact, Dietzen, who was now 11 seconds behind me, was probably my biggest threat because he was dangerous on the rolling terrain and he was decent in the time trials.

The Valladolid time trial was only 24 kilometres long but everyone knew that Herrera would be vulnerable. On a bad day he could lose minutes. Even if he had a good day, I could expect to gain a minute-and-a-half on him if everything went to plan.

We left the Asturias region and headed to La Coruña on the Galician coast, then turned towards Vigo. The race slipped into a sort of lull. Riders from lower down the general classification fought for stage victories and Herrera and I kept a casual eye on each other. Neither of us were going to gain anything on these flat stages. We both knew the time trial would decide the Vuelta.

TO WIN ONE of the big, three-week tours it goes without saying you have to be the strongest, or at least one of the strongest, riders.

But even the strongest riders can have a bad day. The fear is that the bad day coincides with one of the most important stages. If you feel below par on a flat stage, it's easy to get through it. Even if you feel as sick as a dog, you can hang in there. But if you feel bad in the mountains – as I did in the Pyrenees during the 1983 Tour de France – it can be game over.

Luck always plays a part too. Crashes, illness or injury are part of a rider's life. I knew that to win a race like the Vuelta, I needed everything to go my way. And I was about to find out that something as simple as an ingrowing hair can ruin everything.

Midway through the 15th stage I noticed that I had a pain in my groin area. As the day went on, I was shifting my weight in the saddle, trying to avoid putting pressure on it.

The doctor said there wasn't much he could do. He suggested I slather on the chamois cream to keep the area lubricated so it didn't rub too much.

The following day's stage was from Ponteareas to Ponferrada. Just when I needed a shorter stage, we faced 237 kilometres and more than six-and-a-half hours in the saddle.

At the end of that day the lump was bigger and harder, and it was really beginning to smart.

The cyst was in the worst possible place. Dead centre, right under the perineum where the whole weight of my body rested on the saddle. I wriggled left and right to try to ease the pain but it didn't help at all.

There was no respite. Stage 17 from Ponferrada to Valladolid was another 221 kilometres. Another five-and-a-half hours of shifting around like I had a bad case of piles.

The final hour of that stage to Valladolid was agonising. My eyes were watering. The pain was immense. It was like trying to ride a bike with a marble trapped in my shorts. It was such a relief when I could get up on the pedals and take the weight off my arse for a bit.

That's probably why I was up at the front, taking seventh place in the bunch sprint. I took the chance to get out of the saddle for a few minutes. My legs felt absolutely fine but sitting down was becoming impossible. I was starting to wonder if I'd have to ride all the way to Madrid out of the saddle.

That night in Valladolid, Ruperez and I weighed up the situation. No one else on the race knew anything was wrong with me and we wanted to keep it that way. We didn't want Herrera finding out that I was struggling and getting a huge psychological boost.

But with the time trial to come the following day, I had to do something to ease the pain. Although I was confident of beating Herrera by a minute-and-a-half and taking the yellow jersey, I was concerned about the stages to come afterwards.

I knew I had no chance of making it to Madrid with the cyst continuing to grow. By now it was the size of a pea and even sitting on a normal chair was uncomfortable.

The decision was taken to cut out the cyst, ride the time trial and then grit my teeth for the final four stages.

Mendiburu was good friends with the Vuelta's race doctor so he was asked to come to the hotel to do the operation. He was sworn to secrecy because we didn't want anyone finding out.

We did the operation in my room. I got up on the soigneur's massage table and I was given an anaesthetic injection. The doctor lanced the boil, drained it, and stitched up the wound. It was quite an awkward place to stitch so he had to use five stitches to hold the skin together.

At first everything felt great. I slept well for the first time in a few days but then the anaesthetic wore off.

When I woke up in the morning, I felt very nervous because although the cyst had gone, the pain had not.

The time trial was 24 kilometres long. I calculated that would mean about 30 minutes of agony and I knew I could cope with the pain for that long. I could do no more than take it one day at a time. I got onto the rollers so I could warm up before the time trial. I took a deep breath and braced myself for the pain as I sat down on the saddle. I had taken some painkillers to try to make it better but I'm not sure it made any difference at all because it was such intense agony.

I warmed my legs up slowly but all I could think of was the pain between my balls and my backside. It was as if I couldn't feel anything else but the pain in my groin.

I sprinted out of the start house and got the big gear up to speed. I must have ridden about three-quarters of the way out of the saddle because sitting down was like sitting on nails.

Knowing I was setting a good time was the only thing that kept me going. I gained time on Herrera all the way and at the finish my 39-second overall deficit had been converted into a 42-second lead. I went to the podium to get the yellow jersey but I didn't feel much like smiling. I wanted to get back to the hotel and ask the doctor to examine my wound.

IT WASN'T PRETTY. The doctor confirmed the worst. The effort of putting everything into the time trial had burst the stitches. The wound was a real mess and he had a real job trying to stitch the skin back together.

That night, I didn't sleep well. I was four days from winning the Vuelta but every minute in the saddle had felt like an hour during that time trial. The road stages were going to be even tougher to endure.

The 19th stage to Avila scared me. There were two first-category climbs and a couple of second-category climbs for good measure. That, at least, would give me the chance to ride out of the saddle for a while.

With Herrera and Dietzen still within a minute of me overall, I knew they would try to make life hard.

Mendiburu told me to take it one day at a time. Survive today and don't think about tomorrow. Ruperez was very encouraging too, saying that it was bound to get easier as we went on, but I knew how much pain I was in and so I wasn't convinced by either of them.

I was nervous because the pain was constant and the prospect of riding 213 kilometres frightened me.

We tried everything to make it easier. I cut a hole in the padding in my shorts hoping it would ease the pressure but it didn't really work. We talked about cutting a hole in the top of the saddle, directly under the wound, but I was worried it might make things worse.

To have the yellow jersey in the Vuelta, with four days to go, and know in my heart of hearts that I probably wasn't going to make it was extremely difficult to take.

I was worried that this might be my one and only shot at winning one of the grand tours. There was no guarantee I'd ride this well again.

That morning, I was in agony before we even left the neutralised zone at the start of the stage. Every time I sat down, I could feel the tears welling up in my eyes. Each bump in the road made me wince and every muscle in my body tensed.

I dropped back to the team car. Ruperez was putting a brave face on things. 'Just get through the first hour and it'll get easier.'

Time was passing slowly and I just couldn't imagine getting to the finish.

'Once they start racing, you'll forget about the pain a bit,' Ruperez said, but I still wasn't sure.

I know he was trying to help but all I could think about was pulling over to the side of the road, getting off the bike and making the pain stop.

I could usually hurt myself on the bike. I could ride until my legs and lungs burned but this was a totally different type of pain.

In the first 20 kilometres, I dropped back to the team car four or five times and each time I returned to the bunch I could feel the other riders looking at me.

A bike rider can sense weakness in one of his rivals. They knew something was up.

Someone asked: '*Mal au cul?*' Have you got a pain in the arse?

I tried to make light of it.

But by then, I knew my race was over. I wasn't going to get through the next 20 minutes, let alone the next four days.

The bunch was just rolling along at a really easy pace. Normally I wouldn't even feel the pedals at this speed, but every pedal stroke was draining me. I felt weak from coping with the pain.

I knew it was futile and I dropped back to the team car one last time. Ruperez didn't bother to say anything this time. He knew I was done. The colour had completely drained from my face.

I slowed down, got off my bike carefully and climbed into the back of the car.

Pulling out of the Vuelta while wearing the yellow jersey and so close to the finish was terrible, not that I wanted anyone feeling sorry for me. That would have made it worse.

I've been asked whether I'd have won that Vuelta had it not been for the ingrowing hair.

I'm not even going to answer the question because it's a pointless one. Luis Herrera won the race, and he was a worthy winner, because he got through to the end and I didn't. That's what the big tours are all about. They are the biggest test of a cyclist's ability and stamina. One of the requirements is that a rider stays free of injury and illness. I was unlucky, yes, but I hadn't managed to do that.

I saw Herrera at a race shortly after the Vuelta and I congratulated him. He was sympathetic about what had happened to me, which was nice of him, although he didn't need to be.

Bike racing is an unforgiving business. We can discuss what might have happened had I been injury free but it's irrelevant. All that matters is the name in the record books.

Six weeks later, Ireland had its first grand tour champion. Stephen Roche won the Giro d'Italia. And as Roche enjoyed the greatest summer of his career, I suffered my most disappointing.

25. A bittersweet summer

Roche's triple

The 1987 Tour de France was the most open since Bernard Hinault's absence in 1983. Hinault had retired, leaving the peloton without its patron, its figurehead. Not only that, but the defending champion, Greg LeMond, was also missing. He had been the victim of a freak shooting accident while out hunting during the winter and his entire career hung in the balance.

So, the list of contenders for the 1987 Tour was longer than ever. I considered myself to be among them, not least because I had come so close to winning the Vuelta.

But there were so many others who believed it was their year. The list of potential contenders was long and had an international flavour. The French thought Laurent Fignon could win his third Tour and they also had Jean-François Bernard and Charly Mottet, who had shown a lot of promise and were tipped for great things. Colombia's Luis Herrera, the winner of the Vuelta, and Ireland's Stephen Roche, who had clinched the Giro, were automatically on the list too.

Urs Zimmermann of Switzerland and Andy Hampsten of the USA had been third and fourth in the 1986 Tour, so they deserved consideration too. Then there were several Spaniards, the best of whom was Pedro Delgado. Phil Anderson of Australia was not as good as he had been in 1982 and 1983 but he still dreamed of finishing on the podium. And then there was me: 31 years old but feeling fit and fresh now the cyst had cleared up.

Having been fifth in 1984 and fourth in 1985, I believed I could still improve. If I was being honest, I perhaps doubted whether I could win, but a podium position was within reach.

Since I rode my first Tour in 1978, the race had become a huge event. The field had almost doubled in size. At my first Tour I was one of 110 riders; now there were 207. Once it had been an event dominated by riders from mainland Europe and I, an Irishman, had been a bit of a novelty. Now there were teams from Colombia, the United States and, in the shape of ANC-Halfords, Great Britain.

The accordion music was fading out and the corporate sponsors were coming in. The Tour had become an international sporting event to rival the Olympic Games and football's World Cup. The 1987 Tour was the first of the truly modern Tours. The *Grand Départ* was in West Berlin. The Tour had started on foreign soil plenty of times but this time it would take us five days to reach the French border.

Although I felt I'd recovered fully after the Vuelta, the start of the race was a shock to the system. West Berlin was incredibly hot that weekend and so was the racing. I was 46th in the prologue time trial. Although I was not a prologue specialist I usually did a bit better than that. Then our Kas team was tenth in the team time trial, which was neither a triumph nor a disaster.

My team-mate Acacio Da Silva won stage three in Stuttgart, which was a good result for us but I was beginning to worry that the zip was missing from my legs.

I was getting up there in the sprint finishes but I didn't feel like I was on top of my game. The first week of the Tour is always fast but this time it seemed to be even more competitive. With so many riders, there was always someone willing to attack. Rarely did we get a chance to roll along at a casual pace; the racing started as soon as the flag dropped.

I couldn't understand why we didn't just let them go and reel them in steadily. Instead, it was like being back in the amateurs with everyone thinking they had a chance.

The fact I'd missed the 1986 race made me wonder whether I'd simply forgotten what the Tour was like but a lot of the guys agreed that the racing was much harder than usual.

Fignon was the only former Tour winner in the field but he didn't have the authority of a *patron*. He was yelling to the guys at the front that they should let the lunatics go, but no one was listening.

One day we were next to each other when the bunch began to stretch into one thin line as the attacks kept going off the front. 'If Hinault was here, this would be stopped immediately,' I said.

Fignon replied: 'We're going to kill ourselves if we carry on like this all the way to Paris.'

Hinault would keep a lid on things every now and then. If he decided the bunch should take it easy for the first couple of hours of a stage, that is what happened. He knew how much he'd be suffering in the mountains and during the time trials, so he didn't want to be on the limit in the flat stages too.

Without Hinault, everyone thought they could win a stage or get the yellow jersey.

Most of the riders agreed it was crazy but nothing changed. I would be chatting to someone and they'd be complaining about the relentless attacking and then, ten minutes later, I'd see the guy sprinting off the front.

The fast pace and the big bunch meant there were a lot of crashes too. The Tour had grown so big but they still sent us down the narrow country roads. Some days were total chaos.

And it's a bit unkind to stereotype them but with two Colombian teams in the race, disaster was never more than a moment away. We used to joke that their reaction times were 3.5 seconds slower than the rest of us. That might be a bit unfair but it's true that they were still not used to the style of racing in Europe, where everyone rode so close together. If there was a crash, there was often a Colombian jersey at the bottom of the heap.

The first ten days were fast, hot and stressful and I wasn't feeling confident. Christian Rumeau told me I'd improve once we got to the mountains but I wasn't sure. When I was in top form I could fly over the third and fourth-category climbs without really noticing them. Now, everything felt like more effort than it should. The pedals were not flying round.

THE TOUR IS WHERE a lot of contract negotiations take place. I was already in the middle of discussions with Louis Knorr and although I was happy with Kas, it didn't hurt to keep my options open and find out what else was out there. I wanted a pay rise and was hoping for another million pesetas than Knorr was offering, and he was waiting to see what results I got.

For the first time in 20 years, there was a British team in the race. ANC-Halfords were probably a little bit out of their depth. I tried to have a word with their riders when I saw them because I knew what it was like to be a stranger in the middle of the Tour.

They had some good riders too – Malcolm Elliott was a good sprinter, who went on to win the points jersey at the Vuelta, and Adrian Timmis was a climber who should have had a good career but that Tour probably burned him out. I also knew Guy Gallopin, my old team-mate from the Skil and Kas teams.

Their manager, Tony Capper, was a larger than life guy – in every sense – and he had spoken to me a few times. He didn't know that negotiations were done more discreetly in cycling because he would come over and say, loudly: 'So, are you going to ride for us next year or what? Name your price.'

One day early in the Tour, we were staying in the same hotel as the ANC-Halfords team and Capper arranged a meeting. I went to his room and Phil Griffiths, their *directeur sportif*, was also there.

Capper was very ambitious. He said that now he'd seen the Tour, he knew what it would take to win the race and that he wanted to sign me, Phil Anderson and Stephen Roche, for starters, and win the Tour.

He asked how much Kas were paying me. In discussions like that, it's never wise to give away too much, so I dodged the question. He said: 'Whatever it is, I'll double it.'

I never spoke to Capper again after that – well, apart from small talk at the start of a stage, that is. Before the Tour ended, he had gone back to England leaving Griffiths and four of the riders to soldier on to Paris. Slowly the team disintegrated, ran out of money, and that was the end of them.

THE TOUR WASN'T getting any easier but the alarm bells began to ring more loudly during the time trial from Saumur to the new technology theme park at Futuroscope. The course was brutal. We had to ride 87.5 kilometres on rolling roads that had become sticky in the heat.

There's nothing comfortable about a time trial stage of the Tour de France, especially if you are hoping for a good result in the overall standings, but this was extreme.

A time trial of that length will exploit every weakness in a rider. I was only about 25 kilometres into the stage when Rumeau, who was in the team car behind me, stopped giving me time checks. That's never a good sign. It meant I was losing a lot of time.

I gave it everything I had but the cupboard was bare. I suffered so much for more than two hours that it was like riding through a black tunnel. I ended up 26th, more than five minutes behind the stage winner, Stephen Roche.

If I had been in top form, there was no way I'd have lost five minutes to Roche, even though he was one of the top time trial riders in the world at the time.

Even more worrying was that I finished behind some of the climbers – guys who would take time from me in the mountains. I needed to beat Delgado, Zimmermann and Robert Millar in a stage like this to keep alive any hope of a high placing overall. All of them beat me that day, which was a real blow to my morale.

The yellow jersey was now out of my reach. One bad day in the mountains would make it very difficult to finish in the top ten. And I was already out of contention for the green jersey because I hadn't been going for the points.

The stark reality was that a stage win was now the best I could hope for from the Tour, and even that would be a tall order.

At last, early on the 12th stage from Brive to Bordeaux, common sense prevailed and we took it easy for an hour or so. For almost a fortnight we'd raced as if we could see the Eiffel Tower on the horizon but with the Pyrenees just around the corner everyone was in the mood to knock it back a bit and catch up with their friends in the peloton.

The weather was glorious. We were on a long, straight country road. It wasn't very wide but we were going very easy. I was a little way back from the front of the bunch, rolling along next to Roche, chatting. My hands were on the tops of the bars and we can't have been doing more than about 25 kilometres an hour.

Suddenly the guy in front braked. I reached for my brakes as quickly as I could but there wasn't enough time to avoid him. I went straight into the back of him and then went down.

I fell like a dead weight, landing very heavily on the road. Although we had only been rolling along at a slow speed, those crashes can be the most damaging. If you crash at high speed you slide when you hit the floor and take all the skin off your arse and elbows but you can get bandaged up and go on. However, when you fall the way I did, you land like a sack of potatoes being dropped off the delivery truck.

I knew immediately that I'd broken my collarbone because the pain was intense.

My team-mates gathered round me, hoping to pace me back to the bunch, which was still visible further up the long, straight road. I managed to get back on the bike but I knew I wasn't going to be able to ride on. I couldn't put any weight on my arm when I put my hands on the bars.

Acacio Da Silva and Iñaki Gastón tried to lead me back to the peloton while Gilles Sanders pushed me. The bunch carried on at a very slow pace for a long while, waiting for me to get back to them, but still we couldn't close the gap. I could see the line of team cars up ahead but I could not ride fast enough with only one hand on the bars.

I knew my Tour was over. Eventually I pulled over to the side of the road. The photographers gathered round me. Gerard Porte, the Tour de France doctor, examined me and confirmed my collarbone was broken.

Rumeau helped me off my bike and put his arm around me and that is when the tears came. They weren't tears of self-pity. It had been a terrible year and the emotion of everything caught up with me. De Gribaldy's death, what had happened at the Vuelta and now crashing out of the Tour.

Although things weren't going well, I didn't want to leave the race. The Tour is such a special event and I still hoped I could win a stage. Missing the race in 1986 had been disappointing but watching the circus roll on without me was worse.

I was in the routine of suffering that the Tour brings and to suddenly leave it and find myself on the way to the hospital was a big shock. Instead of bracing myself for the Pyrenees and the Alps, I was on my way home.

The doctor told me I should stay off the bike for five weeks because as well as the fractured collarbone, I'd torn my ligaments quite badly. The World Championships were only seven weeks away so I knew I couldn't afford to follow the doctor's advice. I was back on the rollers within three weeks.

I didn't watch much of the Tour on television, even when Roche got into the yellow jersey. I watched the time trial at Mont Ventoux and the day when Roche fought back on La Plagne to limit his losses to Pedro Delgado.

I can't lie. It was difficult to see Roche win the Tour. I certainly didn't want Delgado to beat him but it was hard to see another Irishman win the yellow jersey. It wasn't that I was jealous of him, but Stephen was achieving something that I knew I could never do. He was going to be the first Irishman to win the Tour de France.

ONCE I WAS BACK on my bike, I needed to get my sharpness back if I was going to challenge for the rainbow jersey at the World Championships, which were to be held in Villach, Austria.

I had been booked to ride a couple of criterium races in Ireland at the end of August, one in Dublin and another in Cork two days later. Knowing that a lot of riders would be hanging around between the two, a group of businessmen in Wexford put up the money to organise a race on the day in between.

Initially I was only booked to ride in Dublin and Cork but my manager, Frank Quinn, said: 'They've gone to a lot of effort in Wexford and they're expecting you to put on a show. What are you going to do with a day off anyway?'

The money was quite attractive and so I decided to race at Wexford too.

I didn't realise it then, but I'd just signed up for a best-of-three clash between the British and the Irish.

In Europe, some of the criterium races are exhibition events designed to bring in the crowds and show off the stars. Sometimes the organiser would have a say in who he wanted to win because he was putting up the money.

But the British races didn't work like that at all. They had an established series of city-centre races, sponsored by the cereal company Kellogg's. And these races, held on short, tight circuits, were their staple diet. The Brits were very good at them and they were extremely competitive.

I remembered my first few times racing the Kellogg's series in Britain. The organiser, Alan Rushton, signed me up and asked if I could recruit a few riders from Europe. At one race, the Belgian, Frank Hoste, rolled up to the start line quite casually and, assuming that the race would work like they did in Belgium or Holland, said: 'Okay, what's the story? Who's winning here?'

I nodded in the direction of some of the British guys. They were lined up on both sides of the road, holding onto the barriers with their feet already clipped into their pedals so they could sprint away from the line as soon as the gun went.

'It doesn't work like that here,' I said. 'You're going to earn your money tonight.'

The Brits would start on the 'g' of 'go' and give it everything for an hour or an hour-and-a-half, depending how long the race lasted. They were fast through the corners, their bike-handling skills were impressive and they could be cut-throat too.

Malcolm Elliott, John Herety, Mark Walsham, Steve Joughin and Phil Thomas were among the best in the business at the time. And although he was an Aussie, Shane Sutton was an honorary Brit. He still is today, having worked for British Cycling for so long. Sutton was like a terrier on wheels. They all were.

I quickly found that if I backed off through the corners, half a dozen of them would swarm past.

The first race was in Dublin, home town of the Giro d'Italia and Tour de France champion Stephen Roche. We had a chat with a group of riders led by Phil Thomas and quickly got the impression that there was no way they were going to give Stephen a homecoming celebration. He would have to earn it.

There were four of us – Stephen, Martin Earley, Paul Kimmage and me – against the British guys. It rained in Dublin that evening, which made the corners slippery and the cobbles in the castle grounds treacherous. There were a lot of crashes and I went down a couple of times. We took a lot of risks but towards the end, Stephen got away and won the race.

I'm sure the British riders wanted to beat us the next night in Wexford, and we wanted to beat them.

Dublin had been crazy because of the rain but the Wexford circuit was like an obstacle course. It was very technical, with some tight corners. The race went down by the quay, with riders having to dodge bollards and the kerb. There were crashes every lap and every time I went down the finishing straight it was like a scene out of a war film, with people bleeding, holding their heads and carrying their bikes. No one backed off at all and there were a couple of moments when I thought I was going to end up sliding out of control. But I stayed upright and managed to win.

Everywhere we went, we were mobbed. I had been worried that I might be gatecrashing Stephen's party. After all, he had won the Giro and the Tour and was the returning hero, but the people were fantastic towards all of us.

We went to Cork for the final race determined to complete the clean sweep. Again, it was a real battle and although we worked together during the race, the way Stephen dived into the final corner showed that he had every intention of winning the sprint, so I had to work pretty hard to get past him.

I can't honestly say the British were happy at the finish but if anyone had started anything they wouldn't have got out of Cork in one piece.

The thing about that series of races was that it brought us all closer together – Stephen, Martin, Paul and me – just before the World Championships, which is the only race of the season contested by national teams instead of sponsored squads.

I headed to Italy to ride three races in four days and after the final one, I started to feel like my old self again. I thought that missing the second half of the Tour de France might work to my advantage at the World Championships. Our big handicap was that we'd be heavily outnumbered by the Belgians, French, Italians and Dutch, who'd all have 12 riders in their teams. We had just five – the other rider being Alan McCormack, who raced as a professional in the United States.

After the final warm-up race in Italy, the Giro del Friuli, Stephen, Martin and I rode up to southern Austria. It was a solid five-hour ride but we took it nice and easy, just putting the miles in the bank. The World Championships is like a Classic – 250 kilometres of racing that gets harder and faster in the closing stages so that only the very strongest can survive.

Moreno Argentin was the defending champion and the clear favourite. The Italian press had made up their minds that he would win. And, seeing as we were not far from the Italian border, it was almost like a home race for him.

Before the race, everyone had assumed that the circuit in Villach was flat and that the race would suit a sprinter. But after we rode the course I knew it would be a lot more selective in the closing stages.

We always felt like we were racing against the odds at the World Championships. The Irish Cycling Federation was not a wealthy organisation. We didn't have a team manager or much back-up because the federation simply didn't have the resources, so we relied on support from our sponsored teams.

A mechanic from Kas came to help us and Stephen had a couple of people from his Carrera team. We had to get our own green jerseys made, which explains why they were often different shades.

Our jerseys may not have matched but the spirit in the team was excellent. Stephen had won the Giro and the Tour and he gave an interview to the press in which he said that he'd try to help me win the world title.

It's probably fair to say the course suited me slightly better, and I knew I could beat Argentin if it came down to a sprint, but we had two very strong cards to play. Stephen was always happier talking to journalists than I was and I was happy to stay out of the spotlight as the race got closer.

The Italian press – keen to play up the rivalry between Stephen and I – refused to believe that we got on. We were room-mates that week in Austria. They couldn't imagine two Italian stars sharing a room the week before the World Championships.

We didn't really have a plan for the race, other than to make sure one or other of us – or preferably both – went with the moves during the final couple of laps. Earley and Kimmage did some very good work to chase the break early on. The latter stages turned out as we expected. With two laps to go, there was a crucial split. Both Stephen and I made it. By now, the big nations were also down to two or three contenders, so we'd evened the odds.

On the final lap, everyone was nervous and tired. We knew that it might take just one well-timed attack to win the race.

Argentin was glued to my back wheel. He would have got into my back pocket if he could. He was following me everywhere and I knew he'd react if I tried anything. I rolled alongside Stephen and we agreed to take turns following the attacks.

If one of us got away in a smaller group, we'd take our chances but if nothing stayed away, it would come down to a sprint, most probably between Argentin and me because we were the two fastest finishers.

We hit the last climb with about three kilometres left and I was in a group of a dozen or so that was still together. Every time there had been an attack, a green jersey followed. We'd played it perfectly; now we just had to see out the finish.

Then Teun Van Vliet of the Netherlands tried something and there was a hesitation.

Stephen reacted and joined Van Vliet. One by one, Rolf Gölz of Germany, Guido Winterberg of Switzerland and the Dane Rolf Sørensen went across to them. Argentin and I sat tight, each waiting for the other to respond. There was no way I was going to tow Argentin across to Stephen's group. It was up to him to chase and if he did, I'd have an armchair ride up to the leaders.

In the final two kilometres, they were never more than a few hundred metres ahead. We could see them all the way to the finish but no one in my group was prepared to make the crucial effort to close the gap.

I felt comfortable. Stephen was up the road and had a good chance of winning, while I could afford to wait. If it all came back together at the last moment, I still had a chance in the sprint.

Eventually, Canada's Steve Bauer went to the front of our group and began to chase them down. Bauer was very strong and he closed the gap a lot. As we swung into the finishing straight we were almost upon them.

I was beginning to think about the sprint when suddenly Stephen jumped away. His timing was perfect. Tactically he couldn't have played it any better.

As Stephen crossed the line – the new world champion – I put my hands up to celebrate too. It wasn't a gesture for the cameras; it was a genuine show of delight. Our little gang from Ireland had beaten the best in the world. It wasn't me that would pull on the rainbow jersey but it was still a magnificent feeling.

Our hotel was full of happy Irish supporters that night and they stayed up very late singing and knocking back the drink.

I was exhausted but managed to stay up until about midnight when I left Stephen at the bar, wearing his rainbow jersey, a smile as wide as the Liffey on his face.

The next morning the alarm went at six. An indecently early hour but we had to make our charter flight to Brittany for a lucrative criterium appearance. I have no idea what time Stephen made it to bed but he was still wearing his rainbow jersey. To be fair to him, I think I'd have done the same.

26. El Rey

The 1988 Vuelta a España

The spring of 1988 was all about preparing for the Vuelta a España. If I was going to win a grand tour, this was it. This was my time.

Although Jean de Gribaldy was no longer with us, we followed his hectic schedule. A few hours after finishing fourth behind Eddy Planckaert, Phil Anderson and Adri Van der Poel at the Tour of Flanders I got on a charter flight to Spain ready for the five-day Tour of the Basque Country.

The race was always important to our Spanish sponsor, Kas, so there was never any opportunity for me to remain quietly in the bunch. I had to show my face at the front and be competitive.

That week I was riding very well. I won a stage and was in the top three in all the others, although as the week went on I was developing a tickly cough.

On the final day, there were two stages. I was third in the road race stage that morning, which meant I was 40 seconds behind the Dutchman Erik Breukink overall going into the afternoon's time trial. I gave it everything but the gap was too much to make up, although I was pleased to make it onto the podium.

After the stage my cough was worse, so I took a swig from a bottle of cough medicine I'd bought from a pharmacist near my home in Belgium.

The pharmacist was a friend of mine and he was involved in cycling at a regional level, so I trusted him to know what I could take safely when I was racing. He kept up to date with which substances were on the banned list.

Then I went to the dope control to give a urine sample before flying to France for Paris-Roubaix.

I took a back seat that day because my team-mate Tommy Wegmüller got into a break that went all the way to the finish. He should have won that race but he suffered some terrible luck when a plastic bag blew across the road and caught in his rear derailleur, jamming his gears. It meant he couldn't change gears for the sprint, which gave a big advantage to Dirk Demol.

After finishing fifth at Liège-Bastogne-Liège, I got a rare chance to ride Ghent-Wevelgem. Normally, it was held on the Wednesday between the Tour of Flanders and Paris-Roubaix, while I was racing in the Basque Country, but because the organisers had switched the date, I was able to ride it before flying to Tenerife for the start of the Vuelta.

Ghent-Wevelgem was a really hard race. The wind blew all day, which suited me because I was good at reading the conditions and ensuring I was in good position in the bunch. The Norwegian rider Dag-Otto Lauritzen had been away on his own for almost 60 kilometres when I rode across to him, together with Ron Kiefel of the USA, Gianni Bugno of Italy and the Belgians Ludo Peeters and Claude Criquielion. The sprint was pretty straightforward and I went home to get ready for the Vuelta feeling very confident.

THE DAY BEFORE I was due to fly to Tenerife for the start of the Vuelta, Ramon Mendiburu called me to say I'd tested positive at the Tour of the Basque Country. He told me the drug was codeine and as soon as he said that I knew it had to be the cough medicine I'd taken.

It was one of two occasions when I had a problem with the dope control. The first time was after Paris-Brussels in 1984. I had finished third behind Eric Vanderaerden and Charly Mottet and I went to the dope control. The doctor took me into a small toilet so I could urinate into a container. That sample was then split between two smaller jars, sealed with wax and labelled.

A few weeks later, there was a story in the French newspaper *L'Equipe* saying that one of the first three at Paris-Brussels had tested positive for a substance called Stimul. I asked my doctor what it was and he said it was something students took to help them concentrate when revising for exams.

I had not taken anything, so I asked for the second sample to be tested and I asked Karl McCarthy from the Irish Cycling Federation to be my witness at the second test because I was busy racing.

He said that there was a tiny amount of urine in the jar, less than the minimum required. I went before the Belgian Cycling Federation and they gave me a three-month suspended ban, which meant that if I had another problem within two years, I'd be in trouble. I paid the fine in Swiss francs but I felt aggrieved because my reputation had been damaged.

I appealed to the UCI and they agreed that although there were grounds for making a case that protocol had not been followed, they wouldn't overturn the Belgian federation's decision. I considered appealing but I didn't want the case to drag on. The suspended ban wasn't going to stop my career.

The case at the Tour of the Basque Country was different because once I discovered that codeine had been in the cough medicine I knew there was no point asking for the B sample to be tested.

I explained the situation to Mendiburu and to Louis Knorr, the boss of Kas. Knorr understood but he wasn't happy because they made soft drinks so they didn't want any association with doping, but they understood it had been an accident. Louis Knorr wasn't angry but he was concerned.

He said: 'Don't worry, the press is on our side.'

If it had been a case involving steroids or a performance-enhancing drug rather than something that was in a cough medicine the situation would have been very different.

But it still wasn't something I wanted to be involved in. I was penalised ten minutes in the overall standings at the Tour of the Basque Country and I accepted the result.

There wasn't a big controversy. It certainly wasn't like it is today. There was a story in the paper announcing the result and that was it. The organisers of the Vuelta and the Spanish Cycling Federation supported me. There was never any suggestion that I'd have to miss the Vuelta.

It was a small distraction in the days leading up to the Vuelta but I was still focused on having a good start to the race to ensure I was in the hunt for the yellow jersey in the mountains.

MY STRATEGY FOR THE Vuelta was exactly as it had been the previous year. I knew I was not the best climber in the race but I was the strongest all-rounder. I could gain on my rivals by winning the time-bonus sprints, doing well in the time trials and riding carefully in the mountains.

I was worried about the climbers because they could gang up on me and make life very difficult. Luis Herrera, the defending champion, would be a threat but I was more worried about the combined strength of the BH team.

They had four potential winners. Their leader was Alvaro Pino, who had beaten Robert Millar to win the 1986 Vuelta. They also had Federico Echave, Anselmo Fuerte and Laudelino Cubino, who were excellent in the mountains. Together they would be a very big threat.

The Vuelta started on Tenerife, which is a rugged, mountainous island. We almost lost the race before we flew back to the mainland. The first stage was unusual. The organisers split the bunch into groups of 36, with two men from each team per group. Each group then did a separate road race over a 17-kilometre circuit, with the winner of the fastest heat declared the winner of the stage.

I had never done a race like it. I was in a heat with several of the favourites for the Vuelta and there was a chance to gain a few seconds over everyone else if our heat was the fastest, so we went flat out as soon as the flag dropped.

We gave it everything and at the finish, an Italian called Ettore Pastorelli took the sprint, so he was the stage winner and the first yellow jersey holder of the race.

The following day was a real dog of a stage and one of my worst days on a bike. Cubino, one of the dangerous men from the BH team, got into a small break and they gained a lot of time.

My team-mate, Iñaki Gastón, was in the leading group but he was not a serious contender for the Vuelta so there wasn't any great tactical advantage to having him up there – not when BH were represented by Cubino. We were in two minds what to do. Usually we would not dream of chasing down a break with a team-mate in it but we didn't want to give Cubino a present.

The rest of the Kas team was a shambles. We were falling apart. I dropped back to the team car at one point and passed Wegmüller, who was bent over by the side of the road. I asked him what the matter was. He groaned and said he had terrible stomach cramps, probably from drinking tap water. He pulled out of the race and it turned out he had dysentery.

Acacio Da Silva was in all sorts of trouble too. He said he had the same problem as Wegmüller and that was the last I saw of him until we got to the finish.

The rest of us had to do something to prevent Cubino from gaining a lot of time. None of the other teams were in a hurry to help us so we left it as late as we could, then got on the front and began to chase. At the finish, we'd cut the gap right down to a minute and 14 seconds, which wasn't ideal but was a lot better than conceding three or four minutes.

As it turned out, Gastón won the stage and took the yellow jersey so the bluff worked out pretty well for us.

About 25 minutes later, Da Silva crossed the line, holding his stomach and complaining. I could never be sure with Acacio. He was such a talented rider but he would stay at home in Switzerland and leave his bike untouched in the garage for days. Then he'd turn up for a major race like the Vuelta and suffer terribly for the first few days because he hadn't been training.

So I wondered if it was a bit of an excuse because he was the sort of guy who complained of a stomach ache one minute and downed a can of Coke in one the next.

Our team was in a bit of a state during the team time trial around Las Palmas. We had lost our big engine, Wegmüller, and Da Silva was riding on one leg, so we did pretty well to finish sixth, although we lost another 1-11 to BH.

That meant Cubino was in yellow, 1-28 ahead of his team-mate Pino. I was another minute behind Pino. My plan to gain time early in the race so I'd have a bit of a buffer in the mountains had not worked at all.

Once we arrived back on the Spanish mainland, Faustino Ruperez and I sat down to plan our strategy. We looked at the overall standings and the stages to come and decided I had no option but to sprint for every time bonus there was.

Recovering the deficit six seconds at a time was going to make it a long, hard slog, but if I wanted to win the Vuelta I had to get back on terms before the mountains.

To complicate matters, BH also had a pretty handy sprinter, Jorge Dominguez, who was always in the way, trying to stop me picking up the time bonuses. So, while I was battling for seconds here, there and everywhere, Cubino was enjoying a comparatively stress-free ride in the bunch.

It took me four days to claw back a minute but by the time we reached the first proper mountain stage, to Branillin, at the end of the first week, I was right back in the picture.

That was when the BH team tried to work me over. Pino attacked on the penultimate climb, the Puerto de Pajares, and gained more than four minutes while his team-mates watched me, waiting for a response. It was a smart tactic by BH because Pino was better at the time trials than Cubino.

I was short of team-mates to help me in the mountains. Only Eric Caritoux could stay with the leaders, so I had to rope in a bit of help from elsewhere. Robert Millar and I were both managed by Frank Quinn, and his chances of winning overall were slimmer than mine, so he was happy to give me a hand in the mountains.

Millar was a pure climber who liked to make sudden darting accelerations, but he could also ride at a very even tempo, which I preferred.

I would lead on the descents and the flatter roads and Millar would take over on the climbs. Without him setting the tempo on the climb to Branillin, Pino might have gained five or six minutes but as it was we limited him to 2-29.

The BH team really played their cards well that day because close to the finish both Cubino and Fuerte attacked and gained a minute over me. I couldn't chase them because I was already at my limit, so all I could do was dig deep and hope I didn't blow up and lose even more time.

The following stage was a 6.8-kilometre mountain time trial at Alto Naranco near Oviedo. I was relieved because if we'd had another long stage, I might have found myself in serious trouble.

Instead, I had almost the whole day to rest and recover a bit of energy. Because it was such a short time trial, I could give it my all without doing myself too much damage.

Pino won the time trial but I was second, which moved me up to second place overall, still 2-10 behind Cubino.

With more mountains to come, two minutes and ten seconds was beginning to look like a worrying gap, particularly as Cubino was showing few signs of weakness.

A couple of days later at the Alto de Valdezcaray, I found my climbing legs. At the finish, having crossed two very difficult first-category mountains, I started my sprint very early and caught Mariano Sanchez, a Spanish rider who had been out in front all afternoon, just before the line.

Still I couldn't shake off Cubino, though.

THERE WERE TEN STAGES to go, but only one of them finished at the top of a mountain. I knew that if I could survive stage 13, which finished at the ski station at Cerler, I would be in with a chance of winning the Vuelta.

Things swung in my favour that day because Cubino finally faltered. The only problem was that I now had another BH rider to worry about.

Anselmo Fuerte broke away with Colombia's Fabio Parra on the climb to Cerler and began to gain a lot of time. It was every man for himself on the mountain. Fuerte was gaining time over me but I was stretching ahead of both Pino and Cubino. It seemed that whenever a BH rider was stronger than me, it was the wrong man.

I remember going round a hairpin bend and looking up to check how ahead Fuerte was, then looking down to see Pino and Cubino behind me.

At the finish, Cubino was still in yellow but only just. Fuerte was now only three seconds behind him and I was third, 33 seconds adrift but well within striking distance with a time trial to come. Pino, BH's best time trial rider, had slipped back.

All of a sudden, I felt very confident although I refused to take anything for granted. The big mountains were behind us but there were still some awkward days ahead.

Stage 16 to Albacete was a day to be wary. Every time we went to Albacete the same thing happened. It was like the wild west. The whole area was like a desert. The bunch would get about 30 kilometres from the town and the wind would pick up until the cactus plants and bushes were blowing sideways.

The crosswinds made everyone nervous but I was always quite comfortable riding in those conditions because it was just like the weather we had during the Belgian Classics.

It's fair to say the Spanish riders were not so happy. They didn't know where they should position themselves in the bunch so they were vulnerable.

The wind cut the bunch to ribbons. There were groups of riders scattered all across the plains and the crosswind was so strong it was almost impossible to close the gaps.

When the gaps started to open up, Fuerte managed to hang on at the front but Cubino found himself in the wrong place at the wrong time and lost almost two minutes. That gave Fuerte the overall lead and made me feel even more confident of victory.

The next day at Toledo, I rode the final three kilometres with the air rapidly escaping from my rear tyre. I knew I'd picked up a slow puncture but there wasn't time to stop and change my wheel. I knew I could ride to ride to the line on the rim if I had to.

Malcolm Elliott won the stage and I hung on for second place and another critical time bonus.

By the time I'd ridden the few hundred metres back to the team car, my tyre was completely flat.

Looking back at those two days, it's easy to see how fine the margins between winning and losing can be. One day the wind blew and caught out my major rival. The next day I punctured at the wrong moment but just about got away with it.

And so we came to the decisive time trial from Las Rozas to Villalba, which was on the penultimate day of the Vuelta. I knew it was a case of now or never. Anselmo Fuerte led me by 21 seconds.

In normal circumstances I would be absolutely certain of beating Fuerte by 22 seconds over 30 kilometres.

In the morning, I went out to ride the course. The first part was a very light drag, which was a bit deceptive. After that it was just about getting up to top speed and holding it. There was nothing technical about the course. Just put it in a big gear and go. This was a course for a powerful rider and I knew Fuerte wouldn't be able to match me.

At the first time check, I was well up on Fuerte but I kept pressing on. I knew I had won the stage well before the finish and at the line, my margin over Fuerte was 1-57.

That put me into the yellow jersey by a minute-and-a-half with just the final stage to Madrid left. The Vuelta was mine.

After I'd been to the podium to receive the yellow jersey I went into a trailer near the finish line to do an interview with one of the radio stations.

I did the interview in my best Spanish when a guy opened the door and said, while we were on air: 'Kelly – dope control.'

The interviewer was livid. He pressed the red button that took us off air, ran the length of the trailer and booted the guy up the backside before shouting at him: 'You've ruined my programme!'

Then he sat down, pressed the red button, apologised very calmly to the listeners for the technical problem and carried on with the interview.

When I went to dope control, the guy looked a bit sheepish.

Riding into Madrid on the final day with the yellow jersey on my back was a special moment – one of the best memories of my career. Being part of a Spanish team made it particularly enjoyable. It was like being the King of Spain for the day. Louis Knorr was extremely happy that I'd been able to win the Vuelta for him.

There was still more than half of the season to go, with the Tour de France to come in July, but after the Vuelta there were a lot of distractions. I had to go to functions in Ireland and Spain to celebrate my victory, which was very nice to do but I knew it would have an effect later in the year.

One day in Ireland we had a couple of things to attend – there was a lunch in Cork followed by a dinner in Carrick-on-Suir.

The function in Cork overran, so Martin Earley, Frank Quinn and I were running late for the do in Carrick. I was driving and I put my foot down. I was going well over the speed limit when I saw the flashing blue lights behind me.

I kept on for a bit but eventually let the police car pull us over. I wound down the window and could smell the police car's engine almost burning.

I though I was in trouble but the officer said: 'We heard on the radio that you had to get from Cork to Carrick so we were looking out for you. When we saw the car go past we knew it was you. But take it easy, will you? They'll wait a few minutes for Sean Kelly.'

BY THE TIME I got back into the racing, I was playing catch-up. With the Tour de France only a few weeks away, I felt I was way off where I needed to be. I had a problem with my sinuses but I rode the Tour of the Asturias stage race in Spain anyway because I thought I needed the miles to get ready for the Tour.

I was bunged up and could hardly breathe, so every day was miserable. There was a horrible gunge coming up from my lungs but I didn't quit the race, even though I was probably doing more harm than good.

From there I went to the Tour of Switzerland and I was still feeling below par.

The Tour de France was not a memorable one for me. I finished 46th, an hour behind the winner, Pedro Delgado.

During the first week, there was a finish at Evreux, an uphill sprint that was tricky to judge. My team-mate Acacio Da Silva and I were both going for it. I could see Acacio had gone for a long one and he was just ahead of me, so I backed off a little. Then Acacio stuck his arms in the air to celebrate and Steven Rooks almost got him on the line.

Even though he'd won, I was really pissed off with him because he'd nearly blown it. I gave him a bit of a bollocking but he had this big smile and said: 'Hey, Sean, no problem. I won.'

On stage ten to Besançon, we were riding at quite a fast pace when suddenly there was a crash. I went down with Da Silva. I picked myself up and saw Da Silva had one of the Colombian riders by the throat. He was going to whack him so I had to run over and say: 'Hey, Acacio, leave it.'

Although I was in ninth place overall when we reached the Alps, I knew I wasn't riding well enough to challenge. The stage from Besançon to Morzine was hellish. I suffered all day and lost a couple of minutes. The next day finished at Alpe d'Huez and I blew completely. I've never enjoyed that climb at the best of times. There's something about the ever-changing gradient that makes it hard for me to get into a rhythm. I was almost 24 minutes behind the winner. We weren't even in the so-called laughing group – the last group on the road where they're concerned about making the time cut. It was worse than that. We were stuck in no man's land.

After the high of winning the Vuelta, I felt like my good form had drained out of my body and through the soles of my shoes.

Then something happened to put the struggles of the Tour de France into perspective. We were in Grenoble, preparing for the time trial to Villard-de-Lans, when we heard that Louis Knorr, the cycling-mad boss of the Kas company, had died from a heart attack. It was very sad news and it cast a long shadow over the team for the rest of the race.

We hoped we might be able to win a stage to honour his memory but there are no gifts in the Tour and I was simply not able to win.

There was some uncertainty in the camp towards the end of the Tour because no one knew if the team would continue. Louis was the man who made the Kas team happen. It was his passion. We weren't sure there was the same interest from others in the company. In late August, we heard that Kas would be pulling out of cycling at the end of the year.

I was glad that I had managed to give Louis the victory in the Vuelta a España that he desperately wanted to see and at the same time sad at the way the team was ending. But I knew that the Kas team without Louis Knorr would not be the same.

After three years with a Spanish team, I was ready for a change and I was not short of offers.

27. Going Dutch
1989

As soon as the cycling world knew I was available the offers came in. I was 32 years old but having won the Vuelta a España, I was still the world number one-ranked rider and I thought I had another three good seasons in me.

Most of the top teams had already put their plans in place for 1989. Their rosters were full and their budgets spent but there were still many teams interested in making room for me.

Frank, my manager, did most of the negotiating. We spoke with the Spanish Teka team and their offer was good but it wouldn't have given me the change of routine I was looking for.

I wanted a break from Spain. At the time, the Spanish calendar was packed with stage races and Teka's management would expect me to do them all. And they would want me to do the Vuelta. I wasn't keen on that at all. I'd won the race and didn't feel I needed to go back. I wasn't sure how many years I had left at the top but I knew that for whatever time remained I wanted to concentrate on the Classics and the Tour de France.

The weeks passed by, the season ended and still nothing was signed. The sports pages were filled with rumours linking me to every team. At one point the papers said I was joining the American 7-Eleven team or the Café de Colombia squad led by Luis Herrera. There was even a story that I'd go to Fagor to ride with Stephen Roche. I wondered where the journalists got these ideas.

Despite the rumours, only three teams were ever strongly in the hunt. We decided to keep Teka's offer on the back burner as insurance in case everything else fell through.

The Belgian ADR team, which was run by Jose de Cauwer,

made an interesting offer. With all the bonus clauses they had included it could have been very lucrative but I had heard there were a few organisational issues with them, so we asked them to provide a bank guarantee to cover a year's salary. I didn't want my pay cheque arriving late. Unfortunately, they weren't able to come up with a bank guarantee.

ADR was not a big team. Although they had ridden the Tour de France in 1988, and Eddy Planckaert had won the green jersey, they would be relying on a wild-card invite to the 1989 race.

The other team that was interested in signing me was the Dutch PDM squad.

But they could not commit to signing me because they had Greg LeMond tied to an expensive contract. LeMond had barely raced for PDM in 1988 because he was still recovering from the effects of the gunshot wounds from his shooting accident.

Both LeMond and PDM wanted out but until LeMond could find a team willing to take a gamble on him, he was stuck at PDM. And that's where ADR came in.

The negotiations went on for several weeks. I was waiting for ADR and LeMond to come to an agreement so that PDM had the space and budget for me. It wasn't until November that it all got sorted out but I was prepared to wait because I knew PDM was the best option for me.

The man in charge of PDM was Manfred Krikke, while Jan Gisbers ran things at the races. The team was one of the strongest in the world. They were led by two Dutch climbers: Steven Rooks, who had been runner-up to Delgado at the 1988 Tour, and Gert-Jan Theunisse. They had also signed the Mexican Raúl Alcalá from 7-Eleven, while Martin Earley came with me from Kas.

My job was to share the leadership responsibilities with Rooks, Theunisse and Alcalá. I'm sure you've heard the saying about too many chiefs and not enough Indians.

Joining a Dutch team was like stepping into the middle of a long-running soap opera. I knew what I was getting into because I'd seen how the Dutch teams raced against each other.

The two biggest teams from the Netherlands were Superconfex, run by Jan Raas, and Panasonic, run by Peter Post. Their title sponsors had changed over the years, riders had come and gone, but the rivalry between the two managers remained as hot as ever.

Sometimes it seemed like they were happy to lose as long as the enemy didn't win. If a break went up the road with a Panasonic rider in it but no one from Superconfex, you could be sure that the Superconfex team would be sent to the front to chase it down, and vice versa.

The Dutch press whipped up the rivalry so they were stuck in the never-ending cycle. And, of course, the two other top Dutch teams, PDM and TVM, joined in too. In the spring Classics there were four teams all keeping tabs on each other.

Rooks and Theunisse were good guys but I knew I'd have to keep an eye on them because if I worked for them in one race I couldn't be sure they'd return the favour. They couldn't help it. Dutch cyclists at that time loved a double-cross.

I knew how political it was. I knew that whatever was agreed in the team meeting before a race was not necessarily binding. And I knew that sometimes I'd have to stitch them up before they had the chance to do the same to me.

Gisbers was too nice for it all really. What we needed was someone like De Gribaldy to lay down the law and make sure everyone was pedalling in the same direction. Gisbers wanted to keep all of his star riders happy, so he'd say: 'We'll play our strongest card.'

Of course, when it comes to the biggest races everyone thinks they're the strongest card and that they deserve the support of the rest. Gisbers wasn't strong enough with us. He couldn't issue an instruction and be sure everyone would follow it.

Although I had won the Vuelta a España in the spring of 1988, I'd then gone through the longest barren run of my career. I didn't win many more races that year.

In fact, deep into the spring of 1989 my winless streak had become the longest of my career. I hadn't won a race since the Tour du Limousin the previous August.

PDM rode Tirreno-Adriatico that spring so my run of seven consecutive victories at Paris-Nice had come to an end by default. In the Classics I was consistent enough – fifth at Milan-San Remo and quite active at the Tour of Flanders and Paris-Roubaix without threatening to win either.

But a couple of months into the season, I still had not given my new team a victory.

At Liège-Bastogne-Liège, I felt really good but I knew that Rooks and Theunisse would want to be the protected riders. Gisbers gave his team talk and he said that my role was to follow the wheels and hope the race came down to a sprint from a small group. I could see how this would turn out. If I waited for the sprint, Rooks or Theunisse, or both of them, would be off up the road and I'd be stuck playing policeman in the group behind.

Or, if we missed the move completely, I'd be the one doing the chasing.

So, I decided that I'd have to give them the flick, which is what I did.

We were about 55 kilometres from the end and the front group had been thinned down to about 70 riders as we hit the climbs. All the favourites were there – Roche, Criquielion, Anderson, Millar and Rooks and Theunisse, of course.

On the Côte de Chambralles, which is quite a steep climb, a French rider called Fabrice Philipot attacked. He was not a well-known rider and he certainly wasn't considered a potential winner of Liège-Bastogne-Liège.

Ordinarily, he was not the sort of rider we'd need to mark, but I went after him anyway. Then Pedro Delgado and Phil Anderson came with us and that gave me my alibi, so to speak.

Anderson rode for TVM, one of the other Dutch teams, so I could say that I was marking him.

I was careful to make sure it didn't look like I was attacking but I was desperate to get away in a smaller group and take my chances from there.

As soon as we got over the hill and out of sight, I went to the front to make sure we opened the gap. The other three worked as well and we were away. Rooks and Theunisse were now stuck in the chasing group hoping someone else would work to bring us back. They didn't chase me themselves but you can bet they wanted to.

It was only in the final 15 kilometres that it got close. The chasers got within 15 or 20 seconds of us and when I looked behind I could see they were catching us.

That actually worked out quite well for me because it ensured the other three kept co-operating deep into the final kilometre. I was worried that Anderson would be strong in the sprint but he decided to open it up early so I was able to latch onto his wheel and then power past to win Liège-Bastogne-Liège for the second time. Afterwards Gisbers slapped me on the back and told me what a great move it was.

Even Rooks and Theunisse seemed pretty happy at the finish although they were probably thinking: 'Hmmm, we'd better watch the Paddy from now on.'

THE 1989 TOUR de France is considered by many to be the greatest of all time because of the time trial showdown between Greg LeMond and Laurent Fignon on the Champs-Élysées on the final day. It was certainly dramatic.

LeMond used his special triathlon handlebars to overturn a 50-second deficit in just 26 kilometres. After three weeks only eight seconds separated them. It was the closest Tour ever.

PDM was the strongest team in the race, with four riders in the top ten overall. Theunisse was fourth, Rooks was seventh, Alcalá was eighth and I jumped above Robert Millar in the final time trial to finish ninth. Theunisse won the king of the mountains competition and I took the green jersey for the fourth time, which was a new record.

But although we won stages, a couple of jerseys and were grouped in the top ten, we were criticised by the press in Holland for not managing to get a better result overall.

They thought that Theunisse could have been higher but the tactic was never for the rest of us to support one guy. We all rode our own race. Theunisse and Rooks were inseparable. They were like brothers on and off the bike and rode like the Schlecks, Fränk and Andy, have done in recent years.

Alcalá was a great talent but he wasn't disciplined enough, and I had given it everything and ended up ninth. It's easy to say we should have done better but having four riders capable of finishing in the top ten is not the same as having one guy capable of winning. Theunisse, our best rider, was seven-and-a-half minutes behind LeMond.

Having watched with amusement from the outside, I hadn't realised how much pressure there was on the Dutch teams at the Tour until I was part of one. Erik Breukink, riding for one of our big rivals, Panasonic, won the prologue time trial in Luxembourg to take the yellow jersey. Then Fignon's Super-U won the team time trial, with Panasonic and Superconfex second and third. We were fourth, third of the Dutch squads, so there were long faces all evening after that.

Alcalá won a stage on the motor racing circuit at Spa in Belgium which eased the pressure, then Earley won for us in Pau, by getting in a break and finishing it off really well, so the mood was good before we reached the mountains. By the time we hit the Pyrenees, the race was already shaping up into a battle between LeMond and Fignon.

I was climbing better than I had at the Tour since 1985 and on the first day in the Pyrenees, I finished ahead of Rooks, Theunisse and the other favourites to take a big step towards winning the green jersey.

JULY 14 IS Bastille Day, the French national holiday. It's a day when the whole country stops and most of the population watches the Tour. And boy, did we give them a show.

Fignon was in yellow, seven seconds ahead of LeMond, with another Frenchman, Charly Mottet, in third place, 57 seconds, back. Our PDM boys were stacked up from ninth to 12th and the pressure was on us to move up the standings before the Alps.

The 13th stage went from Montpellier to Marseille in the south of France, a region famous for the Mistral winds, which can blow hard even in summer.

Gisbers said the forecast was for strong winds, picking up in the afternoon. He looked at the map and worked out that when we changed direction, shortly after the feed zone at Mouriès, around halfway through the stage, we'd have a howling cross-tailwind.

He thought that if we attacked en masse through the feed zone, we could catch Fignon, LeMond and some of the others by surprise and leapfrog a few places up the overall standings.

As Gisbers explained his idea, I was wincing because attacking in the feed zone is a definite no-no. It's one of the unwritten rules because it's hectic enough there when 200 riders are trying to grab their bags of food from the team helpers without some idiots attacking off the front.

I looked around at my team-mates and could tell there wasn't much enthusiasm for Gisbers' idea but team orders are team orders, even if I knew it would make us unpopular.

As we approached the feed zone, we gathered at the front. The plan was for Martin Earley and Marc Van Orsouw to open it up and for me and a couple of the others to then attack over the top and try to get a break going with the help of the wind once we'd changed direction.

Understandably, Earley and Van Orsouw were reluctant. We were looking at each other and the feed zone was coming up so I decided to take matters into my own hands.

Instead of slowing down to pick up my bag, I sprinted for it and didn't look back. I knew it would be murder behind, so I just kept going.

A few of us rode hard for a couple of kilometres. Then we reached the turn in the road and quickly realised the wind was nowhere near strong enough to do any damage to the bunch.

We eased up, the bunch caught us and as we slipped back among the other riders, I was getting a fair bit of abuse. I tried to make a joke of it, saying: 'Hey, *desolé*, team tactics *Hollandaise*.'

I thought I'd just about got away with it when I saw Fignon. He was mad as hell and gave me an awful bollocking, calling me every word under the sun in French. It was a real telling off and it was all the worse because I knew he was right. I said: 'Laurent, I'm sorry, we were told to attack,' but he just waved his hand dismissively, swore again and moved off up the bunch.

I was feeling pretty bad about myself because I wasn't the type of rider to pull a stunt like that. I respected the other riders and the way we were supposed to race.

Things calmed down for a few kilometres but then a murmur went through the bunch and everyone was shouting at us again.

It took us a few minutes to work out what was going on but we realised that Fignon and Mottet had attacked and were getting away. That was an awful moment because the whole peloton was looking at us. We'd made Fignon mad, now it was up to us to chase him down and get everything under control. We went to the front and started to ride hard on the front of the bunch but we couldn't catch Fignon and Mottet.

Perhaps they were inspired because it was Bastille Day but they took a lot of catching.

In the end, we had the whole PDM team on the front, taking turns, riding like it was a team time trial and we were barely denting their advantage. LeMond, who stood to lose the most because of us, and his team-mate Johan Lammerts did a lot of work too. It was a long, long chase. Far too long. It was hot and we were racing like lunatics. I was in my biggest gear and it was spinning out. By now, the peloton was in a terrible mood.

We could see Fignon and Mottet on the horizon, surrounded by cameramen on motorbikes, and they were absolutely flying along. It took almost an hour, and a lot of energy, but eventually we got them back and the angry peloton calmed down a bit.

It was then the PDM riders turned on each other. We'd all been at the front, riding bloody hard, but Theunisse was not happy with Alcalá, accusing him of 'glass-cranking', which means soft-pedalling when it was his turn on the front.

On occasions Alcalá could go missing when there was work to be done but this was not one of those days. He'd been riding as hard as anyone and he was just as angry as Theunisse.

They almost came to blows and I had to get between them and calm them down.

I regretted that attack for a long time and the next morning I apologised to a few people because they had every right to be annoyed with us. It wasn't a clever tactic and not just because it didn't work. We got a lot of grief from the other riders.

The rest of the Tour was a ding-dong battle between LeMond and Fignon. The yellow jersey swapped from one to the other as we hit the Alps. Fignon was the more aggressive of the two but LeMond refused to give up and he judged his effort brilliantly.

We knew by now that Theunisse was too far back to win, but he had the king of the mountains competition sewn up and I was on course to win the green jersey.

THE 18TH STAGE from Bourg d'Oisans to Villard de Lans was only 91.5 kilometres but it was an explosive stage and at the end of it we found we had some more explaining to do, this time to Fignon.

It was a really hard route. We went over the Côte de Laffrey, an unpleasant climb with a false flat at the top, and the first-category St Nizier de Moucherotte. Fignon launched a powerful attack on the lower slopes of the St Nizier. This was his bid to win the Tour. He did some real damage to us behind.

Mottet was dropped and a group of only eight was left, with four of us from PDM in there – me, Rooks, Theunisse and Alcalá. We rode hard all the way and held Fignon's advantage to just 24 seconds. That meant he was 50 seconds ahead of LeMond overall with the time trial in Paris to come. If Fignon had gained another ten seconds, he would have won the Tour.

For years afterwards, Fignon was convinced we had collaborated with LeMond. He thought there was an alliance because LeMond had ridden with PDM the year before.

But Fignon could not have been more wrong. We were not riding to help LeMond or defeat Fignon. If anything we were trying to gain enough time to move Theunisse onto the podium.

I remained good friends with Laurent and it was very upsetting when he died from cancer in 2010, aged only 50. Every now and then, usually after a good meal and a few glasses of wine, he would ask: 'Okay, Sean, it's all in the past now so you can tell me. Did PDM work for LeMond that day? I won't be angry if you say yes, I just want to know the truth.'

And I always told him the truth. 'Laurent, I promise you, we did not have any agreement with LeMond.'

28. The end of the rainbow

The 1989 World Championships

I don't think there's any point regretting things I can't change but if there is one race that causes a knot in my stomach it's the 1989 World Championships, held in Chambéry in late August.

That was the biggest disappointment of my career by far. Worse than losing the yellow jersey after a single day, worse than having to pull out of the Vuelta while leading the race.

It was the day I should have been world champion.

The course in Chambéry, in the French Alps, was going to be a hard one. The Côte de Montagnole, the hill we had to climb 21 times, was not that hard on its own but by the 20th time round it was extremely gruelling.

I knew by now I could never win the Tour but a one-day race like the World Championships was well within my grasp, even if I knew I'd have to be a little bit clever to make up for the significant numerical disadvantage of being in a small Irish team.

The World Championships is always a war of attrition. Lap by lap, strong men weaken until only the toughest are left. But it can also be a very tactical race. When everyone is tired and scared of over-reaching themselves, mistakes are easy to make. A breakaway that looks benign can suddenly become dangerous.

I arrived in Chambéry a couple of days early and rode the course several times to get a feel for it. I was assessing the difficulty of the climb, learning the descents, familiarising myself with the finishing straight in case it came down to a sprint.

But I kept changing my mind about which gears I would need. These days the bikes have 22 different gears, which gives a wide range of ratios. There isn't a big jump between one gear and the next. But bikes then had only seven sprockets, meaning 14 gears to choose from and the selection on a course like the one in Chambéry would be critical. I needed a gear light enough to save my legs on the climb, particularly early on, but I needed a big enough gear to get the maximum out of my sprint.

I couldn't decide what to do for the best.

The day before the race, there was quite a strong headwind in the finishing straight so I opted for a biggest gear of 53x13 – that's a front chainring with 53 teeth and a smallest rear sprocket with 13 teeth. Usually I would go for a 12-tooth sprocket but a headwind would make it a harder sprint, requiring a slightly smaller gear.

By choosing the 13-tooth sprocket I could give myself greater flexibility with my climbing gears, which would be important when we tackled the hill late in the race and the attacks were firing.

The day of the race was dry but relatively cool, which suited me better than a baking hot summer's day. I tried to preserve as much energy as I could in the first three quarters of the race and when the action started on the penultimate lap, I was ready.

With about an hour and a half to go, the sky, which had gradually darkened as the afternoon wore on, went black and we were hit by heavy rain. The temperature plummeted by about eight degrees and the wind picked up.

Steven Rooks, a PDM team-mate for 364 days of the year but a rival riding for the Netherlands that day, attacked on the second last lap. A few kilometres later, once Rooks had got a nice gap, Martin Earley, my Ireland and PDM companion, wanted to go to the front to chase him down for me. I told him to wait and see if any of the other nations reacted because I didn't think it was right for us to work against another PDM rider.

That attack by Rooks set up the endgame. The last time up the Côte de Montagnole was really difficult because Laurent Fignon put in a really hard attack. I was worried that this was going to be the move that decided the race, particularly when Greg LeMond went after Fignon, but there was no way I could follow them at that pace. I had to get over the climb as best I could. One by one, other riders responded to Fignon and LeMond, among them Thierry Claveyrolat of France and Dmitri Konyshev, the Russian. I kept the gap as small as I could and although the descent was hairy in the wet, I got down quickly and joined the back of the group as we reached the bottom, with about two kilometres to go.

I looked at the group and liked my chances if I could get a few seconds to recover. LeMond was the most obvious threat because he had a really good sprint at the end of a hard race like this. Fignon was quick but wouldn't be too much trouble. Rooks and Claveyrolat weren't anything to worry about. I didn't know Konyshev because the Russians had only just been allowed to race with the professionals. He had to be good to be in this company but could he sprint?

I gestured to Rooks, my PDM team-mate, to go to the front of the group and keep the pace high and give me a lead-out for the sprint. Although we were riding for different countries, I would have expected him to take it on because there was no way he was going to win the sprint. But Rooks didn't go to the front, so I knew I was on my own.

Fignon, the fighter that he was, made the only move he could. He attacked with 800 metres to go. It was another huge effort and he got several bike lengths ahead of us while we all watched each other. LeMond blinked first and sprinted after Fignon.

This was perfect for me. I was just behind LeMond and I was able to follow him as he shut down Fignon. He was practically leading me to the line.

But LeMond was incredibly strong. He hesitated only a few seconds after catching Fignon and then opened up his sprint for the line.

He was too strong and I couldn't get past. I gave everything I had but LeMond did not fade. With 850 metres to go I could see the gold medal at the end of the rainbow. With 150 metres to go, it had slipped away.

As soon as I knew I was beaten, I stopped pedalling and Konyshev nipped past me to get the silver medal. You may wonder why I didn't keep going and make sure of second place but for me, that day, it was gold or nothing. I wanted the rainbow jersey. I wanted to be world champion. If I couldn't have that it didn't much matter to me whether I got silver or bronze.

My head dropped as I crossed the line. I had never felt so deflated at the end of a race. I knew just how great the opportunity had been.

I couldn't hide my disappointment on the podium. I tried to take every defeat with good grace and I didn't begrudge Greg his victory but I was crushed.

I wanted to get out of Chambéry and go home but we had to go to Megève for a dinner hosted by our sponsors, PDM. It was the last place I wanted to be that night, stuck in a room with 200 guests who wanted to talk about what a great race it had been.

Hearing people say 'bad luck' was incredibly difficult. I was in a grim mood but I wanted to be polite and friendly because everyone there was a guest of our sponsors.

Rarely did I replay the finish of a race in my head afterwards because there was nothing I could do to change the result but that night I kept thinking about the last lap. Could I have done anything differently? Would I have won if Rooks had given me a bit of help in the final kilometre?

I couldn't say for sure but I felt in the pit of my stomach that I should have been world champion that night.

29. The politics of PDM

1990

Linda and I always agreed that when my career ended, we'd move back to Ireland. She understood that during the season, I had to be based in Belgium.

When we first got married, Linda and I lived with Herman and Elise in Vilvoorde but eventually we got our own place nearby. During the season we lived there and every October we packed up and drove back to Carrick-on-Suir for the winter.

It was hard for Linda living in Belgium. She never loved it and because I was often away at races, she was by herself a lot of the time. Back in Ireland she'd had a job and friends and her family and although Herman and Elise were very kind to us, Linda missed home. It was a big sacrifice for her to live away.

She never complained because she knew it was how I earned my living but the deal was that as soon as my career ended we'd go home.

We planned to have a family but we waited because we didn't want their lives disrupted by starting school in Belgium and then moving back to Ireland.

When I knew my career was coming to an end, the time was right have children.

I found the thought of becoming a father exciting but when we were told Linda was expecting twins, it was quite daunting.

They were born in February 1990 and we named them Nigel and Stacey.

We brought two nannies with us from Ireland because there was never any question of me getting up in the middle of the night to do the bottles or change nappies. Linda was okay with that. She knew I needed to rest and concentrate on my racing.

Becoming a father didn't change my outlook on life. I was still a professional bike rider trying to do my best in the races.

To start with, I didn't find it too hard to be away from home but as Nigel and Stacey grew up and began to develop their own personalities it became difficult leaving them.

BEFORE THE 1990 season, Steven Rooks and Gert-Jan Theunisse left PDM to join Panasonic, who offered them a lot of money, and we got Erik Breukink in return. I thought PDM got the better end of the deal because Breukink was only 25 – younger than the other two – and was considered a potential Tour de France winner.

I liked Rooks and Theunisse but I had more confidence in Breukink to be a man of his word. Theunisse was a very individual guy – I never quite knew what he was going to do. He was great fun but quite unpredictable.

My role in the team was changing. I was no longer guaranteed to be a leader. I knew I'd have to work for other riders and I was happy to help Breukink.

PDM also signed a couple of riders from East Germany. Uwe Ampler and Uwe Raab were both very good riders but they had been prevented from turning professional until the fall of the Berlin Wall.

Raab was 27 and had a reputation as a really good sprinter in the amateur ranks but it was difficult to know how good he was until he'd achieved something in the pro races.

During the Ruta del Sol in southern Spain at the start of the season it was decided that we'd work for Raab to give him a chance to show what he could do.

On the first day, the plan was to take up the pace near the end and deliver Raab to the line. I was supposed to be the last rider in the line, with Raab on my wheel ready to unleash his sprint. We got to the front with about eight kilometres to go and had the bunch in one long line behind us. One by one the PDM jerseys in front of me pulled over and I was there ready to take Raab to within a couple of hundred metres of the line. After that, it would be up to him.

I looked round and Nico Verhoeven, one of our Dutch riders, was on my wheel. With a kilometre to go, he shouted to me: 'Go.'

I was on the front of the bunch so I upped my pace. I thought that Verhoeven had made a mistake, got himself in the wrong place in the line and would pass me and do the final stint to set up Raab. But Verhoeven didn't come past me. He left me hanging out there longer than I expected.

My legs were dying on me by the time he finally came past me, with 500 metres to go. Verhoeven did a short turn on the front and left Raab with 350 metres to go on his own. That was far too far for him to hold off the other sprinters, although he nearly did it. Olaf Ludwig got past him and Raab had to settle for second.

There wasn't too much of an inquest afterwards because Raab had done well, Verhoeven had made a simple mistake and it was a relatively unimportant early-season race. I asked Verhoeven what had gone wrong and he said he got blocked in and couldn't get up to the front in time for his turn.

The funny thing was that exactly the same thing happened the next day. Verhoeven was behind me instead of in front of me and he left Raab on his own too far out. Ludwig beat him again.

To do it once was understandable but twice in two days was unforgiveable. On the bus after the stage I sat next to Verhoeven and asked him what on earth he'd been playing at.

Verhoeven's explanation stunned and amused us and said a lot about the Dutch. 'I don't like Germans,' he said. 'During the war, they stole my grandfather's bike.'

A crazy crash at the Tour of Flanders ruined my spring. There was a feed zone at Waregem only about ten kilometres before we reached the first section of cobbles at Wanegem-Lede.

The race to get to the feed station was like something out of Ben Hur. Everyone wanted to get their bag and their bottles and have everything sorted out before we reached the cobbles.

Every year the pushing and shoving seemed to get worse. People were increasingly prepared to take risks because they knew that if they weren't near the front when we reached the cobbles, it would take time and a lot of energy to get up there.

We galloped towards the feed and I managed to grab my bag and sling it over my shoulder. I was in the first 20 in the bunch, where usually things would be a bit calmer than behind. But it was absolute chaos with riders swerving and bags being dropped. There was food and bottles all over the road.

Once we were through the feed zone, the pace slowed down a bit and I was able to take everything out of the bag and put it in my back pockets.

I'd just finished sorting that out when the madness started again because the cobbles were not far away. Riders were jumping up on the pavement, swerving bollards and parked cars before diving back into the bunch. I had to have my wits about me. People were slamming on their brakes and there were a lot of near-misses.

Once we'd done about 500 metres on the cobbles, it settled down a bit. I thought the big panic was over.

I was beginning to worry that I'd not eaten anything for a while because the race had been full-on. Eating and drinking at the right time is vital in a race as hard as the Tour of Flanders. I knew that if I waited until I was hungry it would be too late and I would pay the price.

Although we were on the cobbles, it was fairly calm so I put my hand in my back pocket to get something to eat. As soon as I did that, things jammed up in front of me and I smashed into the guy in front before hitting the floor heavily. I sat in the road with riders swarming round me and knew my collarbone was broken.

After missing the Classics, I had to prove I deserved a place in the PDM team for the Tour de France, so I did a couple of races in Spain at the end of May, then the Dauphiné Libéré in France at the start of June before heading to the Tour of Switzerland.

I was determined to win a stage to give the management no doubts about my inclusion in the Tour.

The first stage was 158 kilometres long, starting and finishing in Winterthur. The weather was filthy so I knew that if a break went early on, it might have a good chance of staying away to the finish. The battle to get into the break was very intense. There were attacks everywhere but eventually five of us got away. Nathan Dahlberg from New Zealand, Roberto Pagnin, Stephan

Joho and Theo De Rooy were the others. It was a good group because we were all committed to making it work. We raced really hard and built a good advantage over the bunch.

Approaching the finish one or two of the others tried to get away a couple of times but they were closed down and then Dahlberg clipped away to win the stage, with the bunch finishing more than a minute-and-a-half behind us.

I got the stage win I wanted, winning a sprint a few days later and then I took the yellow jersey after a strong ride in the mountain time trial, which Breukink won.

We still had the big mountains to come and I was unsure how I'd cope. The last time I'd had to defend a lead on the big climbs had been at the Vuelta a España a couple of years earlier.

I need not have worried because my PDM team was so strong. The biggest threats were Robert Millar and Andy Hampsten, who were both excellent climbers, and they piled on the pressure on the toughest stage of the race, which finished at San Bernardino.

Hampsten won the stage, Millar was just behind but my PDM team-mates did a brilliant job to prevent them from gaining too much time. Seeing Breukink, Alcalá and Ampler just ahead of me all the way up the climb was very reassuring.

People had started to write off my chances, particularly for a stage race as tough as the Tour of Switzerland, but with the help of one of the best teams I'd ever ridden for, I managed to win overall for the second time in my career. After that, there was no doubt I'd be going to the Tour hoping to repay Breukink for all his work.

THE TOUR DE FRANCE started in Futuroscope and after the prologue time trial the race was turned on its head when four riders got clear and gained ten minutes the following morning.

It was a split-stage, with a 138-kilometre road race in the morning and a team time trial in the afternoon. Those days always made the overall favourites nervous because a lot of ground could be lost with a bad performance in the team time trial.

The road stage was very aggressive, with lots of attacks and a nervous bunch that refused to let anyone get away. Four riders got a small gap – Canada's Steve Bauer, who had been fourth in the

1988 Tour, Ronan Pensec, who rode for Greg LeMond's Z team, Frans Maassen of the Dutch Buckler squad, and an unknown Italian called Claudio Chiappucci.

For several kilometres the lead was very small but they refused to sit up and allow the bunch to gather them up. It was turning into a battle of wills and in the end it was the peloton that gave up first and let them go. No one wanted to chase any longer because they knew they had the team time trial in the afternoon and so the door swung open.

Before we knew it, the gap had jumped up to 15 minutes and there was a stand-off between some of the bigger teams over who should chase. Panasonic wanted to chase but would only work if we joined them. LeMond's Z team was reluctant to do too much, and all the while we were hesitating the gap was growing.

Eventually, we got ourselves organised and began to chase them down but at the finish their lead was still ten minutes. We committed to the effort far too late.

That breakaway ended up shaping the whole Tour because it took LeMond almost three weeks to overhaul Chiappucci, the surprise package.

At the end of the first week, Raúl Alcalá won the long time trial from Vittel to Epinal. He trounced us all, beating LeMond by 2-11. If it hadn't been for the four riders who broke away on the opening weekend, Alcalá would have been in yellow.

We now had two genuine Tour contenders in the PDM team – Alcalá and Breukink – although I always worried about Alcalá's lack of consistency. He could be absolutely brilliant but he never got to grips with riding like a team leader. Instead of being up near the front, keeping out of danger, he would drift down to the back of the bunch.

And, for such a gifted climber, he was never really lean. He could have done with going on the De Gribaldy diet.

He could be frustrating to be around because he was so gifted but I never felt he made the most of that talent. I told him a number of times that if he got really serious, he could win the biggest races in the world, perhaps even the Tour de France.

I always tried to avoid sharing a room with him because he

could be a nightmare. Martin Earley was the perfect room-mate because he would be in bed with the lights out at 9.30. But Alcalá would be down in the lobby, chatting up the receptionist until 11.30, then he'd come up to the room, turn all the lights on, put the TV on and start washing his kit in the sink.

One year we did the Paris-Brussels one-day race and had a few days to kill before the Grand Prix Libération team time trial in Eindhoven. Alcalá was going to go straight to Eindhoven and spend half the week living in a hotel instead of going to his home in Switzerland. I was heading back to my house in Vilvoorde and because Linda was back in Ireland with the children, I invited Alcalá to stay with me, although I warned him: 'I'm not cooking for you.'

On the first morning, we got up at 8.30 ready to go training. It was a bit cloudy out so after breakfast Alcalá said: 'Let's wait. It looks like it might rain. We'll go this afternoon.'

We hung around all day, with him saying we'd go out later, until it got too late and we ended up staying in.

The next day, he did exactly the same thing, so the following day I told him I was going out in the morning whether he joined me or not. I went out on my bike for a few hours and came back to find him lying on the couch watching television, eating snacks from the supermarket. The whole time he stayed with me he didn't touch his bike.

We travelled up to Eindhoven for the team time trial and we checked out the course, which was held on a dual carriageway on the outskirts of town. It was a flat course, which meant we would have to power away in the big gears.

On race day, Alcalá was unbelievably strong. In the last 15 kilometres, he was doing some incredible efforts on the front, pulling us along for 500 metres at a time. I was really suffering, thinking: 'This fecker hasn't ridden his bike for three days and he's killing us.'

I knew Alcalá had the talent but he didn't have the mental strength to commit himself when he wasn't on top of his game. He found it too tempting to ease back a bit and let a good result slip away. That's exactly what happened in that Tour. At Alpe d'Huez he lost several minutes because he wasn't in the right place when the attacks started.

It was during that stage to Alpe d'Huez that Breukink made himself our undisputed leader. We had just descended the Col du Glandon and were heading along the valley road towards Bourg d'Oisans and the bottom of the Alpe, when I went back to the team car to get some water bottles.

By the time I got back to the front of the group, LeMond, Pedro Delgado, Gianni Bugno and a couple of other dangerous riders had gone clear on a small climb and everyone from PDM had missed it. We had four riders in the group and there was still a long way to go to the bottom of the mountain. We couldn't give a group of strong climbers a head-start on the Alpe, so we had to get organised quickly.

But we had the same old PDM problem – just with different personnel. Everyone in the group was well-placed overall. Alcalá was fifth, Uwe Ampler sixth, I was ninth and Breukink was tenth.

We had too many chiefs, although it was obvious to me that Ampler and I should do the work because the other two had far better prospects of being on the podium in Paris.

Ampler didn't want to work. Like Raab, he was an East German who had been stuck behind the Iron Curtain for most of his career and now he had the chance to ride the Tour de France he wanted to take the opportunity for himself. In a way, I couldn't blame him for that. He'd been a team leader in the amateur ranks and now he was being expected to sacrifice himself for someone else. He wanted to defend his place rather than ride hard on the flat and then lose five minutes on Alpe d'Huez.

I told him his job was to ride but he refused. Then Jan Gisbers came alongside us in the team car and gave Ampler an earful, telling him that unless he started to help the chase effort, he'd be out of the team. Eventually, Ampler did a few turns, although every chance he had he slipped to the back and stayed there, leaving it to me. Gisbers would bollock him again and he'd do another turn but basically it was up to me.

We had the LeMond group just in sight as the climb started. It was a good thing my job was done because I was cooked.

Breukink won the mountain time trial at Villard-de-Lans and the final time trial at Lac de Vassivière but he lost the Tour at Luz-Ardiden in the Pyrenees, where he had a very bad day and lost four minutes to LeMond.

If he'd been able to hang on there, he could have won the Tour, because he finished only 2-29 behind LeMond in Paris, but I felt he was too nice to turn the screw when it really mattered. He wasn't ruthless enough.

THE POLITICS OF PDM were never dull. At the World Championships in Utsunomiya in Japan, we had three riders in the first five but the Belgians got the better of me.

Dirk De Wolf, one of my PDM team-mates and a Belgian, got in the early break and was still hanging on when we reached the last lap. He was the king of training. He lived not too far away from me and if we trained together, he'd want me at his house for 7.30am. If I needed a pee, he'd give me 30 seconds before we were on our way again. And after we'd done a four-hour ride, he'd do another couple of hours behind a motorbike.

De Wolf was just in front of us as we reached the final lap and I decided it was time to attack and ride across to him, so I went down the right-hand side of the road. There were attacks going on the left and right and out of the corner of my eye, I spotted another PDM team-mate, and another Belgian, Rudy Dhaenens, go on the left. Dhaenens was a friend and a team-mate and we had an unspoken agreement not to work against each other, so I stalled my effort and let him go. I figured someone else would chase them down but no one did, so the two Belgians rode away to the finish to take the gold and silver medals.

I was pleased for Rudy. Besides, if I'd gone with him, I suspect the PDM agreement would have gone out of the window and the two Belgians would have given the Irishman a working over. But it would have been nice to have to find out.

30. Poisoned

The 1991 Tour de France

In 1990 Paul Kimmage wrote a book called A Rough Ride. Paul retired from racing in the middle of the 1989 Tour de France. He stopped by the side of the road one day and decided enough was enough. Paul was an intense character and he still is, but we always got on well.

I never read the book from cover to cover but from the bits I read I knew it would go down badly in the peloton. There was a code in professional cycling and he went over the code, big time. He certainly wasn't going to be welcome at the Tour de France after that.

The book got a lot of press coverage and it caused a storm but most of the people who were angry about it hadn't read it. They were just angry that someone had written about doping full stop.

Shortly after the book came out, riders came up to me in the bunch to ask what the hell Kimmage was playing at. I was getting the big stick because I was friends with Paul. I could see why some people were angry. He'd been looked after and now he was pushing the boat out a bit too far. But I didn't criticise him publicly. I said that it was his book and he was entitled to write whatever he felt he wanted to write. A lot of it was true, so why criticise him?

SOME TIME before the 1991 Tour de France began, there was a meeting between the PDM team management and the riders. They told us they had a liquid food supplement we could use if we wanted to. It was called Intralipid and we could take it intravenously, by injection. The team doctor, Wim Sanders, explained that it would help us recover more quickly and that it was usually used by patients who'd had a major operation and were unable to digest solid food.

I listened to the pitch and I had some questions. I asked Dr Sanders about it and then I asked my doctor back in Belgium. I wanted to know whether it would have any benefits, whether it was safe and whether there were any side effects. Most importantly, I wanted to know whether it was on the banned list. We were told it wasn't.

The plan was to use it every four days during the Tour. The main benefit was that we would be replacing the vitamins and nutrients we lost during the race.

The Tour started well and history almost repeated itself on the opening weekend. The first road stage around Lyon was short, just 114 kilometres, but it was a real humdinger. There were attacks firing off everywhere but, learning the lesson from the previous year, several of the top riders were alert to the danger.

A break of 11 got away and gained 1-44 on the rest of the field. But this time the PDM team made the split. We had three riders in it – Breukink, Alcalá and me. LeMond, the defending Tour champion, also made it.

The fact the bunch let several overall contenders gain so much time was incredible but once we'd been given a chance to do some damage, we took it. Djamolidine Abdoujaparov beat me at the finish, but that was no disgrace because he was so quick.

We were fourth in the team time trial, which pushed me up the leaderboard a bit, not far behind the Dane, Rolf Sørensen, who was in the yellow jersey.

Towards the end of stage five to Valenciennes, Sørensen crashed. He got back up and crossed the line but later we heard he'd broken his collarbone and would not be starting the next morning. LeMond decided not to wear a yellow jersey he'd inherited rather than earned. Stage six was 259 kilometres across the exposed flat countryside of northern France from Arras to Le Havre on the Normandy coast. As we rolled out without Sørensen I knew that LeMond was the *maillot jaune virtuel* and that I was just one second behind him. With time bonuses to fight for, the idea of taking the yellow jersey myself crossed my mind.

The French rider Thierry Marie went on a crazy long escape, which he used to do every now and then. He attacked early in the stage and gained a huge lead. I won a time bonus at one of the intermediate sprints to jump ahead of LeMond, which meant that if we caught Marie, I would wear the yellow jersey.

I went back to the team car to have a chat with Jan Gisbers, the *directeur sportif.* He was keen to organise the chase and bring Marie back and he asked me what I thought. I was reluctant to get the whole team to chase on my behalf for several reasons.

I felt Breukink could win the Tour so I didn't want to tire the team out so early in the race. We didn't want the responsibility of controlling the Tour already. Besides, I thought the teams with sprinters would be keen to chase Marie to give themselves a chance to win the stage, so I told Gisbers we should wait.

But nothing got organised so Marie won the stage by two minutes and took the yellow jersey by a minute.

A few days later, Breukink did well in the time trial at Alençon to move up to second overall and everything was going perfectly, until we got to Rennes, ten days into the race.

THAT EVENING, at the Hotel du Cheval d'Or in Rennes I was resting on my bed when Dr Sanders knocked on the door and took me to his room. Over the course of the evening, every rider on the team got a knock at the door and was asked to walk down the corridor. Dr Sanders told me to hop up on the table and relax while he slipped the needle into a vein in my arm. It was as straightforward as giving blood, but it took about half an hour to inject the Intralipid into my system.

Afterwards I went down to have my dinner. It was the usual things: some soup, then grilled chicken and a plate of spaghetti with vegetables followed by yoghurt.

During the night, I woke up and felt a little peculiar. I didn't feel sick but I did feel uncomfortable, as if I was coming down with something. I managed to get back to sleep but when I awoke in the morning I felt much worse.

I was sharing a room with Martin Earley and he didn't feel well either. I thought perhaps we'd caught a bug.

I went down to breakfast feeling very grim but I managed to force down a bit of food.

One by one my team-mates came into the breakfast room and they all looked how I felt. Pale and shiny. Nico Verhoeven and Uwe Raab were the worst. They both felt very ill straight away.

There was a sense of unease among the riders. We wondered whether it was something we'd eaten at dinner but the staff had eaten the same food and they were fine.

Something was not right.

Gisbers urged us to start the stage in the hope we would feel better. Verhoeven and Raab were really bad, so they stayed at the hotel. The Tour was over for them.

The tenth stage from Rennes to Quimper was horrendous. I don't know how I got through it. Riders were dropping like flies. Martin Earley and Jean-Paul Van Poppel pulled out and Falk Boden finished well behind the bunch, all on his own, and was eliminated because he was outside the time limit.

Breukink, Alcalá, Jos Van Aert and I managed to get through the stage but it was a very, very unpleasant day. Each hour was worse than the last. In the afternoon I thought I was going to faint. It felt like I had flu. My head pounded. I felt burning hot one minute, freezing cold the next. I was shivering but the curious thing was that I didn't feel nauseous. I was sweaty and warm but I didn't have a temperature.

I spent a lot of the day back at the team car. Every time I tried to drink or eat something I felt worse. I dragged myself to the finish and then, on the team bus, there was a big row.

The riders were angry and wanted to know what was wrong. Dr Sanders and Gisbers stuck to their line that it must be food poisoning. I said it couldn't be that because the staff were fine. They said they'd eaten later than the riders so perhaps it was just our food that was bad. He also suggested we'd be more likely to get sick because we were tired after racing hard for ten days, but it didn't add up.

If it was food poisoning why weren't we vomiting or rushing to the toilet?

The food poisoning excuse wasn't going to wash because

journalists were contacting the hotels we'd stayed at and asking if other guests had been ill.

I felt PDM should have issued a statement at this point to say what had happened because it was inevitably going to come out. All that was happening was that poor hotel owners were being accused of poisoning Tour de France riders, which was not right at all. PDM were worried that if they said the riders had used a nutritional supplement it would look like doping.

The next morning I felt no better and there was no way I could ride on. Even if I had been able to get through, the 48 hours I'd gone without eating properly would catch up with me in the mountains.

Our *directeur sportif* Ferdi Van den Haute was the first to point the finger at the Intralipid.

Eventually the doctor checked the fridge in the team's truck and found it wasn't as cold as it should have been.

He thought there'd been a power cut or someone had knocked the switch off by accident and the bags of Intralipid had warmed up. They sent a batch of the stuff to be tested and found it had bacteria in it.

It was a terrible way to go out of the Tour. It could have been extremely dangerous. Someone could have been seriously ill. Verhoeven was the worst. He had to go to hospital but, fortunately, within a couple of days we recovered.

I never used Intralipid again. I'd trusted the doctor that it would be okay and a simple mistake had ruined the entire Tour. We were lucky it wasn't worse.

31. A terrible loss

Sometimes things happen to put sport into perspective. A Sunday afternoon in August 1991 was one of those days.

It was the day after the San Sebastian Classic, which was our first major race since pulling out of the Tour de France. We had a day to wait before the Tour of the Asturias was due to start. It was a routine day on the road. We'd been training, had some lunch and spent the afternoon watching television and kicking around the hotel. A day like so many.

I was sharing a room with my good friend Martin Earley and we were chatting until it was time to go down for dinner. The phone rang, Martin answered it and handed the phone to me straight away. It was Linda.

I could hear the upset tone to Linda's voice. I knew she had some bad news. There wasn't an easy way for her to tell me.

There had been an accident and my brother Joe had been killed. Even now, more than twenty years after it happened, the tears still well in my eyes when I think about that day.

Joe, still a keen cyclist, had been taking part in a leisure ride – we'd call it a sportive these days – called the Comeragh 100.

The route went round all the roads we knew so well from our childhood. They climbed Seskin Hill, which had been made famous by the Nissan Classic. At the top, the lane joins a main road. Joe was alone because he had left the rest of the group behind on the climb. As he turned onto the main road a car hit him and killed him instantly.

As Linda explained what happened, I had a horrible empty feeling in my stomach. Even now, it's very painful to think about.

He was only in his mid-thirties, in the prime of his life, and I feel he should still be here today.

Although we lived very different lives, we were still close. He had been the golden boy back on the farm. He'd been better at school and had made a good career for himself as a sales rep.

To others I was the successful professional cyclist with the glamorous life but he was always my big brother.

He was the one who got me interested in cycling. He was the one who pulled my leg and drove me on when I was just starting to race. He probably didn't realise he was doing it, but he made me want to be better than him.

He was bigger and stronger than me and he'd wind me up, saying: 'Oh, you're going to get a terrible beating in the race tomorrow.' He did it with a glint in his eye, and he was the same with our younger brother Vincent.

It was a terrible accident and it shouldn't have happened, not to Joe. He was always the safe one who stuck to the rules and took care. I can still hear my father warning me: 'You'll kill yourself with that bloody bike of yours.'

But Joe never needed to be warned. He was the sensible one. Somehow, when he was killed the way he was, that made it so much more painful to accept.

32. The final kilometre

The 1991 season would have been a total wash-out but for the final few weeks, when I won the Nissan Classic for the fourth time and the Tour of Lombardy for the third time. At the end of the previous season, I had renewed my contract with PDM for one year, with the option of a second.

Now I was 35 and, having missed the spring Classics two years in a row, I got the feeling PDM thought they might be able to get me on the cheap.

In June, just before the Tour, they offered me a new contract, but for half the salary I'd been on, so I decided to wait until after the Tour and hope that a good performance would get them to make a more realistic offer, or attract the interest of a few more teams. But the Tour had been a disaster, and so my stock was tumbling.

Frank, my manager, handled all the negotiations. We let a few journalists know I was on the market and waited to see who made an approach. I had a couple of offers on the table but they weren't from the sort of teams I wanted to ride for, so I told Frank to sit tight and see what happened in the final few weeks of the season.

As the summer gave way to autumn, Manfred Krikke, the boss of PDM, upped his offer a bit but the envelope kept getting pushed back and forth across the table. He was still a long way off what I thought I was worth.

Then, right at the close of the season, I won the Tour of Lombardy after getting away with a little group then going clear with Martial Gayant and winning the sprint.

Winning that race was like pulling the lever on the fruit

machine and landing the jackpot. All of a sudden PDM wanted to talk, but a much more attractive offer was about to come my way.

The Lotus-Festina team, sponsored by a watch manufacturer based in Barcelona, offered me the payday of my life. Lotus and Festina were two watch companies that had merged. Their watches were sold in Spain under the Lotus brand and everywhere else as Festina. The owner of the company, Miguel Rodriguez, was a cycling fan and had sponsored a small team for a few years.

Now he wanted to take the team to the top and he was getting desperate for a big name to boost their profile. Without a rider with a reputation, Lotus-Festina would struggle to get invitations to the Classics and the Tour de France.

Rodriguez wanted someone who would attract publicity for the team and give him a chance of landing a big result, and he was prepared to pay a lot to get the right man.

Frank and I discussed whether it would be better to wait for an offer from a more established team or take a risk by joining the untested Festina team and the money that came with it.

I would be 36 in May and although I was not planning for retirement I suspected this might be my last contract – certainly my last lucrative one.

Festina's offer was not just appealing because of the money. I needed a fresh challenge. At PDM I had been getting a bit stale, perhaps even a little lazy.

As much as I liked Jan Gisbers, he was too soft with his boys. He was good at making his riders feel valued but sometimes we felt a bit too comfortable. If the boss is telling you everything is going well, it's tempting to ease off a bit. Every now and then a cycling team's manager needs to be a dictator, someone able to lay down the law on the road. That didn't come naturally to Gisbers.

I still had an appetite for racing but I needed a new challenge and a kick up the backside. The pressure of the pay cheque would be plenty of motivation. I felt I had to deliver a good result early on to justify the faith Rodriguez had shown in me.

I knew the clock was counting down to the end of my career but whenever I was asked how long I was going to continue for, I avoided answering. I had signed a one-year contract with Festina, so people assumed I planned to stop at the end of 1992 but I had not made that decision. I wanted to avoid becoming a circus show. My plan was always to reach the end of a season and call it a day, just like that. I didn't want a long drawn-out departure. I didn't want my final season, whenever that was, to turn into some kind of Sean Kelly Farewell Tour with everyone focusing on my final Milan-San Remo, my final Paris-Roubaix and my last Tour. I didn't want any fuss – I just wanted to race.

JOINING FESTINA boosted my motivation, especially for the first couple of months of the season. Domingo Perurena, who I knew from Kas, and Miguel Moreno were the two team managers.

Perurena was from San Sebastián and he was always pretty relaxed. He trusted me to train correctly and he knew I could handle the tactics in the races. Moreno reminded me of De Gribaldy. He was old school.

When we sat down to talk about my race programme for the beginning of the season, he gave me four weeks of stage races in Spain, one after the other. It was like being back at Kas. I told him that four weeks in a row was too much but he was dismissive. 'Oh, it's all in the mind.'

At the training camp at the start of the year, the other riders were trying to rip each other's legs off on the climbs but I knew better than to get involved in all that.

Moreno noticed that I wasn't responding when the pace lifted on the hills and asked me if I was okay. I said: 'I'm fine. We'll see how good they are when the racing starts.'

Cycling was beginning to change. The early-season races were a lot harder and more competitive than they had been when I first started. In the late 1970s, we'd turn up to the Tour of the Mediterranean in mid-February and do the first couple of hours in woollen leg warmers as if it was a training ride.

The early season events were like pre-season friendlies in football. People would race to win at the end of the day but the idea was to gradually build a level of fitness.

But by the early 1990s, everyone was desperate to get some results on the board as early as possible in the season. Riders were training much harder in the off-season and returning to action fitter. The Australians, returning to Europe after their summer, would have 7,000 kilometres in their legs before the first race. When I started, we considered it a big winter if we started the season with 3,000 kilometres of warm-weather training under our belts.

My first victories for Festina were the Trofeo Luis Puig and a stage of the Tour of Valencia towards the end of February but I knew Rodriguez wasn't paying me to win small races. He wanted to make a big impression and that would mean getting a result in one of the Classics.

I had to be quite calculating. I weighed up the spring Classics to see which one offered me the best chance.

Liège-Bastogne-Liège was probably too hard for me by this time, because there were riders who were more explosive than me on the climbs. The Tour of Flanders had always eluded me because it was so tactical. Paris-Roubaix was like buying a ticket for the raffle and hoping my number came up.

That left Milan-San Remo.

I am not saying that Milan-San Remo is an easy race – far from it – but it was tactically quite straightforward. If I could cope with the pace on the Cipressa and Poggio, and read the race well, I knew I could be in with a chance.

And in a way, the strength of Moreno Argentin made it easier for me because I knew that when he made his move I could only allow him so much rope.

Winning Milan-San Remo was pleasing because I felt I had repaid Festina. It didn't mean I could sit back for the rest of the season and say my job was done, but the Classics are so valuable to a sponsor that I knew I'd delivered the goods.

The problem for me, after that, was that I found it increasingly difficult to remain motivated. I still got a thrill from racing, but training was becoming a drag. Over the winter, I'd had a big goal to aim for – I wanted to repay my new team – but now I'd done that, it was harder to drag myself out to do the work that was necessary. The long rides, the bread and butter of a professional's life, were hard to do. I'd set out in the morning, intending to do five or six hours, and after a couple of hours the bike would be pulling me in the direction of home.

I'd had that feeling every now and then during my career, and it never lasted long, but as the weeks wore on I found I couldn't shake it.

Then my morale at the races began to suffer. I was thinking of survival first, not winning. When I crashed, I got fed up. The knocks and bangs took their toll more. The bad weather put me in a bad mood and I couldn't tolerate it as well as I had done.

The week-long stage races were like being on a treadmill. I was just a man in the bunch, making up the numbers. One day I'd make the split, the next I'd miss it but I wasn't bothered either way. Sometimes I thought: 'What am I doing here in the middle of the pack? I used to win this race.'

When the race is on at the front and the bunch is in one long line, with everyone riding in the gutter, fighting to keep the gap to the man in front from opening, you need to be motivated because it's pure suffering. You have to really want it to stay at the front. I found it so easy to let the guys slip by until I was halfway down the field. I'd been racing for 15 years and I was used to giving everything to stay at the front. Now I was hanging on, looking at the backsides of guys I'd never seen before.

For the first time in my career I was going through the motions. The added boost of joining a new team had lasted only so long.

In May, I started the Giro d'Italia – the other grand tour – for the first and only time in my career. I had to go, because Festina's invitation depended on my name being on the start sheet. But I had agreed with Rodriguez and the management that I'd do a week, then pull out because there was no way I could finish the Giro and then do the Tour de France.

Despite everything, the Tour still excited me. I figured that if the Tour left me flat, it would be the time to stop.

Riding a grand tour knowing that I'd be going home after a week was not an enjoyable experience but I liked the atmosphere on the Giro and it would have been nice to ride the race when I'd been at my peak.

I DIDN'T KNOW when I arrived in San Sebastián for the start of the 1992 Tour de France, that it would be my last. If I had thought about it logically, I would have realised that there was a chance I might not do it again but I didn't set off thinking it was the final time I would ride the Tour.

My ambitions for the race had changed. I knew the green jersey was out of my reach because there were younger, faster, hungrier guys like Djamolidine Abdoujaparov, Olaf Ludwig and Laurent Jalabert who would beat me regularly in the sprints. If I had been prepared to chase the intermediate sprints, I might have made myself a contender but I had no motivation to turn myself inside out every day chasing a few points here and there.

I hadn't been a pure sprinter for years – my last bunch sprint victory at the Tour de France had been in 1982. But I didn't feel I had anything to prove to anyone. I had my four green jerseys and I was happy with that. No doubt someone would come along one day and win five or six, as Erik Zabel later did, and that would be fine, because that's sport.

But I still found it hard to accept that my time was done. I didn't have the same feeling I'd had at the Tour before – the sense of being someone who was fighting for the prizes every day, whether it was points towards the green jersey or battling to stay high up the overall standings.

My plan was to get in a break, perhaps around the middle of the race when the bunch would be more willing to let a group go clear, but the opportunity never really arose. Wanting to be in the break and getting in the break are two very different things.

No one was going to let the old man Kelly win anything for old times' sake. There's little room for sentiment in the Tour.

That Tour was incredibly hard. We started in San Sebastián in the Basque Country and had to go through the Pyrenees on the second day. I actually rode pretty well that day and I felt encouraged but then we took a pasting in the team time trial at Libourne. We lost four minutes and finished third from last.

If that brought me back down to earth, the individual time trial at Luxembourg was like a kick in the stomach.

Miguel Indurain, on his way to the second of five Tour de

France titles, slaughtered us that day. Indurain's Banesto team-mate, Armand de las Cuevas, was second on the stage and he was three minutes behind.

I lost nine-and-a-half minutes in 65 kilometres. I tried to convince myself I'd given it 100 per cent but when I thought about it honestly I knew it wasn't like the old days.

I pushed myself until it hurt but I wasn't motivated enough to reach that deep, deep level of pain necessary to compete in a time trial of that distance and difficulty.

At my peak, I'd have pushed until the stars danced in front of my eyes. This time, I could remember glancing at the cows on the side of the hill and noticing the people by the road with their picnic tables. I wasn't in the zone of pure pain.

It is nicknamed the race of truth, and the time trial that day left me with a few home truths.

Although it was a struggle, I was able to finish well inside the time limit in the mountains. I wasn't worried about failing to make it to Paris but it was a relief when I saw the Champs-Élysées for the first time on the final day.

As we lapped Paris, I wasn't thinking that this would be my last Tour. I wasn't emotional about it at all. Although I didn't have a contract confirmed for 1993 I still considered myself a professional cyclist and I didn't feel it was the end just yet.

THE TOUR HAD been hard and motivation to train was not like in the old days but I wasn't ready to stop cycling yet. Bike racing is a difficult habit to kick, especially as I had done almost nothing else for 20 years. When Festina suggested doing another year, I found myself agreeing.

Ironically, PDM had ended its sponsorship, so the man-agement of the Festina team bought out the remains of PDM, which meant I was reunited with Jan Gisbers, Martin Earley and Steven Rooks. In fact, it was a three-way merger because we also absorbed part of the French RMO squad, including their *directeur sportif* Bruno Roussel.

It meant there were a lot of competing agendas in the team right from the start. It was also a huge team, with 31 riders all wanting to ride the big races, and none of the management able to take overall control.

Gisbers was supposed to be the general manager but there was conflict because Miguel Moreno had been in charge of Festina the previous year and Roussel had been running RMO, so they all thought they should be in charge.

I had a disrupted spring. I felt good at Paris-Nice but got a cold before Milan-San Remo, so I wasn't at my best. I crashed at Flèche Wallonne and missed the final two Classics – Liège-Bastogne-Liège and the Amstel Gold Race.

With so many riders all hoping to ride the Tour, I knew I needed a good result or two. Gisbers had agreed that I could follow my usual build-up to the Tour, riding the Tour of Switzerland in June to get ready.

But Roussel wanted me to ride two stage races in France instead, the Grand Prix du Midi Libre and the Tour du Midi Pyrenees. He was going to be our *directeur sportif* at those two races and he said he wanted to get to know me better and see me race.

I told him I knew what worked best for me and that I needed to do ten solid days of racing at the Tour of Switzerland. There was some friction and Roussel wasn't too happy I got my way.

By now, things were starting to fall apart. Some of the riders who had come from PDM had not been paid for a month or two and the atmosphere was sour. There was a division in the camp with Gisbers and Roussel pulling in different directions.

I wasn't at the Giro d'Italia but I heard that things came to a head there and there was a mutiny among the riders when they stopped following Gisbers' instructions.

As far as I was concerned, I was supposed to ride the Tour de France but the day before I was supposed to travel to the race, the phone rang. It was Gisbers, calling to tell me that I had been left out of the team. He said he wanted me to hear it from him before anyone else.

I knew the final places on the team were up for grabs but I thought I deserved to be selected, particularly when I looked at some of the others they were taking. Without being disrespectful, there wasn't much that a guy like Michel Vermote could do that I couldn't. But I wasn't one of Roussel's boys, so I was left out. If I had done as he said and ridden the two races in France, perhaps I'd have been selected, I don't know.

It crossed my mind to pick up the phone and call the boss of Festina, Miguel Rodriguez, but I had never whined about anything in my career before and I wasn't going to start now. The decision had been taken and although I didn't agree with it, I accepted it.

So that was it. The end of my Tour de France career. Deep down, perhaps I was relieved that I didn't have to go through it all again, and happy that the decision had been taken out of my hands.

While the Tour was on, I put my bike in the car and did a few criterium races. The money was good and the racing was fun. It was like the old days.

I thought my days as a professional were drawing to a close. There was no way Festina would be offering me another year and I hadn't given anyone an indication that I wanted to continue.

The plan was to see out the season and then issue a statement bringing my career to an end. For the first time, I felt ready to stop. The victory at Milan-San Remo the previous spring had been the last hurrah. There wasn't going to be a miracle. The biggest races, the ones that made my pulse race, were no longer within my reach and the smaller races and the training didn't excite me.

Seventeen seasons as a professional was enough.

And then the phone rang with an offer that tugged at the heart-strings. Like I said, cycling can be a difficult thing to kick.

33. Encore

As we travelled back to Ireland at the end of 1993, my mind was made up. I hadn't actually announced my retirement but I had decided it was time. The people closest to me knew I was going to stop. I'd already planned to sell the house in Merchtem in Belgium and had my eyes on some land near Carrick-on-Suir on which to build a house.

Then the phone rang. It was Guy Gallopin, who had been one of my team-mates at the Sem team. He and his brother Alain, who manages the Trek team now, were setting up a small professional squad to develop young riders. They'd managed to get a sponsor, Catavana, which was a chain of stores that sold gardening equipment and tools, and had enough money to run a modest programme of races.

They wanted a few 'names' to get a bit of publicity and had persuaded Marc and Yvon Madiot to carry on. Guy called and asked me if I'd join them.

I told him I was done.

Then Alain was on the phone, giving it the hard sell. I kept saying no but the Gallopins worked the old one-two, wearing me down until they sensed I was wavering.

Alain said: 'Do the first six months, help us get up and running, and then stop.'

Eventually I caved in and agreed to join Catavana. It would be a good way to gradually ease into retirement rather than stop suddenly.

There was another reason to carry on. Elise Nys had died in January 1993 and it hit Herman very hard. His soul was totally broken and he was lost without her. They were always together and had been involved in cycling all their lives. For about 40 years they'd been to every World Championships and often they'd take their holiday at the Tour de France. They lived for cycling and had always been so kind and supportive to me, without ever asking for anything in return.

It was painful to see Herman suffering the way he was and I thought that if I stayed involved in cycling for another six months, it might occupy his mind a little bit and help him cope with the grief. So he'd come to the races with me, stay at the hotel with us and be around the cyclists. Then, on the drive back to Belgium, we'd talk about the old times.

I ENJOYED THE racing with Catavana. In the spring we did Paris-Nice and Paris-Roubaix but it felt different to my final year with Festina because I knew for sure that this was the last time I'd be doing these races, both of which meant a lot to me. Having said that, I wasn't sentimental about it. I didn't pin the number on my jersey before Paris-Roubaix and think back to the years when I won the race. I was just thinking about the race ahead, how to survive the cobbles and get as far as I could.

I punctured three times before we reached the Arenberg forest and had to wait a while before I was able to get a replacement wheel. By the time I got going again I was in the fourth group on the road and out of the race. I rode through Arenberg, not because I had any desire to experience it for one last time but because the feed zone was on the other side and I knew I could get into the team car there. I put on the indicators and pulled over to the side of the road.

The Dauphiné Libéré in June was my final major race. Although I was never a dreamer, I felt I was in good enough shape to win a stage. And I came very close at Echirolles. There was a climb near the finish which got rid of most of the sprinters, meaning there was a group of about 50 left to contest the finish. I was in a great position in the finishing straight but a Frenchman called Emmanuel Magnien was a bit too quick for me and he got past me. I was second and Greg LeMond was third. It would have been a nice way to finish but there are few fairytales in cycling. Greg and I were beaten by a 23-year-old who was faster and hungrier than us.

My final race as a professional was on the Isle of Man. The Irish Cycling Federation had permission to hold the national championships as part of the British championship road race. Martin Earley was now racing mountain bikes for Raleigh but he and I lined up for the race knowing that whoever finished first would be the Irish road-race champion. I don't think we were really contesting it. I went to the Isle of Man to race with the British guys one last time.

It was a long race – more than 100 miles – going over the mountain each lap. We knew it would be tough and that if we went too hard early on, it would be carnage at the end, so I had a chat with a few British riders and said: 'Let's take it easy for the first 40 miles.' That gave me a chance to move round the bunch and chat to some of the people I'd raced with over the years.

Graeme Obree was riding. He was a star on the track, having held the hour record and won the pursuit world title on the track, but they were solo events. He was not really suited to racing in a bunch. He kept bumping into people and I could see a crash happening. So I went over to him and said: 'Graeme, you're so strong, you should go on the attack on your own.'

We were going along at a very easy pace but he was bouncing off people like a pinball. I wanted to get him out of the way for a bit. He did attack and he spent a couple of hours out in front before we swept him up.

While the Tour de France was on, I did a few criterium races and began to wind down. We stayed in Belgium until October, tying up the loose ends and then we packed the contents of our house into a truck and headed back to Ireland. My days as a professional cyclist were over, and this time, that really was that.

Every year, just before Christmas, they held a race in Carrick-on-Suir called the Christmas Hamper. That year, they decided to make it my farewell race and although I was initially reluctant to be the centre of attention, I was extremely touched when so many people came over to support me. There were my friends from the professional peloton – including Claude Criquielion, Laurent

Fignon, Acacio Da Silva and Stephen Roche. The Tour de France organisers were represented by Bernard Hinault. Three legendary riders came over from Belgium: Eddy Merckx, Briek Schotte and Roger De Vlaeminck, nicknamed Monsieur Paris-Roubaix after his four victories there.

Thousands of riders from all over Ireland entered the race. It was the biggest peloton I'd ever been a part of. There was a long, unbroken line of cyclists leaving Carrick to head into the countryside before we returned to the town for a few laps. To this day, people come up to me and refer to that day, saying: 'I raced with you once.'

At the end of the last lap, I won the sprint. Well, you have to give the public what they came out to see...

34. Life after cycling

Cycling had been my life for more than 20 years so you might have thought I would struggle to adapt to normal life but, when it was all over, I found I didn't miss the racing and I certainly didn't yearn for the training.

I still rode my bike and I enjoyed the fact that if it was raining I did not have to go out. I was happy to become a fair-weather rider and enjoy cycling as a pastime rather than a profession. Having the freedom to meet up with the riders from the local club a couple of times a week, roll out into the countryside and chew the fat was wonderful, although I spent rather too much time hanging out at the bakery in Clonmel, breathing in the smell of freshly-baked bread and having a cup of coffee. The transition to leisure cyclist was not a difficult one to make.

Life was not suddenly empty. There was plenty to do. Fifteen years before I retired, I'd bought some land near Carrick-on-Suir and always planned to build our family home on it once my career came to an end. I hired an architect and we went to Belgium for a few days, driving round looking at the houses so he got an idea of what I wanted. I always liked the style of the houses in Belgium. Each one was individual and had a character of its own and I wanted to take some inspiration from there and place it in the Irish countryside.

It took four years to finish the place, although I was not in any great hurry. I wanted to get it done right rather than finished quickly. I took the role of site foreman, overseeing all aspects of the work. I got my hands dirty when necessary and did a fair bit of the bricklaying myself. Building the house was the perfect project for me because I didn't want to get sucked back into the professional cycling circuit just yet.

I wanted to take a break from it all, for a few years at least. I knew cycling would go on perfectly happily without me but I didn't want to become one of those old guys who didn't know how to let go. I wasn't ready to pose for photographs or sign autographs for the fans. I didn't want to give my opinion on the races and the riders.

Getting away from it for a while would give me a clean break. I watched some of the races on television and kept up to date with what was going on but I didn't miss being there in the thick of it for a moment.

But whenever I was back in Belgium, I liked to go and watch my old next-door neighbour, Fons, in his old boys races. We had become friendly over the years and he had a passion for cycling that was infectious. Although I didn't want to hang around the professionals, I loved going to watch an evening kermesse race if Fons was taking part. Watching the riders before the start, all nerves and pent-up aggression, took me back to my youth. Seeing how they raced was exciting. There were no tactics, no caution, just the thrill of sticking a number on their backs and racing each other. I'd see a guy misjudge a corner and go straight on and I could sense the combination of fear and adrenaline.

IT'S FUNNY, REALLY, considering cycling was my escape from a life spent on the farm or the building site, that after I retired both featured quite prominently. I used my own hands to build our house and I returned to farming, albeit as a gentleman farmer.

At one point in my life, I'd said 'never again' when it came to working on the land but there I was behind the wheel of a tractor again. I had some land which I loaned to some of the local farmers for them to rear their cattle on, and I did bits and pieces here and there. Farming, like cycling, never gets any easier. It's bloody hard work, especially if your living depends on it. But it's also in the blood and coming from where I did it is part of who I am. We had some horses and donkeys and for a few years I was breeding foals, dreaming of perhaps finding I had a Grand

National winner on my hands.

Although I was not a big fan of horse racing, the thorough-breds are such marvellous, lovely animals and I enjoyed being around them. It's a serious business and I was only playing at it, really, but I always wondered whether I might one day have a champion on my hands.

I liked being at home as my children, Nigel and Stacey, grew up and went through school. I didn't often sit down to help with their homework but I always reminded them to work hard because it would give them more opportunities in life.

In 1997, I went back to the Tour de France for the first time since retiring as a rider and realised what a huge event and spectacle it was. Dublin had won the right to host the start of the 1998 Tour, so I was part of an Irish delegation, along with Stephen Roche, that travelled to the race as part of the build-up for the following year.

The 1998 Tour's second stage from Enniscorthy to Cork went through Carrick-on-Suir and Sean Kelly Square, which was something I could never have imagined all those years ago. That summer David Duffield asked me to join him in the Eurosport studio. I've worked with them, on and off, ever since. If you'd said to me I'd one day end up as a television commentator I'd have been even more surprised than if you'd told me the Tour's peloton would speed through Carrick passing a square bearing my name.

It is fair to say I was not a natural broadcaster. The idea of the man who nodded when asked a question on radio adding colour to a television company's commentary may seem quite amusing but right from the start people seemed to appreciate my insight, even if it was offered very sparingly back then.

People ask me, after hearing my commentary: 'How do you always seem to know what's going to happen?'

I suppose it's because I still think like a bike rider. I can see how a race is panning out and it seems quite obvious to me what will happen, or at least what won't happen. Bike racing is quite simple when you know how it works.

It took me a while to come out of my shell but I've never been someone who's felt the need to speak when there's nothing to say, so even now I only make a contribution when I feel there's a point to make. I see my job as trying to explain to the viewers what is going on in the race and what the tactics are likely to be.

They can be long days in the commentary box though. During the Tour, particularly, it is hot and cramped and we can be on air for hours. Sometimes I look at the roadbook, the manual that everyone working on the race is given, and identify a stage that might be a long slog. Usually it's the flatter stages when the peloton lets five cowboys get away and hangs them out to dry. There can be a lot of air to fill when the time gap between the break and the bunch is constant and nothing much appears to be happening.

As co-commentator on a long stage, I am occasionally left to my own devices while my colleague answers the call of nature. I remember my old colleague David Harmon was ill at the Tour of Flanders once and he had to spend quite a lot of time in the portaloo, leaving me to fill in. It's then that I realise I'm happier as the *domestique* in the commentary box rather than the team leader.

I enjoy the commentary work. It keeps me in touch with the racing and allows me time to work with my professional team, the An Post-Chain Reaction squad. I never wanted to be a *directeur sportif*. I couldn't see myself driving slowly behind the peloton all day, checking the wing mirrors for riders coming up on the left and right. It's never struck me as a very appealing job, although plenty of former cyclists do turn their hand to team management very effectively.

When the opportunity came to be involved in the running of a team, that was a different matter. Cycling Ireland wanted to set up a base in Belgium so young riders could train and race at the heart of the European scene. They asked me if I could help them get it established so in 2006, together with Cycling Ireland, we founded the Sean Kelly Academy in Merchtem.

When I lived in Belgium, people used to call at the house every now and then, sometimes asking for an autograph or souvenir and I was always happy to oblige because they were always friendly and polite.

One evening the doorbell rang and I answered. A kid was standing there. He introduced himself and said he was a junior racer who wanted to improve because he dreamed of becoming a professional. He said: 'Can I come training with you?'

He seemed like a decent kid, and it took courage to knock on my door and have the front to ask me to go training with him so I said: 'Okay. Tomorrow morning. Nine o'clock,' and shut the door.

His name was Kurt Bogaerts and the next morning he was there just before nine to go training. He was a good training partner. For a start he didn't irritate me by asking a lot of questions and he seemed keen to listen to anything I had to say.

We became good friends and when we left Belgium to return to Ireland it was Kurt's dad who loaded all our furniture into a truck and brought it back for us. The Bogaerts family have always opened their doors to Irish riders in need of a place to stay or a meal, just as Herman and Elise Nys did for me. In Belgium people bond over cycling.

Kurt didn't make it as a professional rider but he remained passionate about the sport. Once the Sean Kelly Academy was up and running and we set up a small professional team, Kurt was the perfect man to become *directeur sportif.*

The Sean Kelly-M. Donnelly team was founded in 2006, with a roster of Irish and Belgian riders. Gradually the team grew, attracting more sponsors such as Murphy and Gunn, a Dublin-based car dealer, and then An Post, the Irish postal service.

Our aim has always been to give young riders, predominantly Irish riders, an opportunity to gain experience and catch the eye of one of the bigger teams. For all but the most obviously gifted, it is incredibly difficult to become a professional cyclist and competition for places among the elite squads is fierce. When I went to France, I was something of an oddity because I was Irish in a world dominated by the French, Belgians, Italians and Spaniards. Now riders come from all over the world – Australia, South America, the United States, eastern Europe and Scandinavia.

We've had some success in recent years. We had Daniel Lloyd on our team for a couple of seasons before he moved to Cervélo and then Garmin. Matt Brammeier joined us and then moved on to HTC-Highroad, where he rode with Mark Cavendish, and then Omega Pharma-Quick Step, two of the biggest teams in the world. Andrew Fenn, a young British rider, learned the ropes before he too moved on to Omega Pharma-Quick Step and later Sky, as did the Lithuanian Gediminas Bagdonas.

But it's a hard road these boys are setting out on although we try to prepare them for the step up. We're very fortunate that our sponsors, An Post, have bought into our vision and understand what we're trying to do but nevertheless it is hard to keep attracting that investment knowing that as soon as we uncover a talented rider he will move on. I've often thought it would be fairer if there was some sort of transfer system so that small squads like ours could be compensated when a bigger team takes one of our riders. It's not quite as straightforward as that because very few of our riders have more than a one-year contract. We simply can't guarantee them any more than a season at a time, so they are free to move on if a better offer comes along. Of course, we want them to go on to be successful but every year it's like the reset button is pressed and we start again from scratch.

I know Kurt would love the opportunity to take the team to the next level, and we're always on the look out for sponsors who want to help us do that to join forces with An Post. My name and my contacts in the sport have helped us gain invitations to races that we might not otherwise have had the chance to do – such as the Tour of Qatar and the Tour of Oman, which are run by the same company that organises the Tour de France and features some of the biggest teams. It was a great experience for our riders but those opportunities are hard to come by.

Our goal remains the same – to spot the next talented young Irish rider and set him on the path to a great career.

My time has been over a good few years now but the races I won are in the record books. That is the nature of sport. All anyone can ever do is set a benchmark for others to take aim at and, possibly, better.

In spring 2013, Daniel Martin – Stephen Roche's nephew – won the Tour of Catalonia and Liège-Bastogne-Liège. Dan was born in Birmingham and has a British father, the former professional rider Neil Martin. Dan's mother is Maria, Stephen's sister, and so Dan opted to represent Ireland.

The newspaper reports all mentioned that he was the first

Irishman to win those races since I had done it back in the 1980s. The sport has changed a lot between those two eras but whether you won Liège-Bastogne-Liège in the 1890s, 1980s or the 21st century it has always been one of the toughest one-day races. The winner is very rarely anything other than the best rider on the day.

Cycling has given me a very good life and it offered my family security. I made some great friends and that, above all, is what I value: the sense of respect and friendship that we shared.

I look back and I feel fortunate that I had the best of it. Maybe the era when I raced was one of the best times to be a professional cyclist. We took the racing seriously but the pressure wasn't as great as it seems today.

Sometimes I see the riders and wonder if they're enjoying it. Dinner time used to be a time for everyone in the team to bond and talk about what had happened that day. You look at some of the teams and half the guys are texting on their phones rather than talking to each other. You can tell the good teams to be in are the ones where the riders get on well.

There's a shared sense of suffering, survival and achievement that, to me, is what cycling is all about. When all is said and done, everybody's legs hurt on the most difficult days and it is that which binds the peloton together.

I still love to ride my bike. I enjoy taking groups of amateur cyclists on their spring training camps in Majorca. I make a point of riding with each group so that I get to know them all over the course of a week. Some of the faster ones want to race me, so they can say they've beaten Sean Kelly. Sometimes I put in a bit of an effort to see what they're made of, other times I let them have their moment.

I don't feel the need to prove myself any more, it's just that sometimes the spirit of competition comes to the fore and the old feeling of hunger that used to gnaw away at me returns. When it does, I can't resist the temptation to push a bit harder on the pedals until some of those old sensations come back.

But I've never romanticised cycling. When I ride my bike today my mind doesn't drift back to moments in my career because that part of my life ended long ago. Perhaps sentiment doesn't come into it because I know how hard bike racing is. The mental and physical toll on the riders make it one of the hardest sports in the world. I know how hard I had to push myself to achieve what I did. I can remember the pain and suffering of slogging over the mountains in the fierce mid-afternoon heat of a July in France. I can remember the times when my fingers and toes went numb in freezing rain and the pain of hitting the ground and breaking bones in a crash.

Bike racing can be a tough life. When it's all on the verge of becoming too much the exhaustion is worsened only by the fear of going through it all again the following day.

And yet, I wouldn't have changed anything because, compared to a life toiling on the farm or heaving on the building site, cycling is a beautiful, glorious and fulfilling pursuit.

Respecting Sean Kelly
by Robert Millar
King of the mountains, 1984 Tour de France

It's a dour December morning and I'm standing by the window looking at the rain, wondering if I ought to go training or not.

I try to convince myself it doesn't look too bad until I leave the comfort of the radiator and stick a hand outside. Bloody hell it's cold, what did it say in the diary for today's schedule? Three hours not messing about with a few decent hills thrown in for good measure. Hmmm maybe I could wait a bit, hope it clears up, but in my heart I know it's set in for the day so I trudge upstairs and get ready. I'd cut short yesterday's training when it started hail-stoning and need to make up some of that lost time therefore arguing with myself is pointless.

Fifteen minutes later, fully kitted in various layers of so-called waterproof gear, I force myself out the garage, and off we go, rain cape flapping in the wind.

First impressions aren't good, it's definitely as unpleasant as it looked earlier from the comfort of the kitchen and I'm pondering if this is good for my health. I decide I'll give it an hour and see how I feel. You never know, maybe I'll get used to the drips of cold water making their way down the back of my neck.

Then a thought occurs to me. Sean Kelly would have left an hour ago, on time, on schedule and probably with no gloves either. I stop whinging to myself and do the three hours.

The impact Sean Kelly had on me was immense. For my first few years I kind of bumbled along without any real direction, relying on a certain amount of talent and a dash of luck to be in good enough form to obtain a few results and justify my place in the pro ranks. Occasionally I'd be fortunate and I'd be able to race with Kelly at the pointy end of the race rather than just seeing him briefly at the start or standing on the podium as I crossed the line much later. Those few occasions made me realise if I wanted to compete more often with him then I'd have to take my job much more seriously than I had been.

Sean was so good a rider that to even have illusions of racing at his level meant I had to look at every aspect of what I was doing. No more excuses, no more lazy days and no more relying on luck instead of planning. Everything needed to be as good as it could because any less than that and he didn't just beat you, he crushed you.

I gradually developed a theory which I called the Twenty Syndrome. It related to Sean Kelly and it directly concerned my chances of beating him. I say my chances but in reality it probably applied to everyone else as well. Twenty degrees, 20 sprocket and the 20th of April.

So any race where it was colder than 20 degrees, didn't have a very long hill which necessitated bigger than a 20-tooth sprocket to get up and was before the 20th of April was a race where I had little chance of beating Sean Kelly.

Experience taught me that unless all of those circumstances lined up it would be unlikely that I'd be racing with Sean Kelly never mind beating him.

Sure, there were riders who were as hard as he was, there were riders as fast as he was and there were riders as talented as he was but for me there was no one who had all those characteristics and did the job of professional bike rider so well. Start of the season to the end of the season, barely a dip in form and never a decline in how tough he was.

No wonder the Belgians adopted him, he was one of those mythical Flandrians you see in black and white photos, covered in mud, growling, being hard. He just happened to be born in Ireland instead of Belgium.

Interestingly, Sean's hardness wasn't the usual aggressive, must-beat-you-into-submission vibe you got from many of the top riders, that wasn't his style. He didn't bounce you out of the way like other sprinters did just because he could, he didn't do you a bad turn for the fun of it and he didn't snarl and intimidate you just because you dared race with him.

He was one of the few people I trusted in the peloton and in fact he was the only top rider I encountered who didn't need to crush you into submission. He raced, he probably beat you and that was it. No bragging, no showing off and no slagging his rivals. It's little wonder the press found him so difficult to interview. Rather than a wordy explanation saying this, that and the other, he would leave all that to other people and let his racing do the talking .

Sean Kelly, who held his place at the very top of pro racing for so many years, is one of the reasons why English-speaking riders get taken seriously nowadays. Before him they were a novelty, an exception to the rule in the established bike riding countries but along with guys like Greg LeMond the ingrained attitudes changed. Speaking English no longer meant you weren't hard enough, or talented enough to deal with the demands, it didn't mean you were likely to be homesick and on the next flight back to where you came from if things got tough.

None of those weaknesses applied to Sean Kelly, not even in the slightest.

Roll of honour

1977 Flandria-Velda
4 victories
Grand Prix Lugano
Circuit de l'Indre
Etoile des Espoirs
Stage 1, Tour of Romandy

1978 Flandria-Velda
4 victories
Stage 6, Tour de France (Poitiers)
Stage 3, Tour of the Mediterranean
Stage 5, Etoile des Espoirs
Stage 1, Setmana Catalana

1979 Splendor
3 victories
Stage 1, Vuelta a España (Seville)
Stage 8a, Vuelta a España (Benicassim)
Grand Prix de Cannes

1980 Splendor
11 victories
Stage 19, Tour de France (St Etienne)
Stage 1, Vuelta a España (Benidorm)
Stage 2, Vuelta a España (Cullera)
Stage 14 Vuelta a España (Orense)
Stage 17, Vuelta a España (Valladolid)
Stage 19, Vuelta a España (Madrid)
Stage 2, Three Days of De Panne
Overall classification, Three Days of De Panne
Stage 3a, Dauphiné Libéré
Stage 4, Tour of Holland

1981 Splendor
7 victories
Stage 15, Tour de France (Thonon-les-Bains)
Stage 2, Dauphiné Libéré
Stage 5a, Tour of Holland
Stage 2, Four Days of Dunkirk
Stage 1, Tour of Luxembourg
Stage 3, Tour of Belgium
Leeuwse Pijl

1982 SEM-Francè Loire
14 victories
Stage 12, Tour de France (Pau)
Stage 3, Paris-Nice
Stage 5, Paris-Nice
Stage 7a, Paris-Nice
Stage 7b, Paris-Nice
Overall classification, Paris-Nice
Stage 3, Critérium International
Tour du Haut-Var
Stage 1, Etoile des Espoirs
Stage 2, Etoile des Espoirs
Stage 3, Etoile des Espoirs
Stage 2, Grand Prix du Mid-Libre
Stage 1, Tour de l'Aude
Stage 2, Tour de l'Aude

1983 SEM-France Loire
14 victories
Tour of Lombardy
Stage 3, Tour of Switzerland
Stage 5b, Tour of Switzerland
Overall classification, Tour of Switzerland
Stage 3a, Paris-Nice
Stage 4, Paris-Nice
Stage 7b, Paris-Nice
Overall classification, Paris-Nice
Stage 3, Critérium International
Overall classification, Critérium International
Stage 4, Etoile des Espoirs
Grand Prix d'Isbergues
Stage 4a, Tour de Lorainne
Stage 2, Paris-Bourges

1984 Skil-Reydel
26 victories
Paris-Roubaix
Liège-Bastogne-Liège
Blois-Chaville
Stage 1, Tour of Switzerland
Overall classification, Paris-Nice
Stage 2a, Paris-Nice

Roll of honour

Stage 7b, Paris-Nice
Overall classification, Tour of Catalonia
Stage 4a, Tour of Catalonia
Stage 4b, Tour of Catalonia
Stage 7, Tour of Catalonia
Overall classification, Tour of the Basque Country
Stage 1, Tour of the Basque Country
Stage 3, Tour of the Basque Country
Stage 5b, Tour of the Basque Country
Overall classification, Critérium International
Stage 1, Critérium International
Stage 2, Critérium International
Stage 3, Critérium International
Stage 1b, Tour du Limousin
Stage 2, Tour du Limousin
Stage 4, Tour du Limousin
Grand Prix Plouay
Paris-Bourges
Critérium des As
Nordwest-Schweizer Rundfahrt

1985 Skil-SEM
15 victories
Tour of Lombardy
Stage 2, Vuelta a España (Orense)
Stage 10, Vuelta a España (Tremp)
Stage 15, Vuelta a España (Albacete)
Overall classification, Paris-Nice
Stage 3, Tour of Catalonia
Stage 3, Tour of the Basque Country
Stage 5b, Tour of the Basque Country
Stage 1, Critérium International
Stage 3, Tour of Holland
Stage 5, Tour of Valencia
Overall classification, Nissan Classic
Stage 1, Nissan Classic
Stage 3a Nissan Classic
Critérium des As

1986 KAS
25 victories
Milan-San Remo

Paris-Roubaix
Stage 10, Vuelta a España (Palencia)
Stage 13, Vuelta a España (Collado Villalba)
Overall classification, Paris-Nice
Prologue, Paris-Nice
Stage 3, Paris-Nice
Stage 7a, Paris-Nice
Overall classification, Tour of Catalonia
Stage 7, Tour of Catalonia
Overall classification, Tour of the Basque Country
Stage 3, Tour of the Basque Country
Stage 5a, Tour of the Basque Country
Stage 5b, Tour of the Basque Country
Stage 1, Critérium International
Stage 3, Critérium International
Stage 1b, Three Days of De Panne
Stage 4a, Tour of Aragon
Stage 1, Tour of Valencia
Stage 3, Tour of Valencia
Overall classification, Nissan Classic
Stage 4, Tour du Limousin
Stage 2, Paris-Bourges
Grand Prix des Nations
Critérium des As

1987 KAS
15 victories
Stage 1, Vuelta a España (Albacete)
Stage 3, Vuelta a España (Valencia)
Overall classification, Paris-Nice
Stage 3, Paris-Nice
Prologue, Tour of Catalonia
Stage 1, Tour of Catalonia
Overall classification, Tour of the Basque Country
Stage 4, Tour of the Basque Country
Stage 5b, Tour of the Basque Country
Overall classification, Critérium International
Stage 2, Critérium International
Stage 3, Critérium International
Stage 1b, Three Days of De Panne
Stage 7, Tour of Valencia
Overall classification, Nissan Classic

Roll of honour

1988 KAS
11 victories
Overall classification, Vuelta a España
Stage 11, Vuelta a España (Valdezcaray)
Stage 20, Vuelta a España (Collado Villalba)
Ghent-Wevelgem
Overall classification, Paris-Nice
Stage 6b, Paris-Nice
Stage 4, Tour of the Basque Country
Overall classification, Setmana Catalana
Stage 5, Setmana Catalana
Stage 2b, Tour du Limousin
Stage 3, Tour du Limousin

1989 PDM
2 victories
Liège-Bastogne-Liège
Stage 4, Dauphiné Libéré

1990 PDM
2 victories
Overall classification, Tour of Switzerland
Stage 4, Tour of Switzerland

1991 PDM
2 victories
Tour of Lombardy
Overall classification, Nissan Classic

1992 FESTINA-LOTUS
5 victories
Milan-San Remo
Stage 7, Tour of Switzerland
Trofeo Luis Puig
Stage 4, Tour of Valencia
Stage 2, Clásico RCN

Grand Tour record & other honours

TOUR DE FRANCE
1978 – 34th
1979 – 38th
1980 – 29th
1981 – 48th
1982 – 15th
1983 – 7th
1984 – 5th
1985 – 4th
1987 – did not finish
1988 – 46th
1989 – 9th
1990 – 30th
1991 – did not finish
1992 – 43rd
Points competition wins: 1982, 1983, 1985, 1989
Total stage wins: 5

VUELTA A ESPAÑA
1979 – did not finish
1980 – 4th
1985 – 9th
1986 – 3rd
1987 – did not finish
1988 – 1st
Points competition wins: 1980, 1985, 1986, 1988
Total stage wins: 16

GIRO D'ITALIA
1992 – did not finish

FICP WORLD NUMBER ONE
1984, 1985, 1986, 1987, 1988

SUPER PRESTIGE PERNOD WINNER
1984, 1985, 1986

UCI WORLD CUP OVERALL WINNER
1989

WORLD CHAMPIONSHIP ROAD RACE
Bronze medal –1982, 1989